THE FRENCH ART NOVEL
1900–1930

LEGENDA

LEGENDA is the Modern Humanities Research Association's book imprint for new research in the Humanities. Founded in 1995 by Malcolm Bowie and others within the University of Oxford, Legenda has always been a collaborative publishing enterprise, directly governed by scholars. The Modern Humanities Research Association (MHRA) joined this collaboration in 1998, became half-owner in 2004, in partnership with Maney Publishing and then Routledge, and has since 2016 been sole owner. Titles range from medieval texts to contemporary cinema and form a widely comparative view of the modern humanities, including works on Arabic, Catalan, English, French, German, Greek, Italian, Portuguese, Russian, Spanish, and Yiddish literature. Editorial boards and committees of more than 60 leading academic specialists work in collaboration with bodies such as the Society for French Studies, the British Comparative Literature Association and the Association of Hispanists of Great Britain & Ireland.

The MHRA encourages and promotes advanced study and research in the field of the modern humanities, especially modern European languages and literature, including English, and also cinema. It aims to break down the barriers between scholars working in different disciplines and to maintain the unity of humanistic scholarship. The Association fulfils this purpose through the publication of journals, bibliographies, monographs, critical editions, and the MHRA Style Guide, and by making grants in support of research. Membership is open to all who work in the Humanities, whether independent or in a University post, and the participation of younger colleagues entering the field is especially welcomed.

RESEARCH MONOGRAPHS IN
FRENCH STUDIES

The *Research Monographs in French Studies* (RMFS) form a separate series within the Legenda programme and are published in association with the Society for French Studies. Individual members of the Society are entitled to purchase all RMFS titles at a discount.

The series seeks to publish the best new work in all areas of the literature, thought, theory, culture, film and language of the French-speaking world. Its distinctiveness lies in the relative brevity of its publications (50,000–60,000 words). As innovation is a priority of the series, volumes should predominantly consist of new material, although, subject to appropriate modification, previously published research may form up to one third of the whole. Proposals may include critical editions as well as critical studies. They should be sent with one or two sample chapters for consideration to Professor Diana Knight, Department of French and Francophone Studies, University of Nottingham, University Park, Nottingham NG7 2RD.

Editorial Committee
Diana Knight, University of Nottingham (General Editor)
Bill Burgwinkle, King's College, Cambridge
Janice Carruthers, Queen's University Belfast
Shirley Jordan, Queen Mary, University of London
Neil Kenny, All Souls College, Oxford
Jennifer Yee, Christ Church, Oxford

Advisory Committee
Wendy Ayres-Bennett, Murray Edwards College, Cambridge
Celia Britton, University College London
Ann Jefferson, New College, Oxford
Sarah Kay, New York University
Michael Moriarty, University of Cambridge
Keith Reader, University of Glasgow

PUBLISHED IN THIS SERIES

www.legendabooks.com

The French Art Novel
1900–1930

Katherine Shingler

LEGENDA

Research Monographs in French Studies 43
Modern Humanities Research Association
2016

Published by Legenda
An imprint of the Modern Humanities Research Association
Salisbury House, Station Road, Cambridge CB1 2LA

ISBN 978-1-909662-23-0 (HB)
ISBN 978-1-781883-21-1 (PB)

First published 2016

Copy-Editor: Charlotte Brown

CONTENTS

For Elliot and Nina

ACKNOWLEDGEMENTS

The research on which this book is based was funded by a Leverhulme Early Career Fellowship, without which I would not have been able to complete it. I would like to thank my colleagues at the University of Nottingham, especially Diana Knight, Christopher Johnson, and Nicki Hitchcott, who have supported me throughout the project. Paul Smith, Richard Hobbs, and Susan Harrow all supported me during my doctoral studies at the University of Bristol, and beyond. Participants in a 2011 conference on 'Art in French Fiction since 1900' at the University of Nottingham helped me to refine some of my initial ideas on the art novel. I am also grateful to Lynsey Russell-Watts for her comments on the first draft, and to Charlotte Brown for her careful copy-editing. Allison Pearson at the Centre for Advanced Studies deserves thanks for her many pep talks. Finally, I would especially like to thank my family for their love and patience.

Earlier versions of some sections appeared in the following publications: 'Saints and Lovers: Myths of the Avant-Garde in Michel Georges-Michel's *Les Mont-parnos*', *French Cultural Studies*, 23.1 (2012), 17–29; 'An Art Novel for the Age of Mechanical Reproduction: Blaise Cendrars's *Dan Yack*', *French Studies*, 67.1 (2013), 47–60; 'Painting and Cinema in Aragon's *Anicet*', in *The Art of the Text: Visuality in Nineteenth and Twentieth-Century Literary and Other Media*, ed. by Susan Harrow (Cardiff: University of Wales Press, 2013), pp. 81–94. I would like to thank Oxford University Press, SAGE, and the University of Wales Press for granting permission to reuse this material.

K.S., Nottingham, February 2016

ABBREVIATIONS

BOC, I, II, III	André Breton, *Œuvres complètes*, ed. by Margueritte Bonnet and others, 3 vols (Paris: Gallimard, Bibliothèque de la Pléiade, 1988–92)
BOC, IV	André Breton, *Œuvres complètes IV: écrits sur l'art et autres textes*, ed. by Margueritte Bonnet and others (Paris: Gallimard, Bibliothèque de la Pléiade, 2008)
D	Paul Bourget, *La Dame qui a perdu son peintre* (Paris: Plon, 1910; fasc. repr. Elibron Classics, 2006)
M	Michel Georges-Michel, *Les Montparnos* (Paris: Livre de poche, 1976)
ORC	Louis Aragon, *Œuvres romanesques complètes*, ed. by Daniel Bougnoux and others, 5 vols (Paris: Gallimard, Bibliothèque de la Pléiade, 1997–2012)
Po	Guillaume Apollinaire, *Œuvres poétiques*, ed. by Marcel Adéma and Michel Décaudin (Paris: Gallimard, Bibliothèque de la Pléiade, 1965)
Pr	Guillaume Apollinaire, *Œuvres en prose complètes*, ed. by Pierre Caizergues and Michel Décaudin, 3 vols (Paris: Gallimard, Bibliothèque de la Pléiade, 1977, 1991, & 1993)
RTP	Marcel Proust, *À la recherche du temps perdu*, ed. by Jean-Yves Tadié, 4 vols (Paris: Gallimard, Bibliothèque de la Pléiade, 1987–89)
TADA	Blaise Cendrars, *Tout autour d'aujourd'hui*, ed. by Claude Leroy, 15 vols (Paris: Denoël, 2001–06)
VL	Camille Mauclair, *La Ville lumière: roman contemporain* (Paris: Paul Ollendorff, 1904)

All translations are my own unless otherwise stated.

LIST OF ILLUSTRATIONS

INTRODUCTION

Art, Authenticity, and the Novel

The 'art novel' may be defined loosely as fiction about art: narratives in which an engagement with the visual arts, and the representation of artists and their creative activity, are central features. In practice, however, it has tended to be defined in rather narrower terms, and to be associated, ever since early surveys of the genre by James Huneker and Theodore Bowie, with a trio of nineteenth-century texts: the Goncourt brothers' *Manette Salomon* (1867), Zola's *L'Œuvre* (1886), and especially Balzac's *Le Chef-d'œuvre inconnu* (1831), the latter often being read as a foundational text from which all subsequent art narratives derive.[1] The narrative tropes that emerge in Balzac's text and are reiterated by the Goncourts and Zola — the central pairing of artist and model, the conflict between romantic love and the artist's devotion to his work, the artist's heroic struggle to create, and his ultimate failure to attain his aesthetic ideals — have frequently been seen to constitute the defining elements, if not the limiting clichés, of the canonical art novel.

The nineteenth-century art novel corpus, with the aforementioned 'big three' at its core, has attracted a good deal of scholarly attention. When it comes to the art novel in the years following 1900, it is not only difficult to think of many clear or well-known examples of the genre (save, perhaps, for Proust's representation of the painter Elstir in *À la recherche du temps perdu*), but the critics also fall strangely silent.[2] It as if, to all intents and purposes, the art novel simply dies out around the turn of the century; as if it suddenly becomes a forgotten species of text consigned to the realm of literary history. The aim of this book is to investigate what happens to the art novel in the period 1900–30, showing that if the genre seems to die out this may simply be because it develops beyond the narrow confines set out by the nineteenth-century canon. Over the course of this study, we will consider the extent to which early twentieth-century fictions about art, by figures as diverse in critical outlook and literary-historical status as Marcel Proust, Paul Bourget, Camille Mauclair, Michel Georges-Michel, Guillaume Apollinaire, Blaise Cendrars, Louis Aragon, and André Breton, consciously rework and even work against the models provided by their nineteenth-century precedents — or, indeed, respond to entirely new concerns.

That the art novel, in the early twentieth century, should move on from the themes and concerns of *Le Chef-d'œuvre inconnu* — a text set in the seventeenth century but reflecting the aesthetic debates of the 1830s — is hardly surprising: art itself had changed almost beyond recognition, with the proliferation of radically new avant-garde movements at the beginning of the new century.[3] Indeed, as Marie Lathers has shown, the artist's model was a central focus of nineteenth-century fiction about art because she functioned as a cipher for debates around mimesis and pictorial realism; by the end of the century, realism was on its way out, and so, correspondingly, was the model in fiction.[4] Furthermore, the painters of the nineteenth-century art novel — Balzac's Frenhofer, Zola's Lantier — had been misunderstood, flawed geniuses, engaged in an impossible creative struggle and inevitably failing to attain the ideal in art — a portrait of the artist that may, as Paul Smith notes, have been 'a sublimation of the tangible alienation experienced by his real counterpart'.[5] But in the early twentieth century the socio-economic position of the artist had changed somewhat, and it finally seemed to be possible to make a living out of avant-garde art. A new optimism developed, fostered partly by the emergence of modern art as an object of financial speculation, with paintings commanding seemingly ever-higher prices and aristocratic patrons often falling over themselves to sponsor the next big thing, as well as by the wealth of expressive possibilities offered by the new pictorial languages that developed in this period.[6] As Emilie Sitzia has noted, twentieth-century fictions of the artist often reflect this optimism: Proust's Elstir or the various fictionalized portraits of Picasso that we will encounter over the course of this study tend to picture the artist not as a *peintre maudit* or damned genius, but as a genial, magisterial figure, confident in his creative powers and easily attaining the glory denied to his nineteenth-century counterparts.[7]

And yet this optimism may only be superficial, masking persistent anxieties about the visual arts, their status, and their capabilities. The myth of the Romantic artist — flawed, misunderstood, often unbalanced — still lingers in many early twentieth-century texts, as we shall see. Moreover, new incarnations of the art novel are frequently haunted by the moment of failure — the key moment of unveiling and disappointment — that was so crucial to Balzac's novella. At the end of *Le Chef-d'œuvre inconnu*, Frenhofer's unknown 'masterpiece', a female nude which the painter holds to be so life-like, so *alive* even, that he has given it a name (Catherine Lescaut), is exposed as a disaster, a mess consisting of 'des couleurs confusément amassées et contenues par une multitude de lignes bizarres qui forment une muraille de peinture' [colours piled up confusedly and contained by a multitude of strange lines forming a wall of paint].[8] The only remnant of Catherine Lescaut's body to emerge from behind this wall of paint is her foot, 'un pied vivant!' [a living foot!] (p. 69), which hints at the perfection that might have been — at the just-out-of-reach attainment of a Pygmalionesque ideal masterpiece which rivals life itself.[9]

Hans Belting has insisted on the crucial role of this fictional failure, not just in terms of its influence over the art novel genre itself, but in terms of the impact of *Le Chef-d'œuvre inconnu* on the theory and practice of modern art. Balzac's novella, he argues, effectively established a myth of modern art based around the idea of the 'invisible' masterpiece, predicated on an ideality or perfection that was inherently unrealizable; that is, failure was an inevitable part of the artist's quest. This conception of the masterpiece or ideal work of art, Belting argues, held sway throughout the nineteenth century and well into the twentieth:

[*Le Chef-d'œuvre inconnu*], though set in the seventeenth century, is about the modern artist's struggle. Perfect art was a shadow, a mere ghost of classical times, and not even Orpheus was able to bring it back into the world because he lost it when he tried to look at it. The ideal of perfection was transformed into an idea of art completely divorced from practice. The contradiction between idea and work could not be resolved, because only the idea could be absolute: the moment it became a work it was lost. [...] Art was a fiction and not a work.[10]

The nineteenth-century artist, then, chased and inevitably failed to realize this ghost-like, fictional masterpiece. In the twentieth century, the spectre of this failure is invoked in Blaise Cendrars's novel *Dan Yack* (1929), where the sculptor Sabakoff fails — just like Frenhofer — to attain the Pygmalionesque dream of ideal, life-giving creation. But while failure is certainly a recurrent theme in some of the texts under consideration here, we will find that the nature of this failure is often of a different order. Rather than reaching a transcendental ideal via the 'masterpiece', the early twentieth-century artist seems more concerned with rendering his (or, occasionally, her) unique vision, or with casting off previous pictorial codes in order to express his personality more directly and authentically. Failure, correspondingly, consists not in an inability to reach the ideal or to express this ideal through a perfect work, but rather in a corruption of art's essential values: a betrayal of oneself and one's own unique artistic vision.

If the early twentieth-century art novel, and early twentieth-century art discourses more generally, conceive of artistic failure in terms of a lack of authenticity, then this is complicated by the fact that that term was understood in a number of senses. The first of these was closely related to the unique, original work of art — a notion that had come under pressure since the advent of photography, which allowed the potentially infinite reproduction of images.[11] At the same time, this notion of the unique original was felt to be more important than ever, with the rapid expansion of the art market around the turn of the century: as paintings and sculptures became objects of private speculation, buyers needed to ensure that what they were getting was the genuine article — indeed, the fear that they could be duped was heightened by several high-profile forgery cases.[12] But anxieties around authenticity were also bound up with a perceived crisis in aesthetic value. Under the Salon system which had previously dominated the production and consumption of visual art in metropolitan France, works of art were assessed and sanctioned according to aesthetic values transmitted by the École des Beaux-Arts, and artists trained within this system tended to make a living from state commissions for works corresponding to these (classical) values. The demise of this system at the end of the nineteenth century meant a shift towards a more open art market, driven by independent dealers and critics; towards a plurality of venues and mechanisms for exhibiting and publicizing art (through private galleries but also via new 'Salons', some of which were open to all artistic persuasions, and some of which remained tied to academic values); and, ultimately, towards an effusion of avant-garde activity, since, in theory at least, artists no longer had to shoehorn their creativity into an academic mould in order to gain success.[13] All of this meant, of course, that works of art could no longer be judged against a single, stable set of academic criteria. Some avant-garde figures deliberately added fuel to the fire: works such as Duchamp's ready-mades (everyday, found objects in which the artist's hand had scarcely intervened), and notorious hoaxes such as the painting by a certain Boronali, which was exhibited at the 1910 *Salon des indépendants* and fêted by critics, and which turned out to have been painted by the donkey at the Montmartre cabaret *Le Lapin agile*, roused suspicion that what exhibition goers were lapping up as the latest in artistic experimentation was not, in fact, art, but rather an elaborate joke at the spectator's expense.[14] This is where a second, broader notion of authenticity comes into play: in these circumstances, the concern becomes not just how to identify works by an individual artist (distinguishing them from copies, forgeries, and works by other artists), but also how to identify art *tout court*: how to say what does and does not have aesthetic value.

The key text of the period that registers this crisis of authenticity is André Gide's 1925 novel *Les Faux-monnayeurs*, in which the emblem of the fake gold coin, while not itself central to the novel's plot, stands for the erosion of values of various kinds. The forged coin works by duplicity, or by virtue of appearing to be genuine: as Édouard (novelist and fictional double for Gide himself) explains, 'Elle ne vaut en réalité que deux sous. Elle vaudra dix francs tant qu'on ne reconnaîtra pas qu'elle est fausse' [It is only really worth tuppence. It will be worth ten francs as long as no one realizes that it is false].[15] As Jean-Joseph Goux has demonstrated, *Les Faux-monnayeurs* responds to the early twentieth-century shift from gold coinage, via the 'gold standard' system (in which coins were made from non-precious metal, but their value was guaranteed by their convertibility into gold) to — from the First World War onwards — a system of inconvertible 'papier-monnaie conventionnel' [conventional paper-currency] within which the value of the coin or banknote is 'une pure fiction' [a pure fiction].[16] Now, in the pre-war fictional world of Gide's text, there are still gold coins, but what the forged coin draws attention to is the fact that *they need not be gold*. That is, it relates the post-war fact of the matter — the fact that any coin, after the abolition of the gold standard, is a purely arbitrary token, gaining its value by virtue of a collective agreement or mutually agreed fiction rather than thanks to any inherent quality. This exposure of currency's lack of inherent value in turn leads Gide into a broader interrogation of values exposed as fictions: paternal authority, indeed *authorial* authority, and, finally, aesthetic value. While Gide's text is primarily concerned with the implications of this for the novel form itself, he does refer, albeit fleetingly and elliptically, to the visual arts. One such reference is to a work which is to be reproduced in an avant-garde review, the *Fer à repasser*, masterminded by the rich society writer Passavant but fronted by a series of interchangeable young protégés. The purpose of the review, the newly-minted editor Armand proclaims, is to investigate the very nature of aesthetic value:

> — Il s'agirait de savoir ce qu'on entend par 'chef-d'œuvre'. Précisément le *Fer à repasser* s'occupe de tirer ça au clair. Il y a des tas d'œuvres qu'on admire de confiance parce que tout le monde les admire et que personne jusqu'à présent ne s'est avisé de dire, ou n'a osé dire, qu'elles sont stupides. Par exemple, en tête du numéro, nous allons donner une reproduction de *La Joconde*, à laquelle

on a collé une paire de moustaches. Tu verras, mon vieux: c'est d'un effet foudroyant.

— Cela veut-il dire que tu considères *La Joconde* comme une stupidité?

— Mais pas du tout, mon cher. (Encore que je ne la trouve pas si épatante que ça.) Tu ne me comprends pas. Ce qui est stupide, c'est l'admiration qu'on lui voue. C'est l'habitude qu'on a de ne parler de ce qu'on appelle les 'chefs-d'œuvre' que chapeau bas. Le *Fer à repasser* (ce sera d'ailleurs le titre général de la revue) a pour but de rendre bouffon cette révérence, de discréditer... Un bon moyen encore, c'est de proposer à l'admiration du lecteur quelque œuvre stupide (mon *Vase nocturne*, par exemple) d'un auteur complètement dénué de bon sens.[17]

['We need to figure out what is meant by the term "masterpiece". That's just what the *Iron* will try to clarify. There are loads of works that we admire automatically because everyone admires them and no one has ever thought or dared to say that they're stupid. For example, on the front page of the issue, we'll reproduce an image of the Mona Lisa with a stuck-on moustache. You'll see, my old chap: the effect will be startling.'

'You mean that you consider the Mona Lisa to be stupid?'

'Not at all, old chap. (Even if I don't consider it to be as great as all that.) You've misunderstood me. What's stupid is people's admiration for it. It's the habit we have of doffing our caps when we talk about so-called "masterpieces". The *Iron* (this will be the general title of the review) aims to mock this reverence, to discredit it... Another good way of doing this would be to offer for the reader's admiration a stupid text (my *Nocturnal vase*, for instance), by an author completely devoid of common sense.']

Just as the false coin continues to have value as long as no one queries its authenticity, so the masterpiece is held to be such thanks to a long-standing, mostly tacit agreement: no one ever questions its inherent value, but accepts it as a matter of course. The iconoclastic review thus aims to expose the role of convention in aesthetic judgements, and to reveal the true basis of aesthetic value (if there is one at all). Indeed, Armand's *Vase nocturne* (an ode to a chamber pot), while a humorous parody of poetic convention, is also conceived here as part of a generalized attempt to shock the reader into questioning his or her assumptions about aesthetic value: to think, in this instance, about what qualifies as a poem — or what qualifies as a *good* poem.

Superficially at least, the art practice of Marcel Duchamp does something similar, and we might think of his inverted urinal (known as the *Fountain*, Figure 0.1) as a direct point of comparison with Armand's poetic chamber pot: the artist takes something conventionally understood to be worthless (indeed something more often treated as an object of disgust than of aesthetic appreciation) and presents it as art, in a bid to lead the spectator into a reflection on the nature of the art object and of aesthetic value. However, the specific work referred to in the above passage (although both artist and work go unnamed) is in fact Duchamp's *LHOOQ* (Figure 0.2), the choice of which is highly significant — not just because of the special 'masterpiece' status of the work of art which Duchamp subverts through his act of appropriation, but also because of how the work relates to Gide's own interrogation of authenticity and aesthetic counterfeiting, both within the novel as a whole and

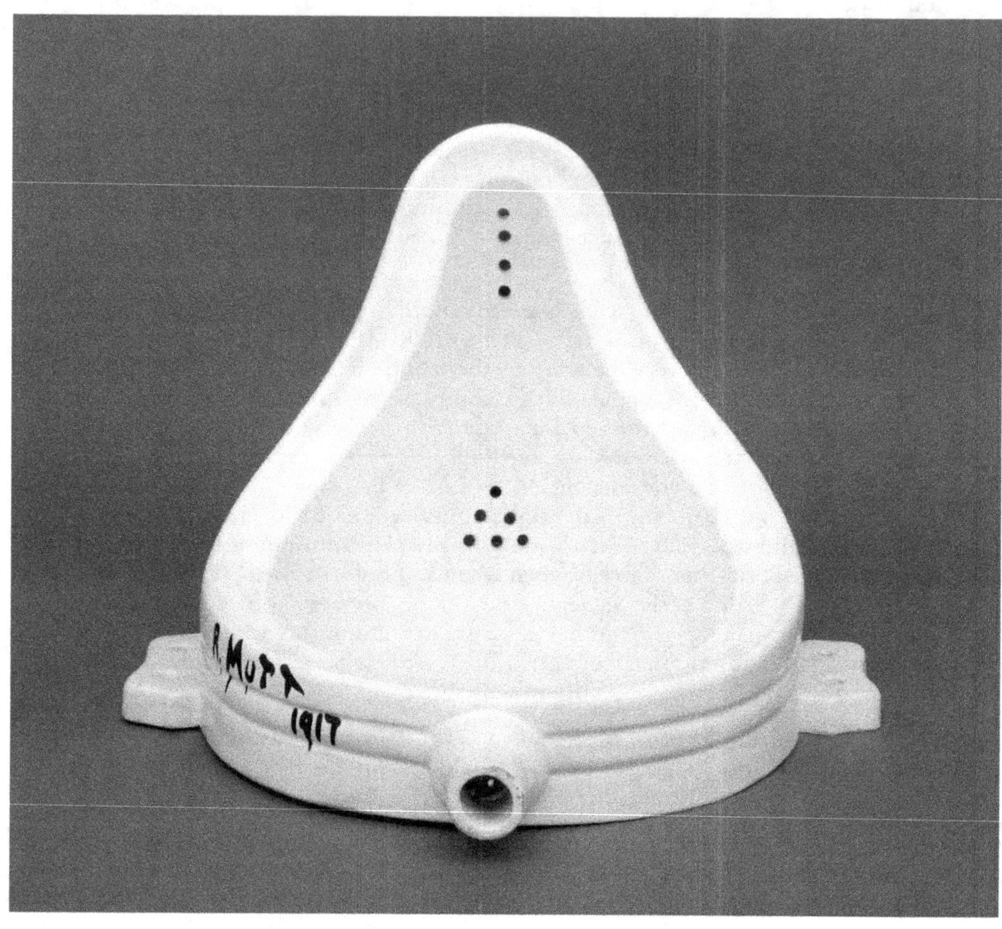

FIG. 0.1. Marcel Duchamp (1887–1968), *Fountain*, 1917, replica 1964.
Tate Modern, London. Photo © Tate, London 2015.
© Succession Marcel Duchamp/ADAGP, Paris and DACS, London 2015.

FIG. 0.2. Marcel Duchamp, *LHOOQ*. Milan, Collection Schwarz — courtesy Mudima.
© 2015. White Images/Scala, Florence. © Succession Marcel Duchamp/ADAGP,
Paris and DACS, London 2015.

in this specific passage, as Jonathan Romney has noted:

> The mustachioed Giaconda is Duchamp's *LHOOQ*, but by removing its name and origin, Gide places it in the market of infinite circulation, where it is entirely authorless and open to re-appropriation. Just as Duchamp 'stole' the original, 'forging' it with a glaring imperfection in his own name, Gide's counterfeiters go one step further by merely appropriating this already second-hand work and placing it in a new frame. The work's familiarity is itself highly ambiguous — there is the irresistible suggestion that Passavant's project is entirely second-hand and spurious; and yet, in another light, it fulfils perfectly the radical ploy of Dadaist representation.[18]

LHOOQ is especially interesting to Gide because it addresses questions of originality and authorship, perhaps even more acutely than the *Fountain* and other ready-mades. Is this a work by Leonardo, or is it by Duchamp? Does Duchamp's appropriation of Leonardo's work count as a genuine act of artistic creation — giving rise to a unique original in its own right — or is it merely a counterfeit, a duplicitous going-through-the-motions which exposes the emptiness of the very notion of artistic authenticity? Is *LHOOQ* comparable to the various acts of appropriation and plagiarism committed by Passavant, or indeed by Gide himself in this very passage when he uses Duchamp's work without explicitly acknowledging it?

These issues might be usefully framed in terms of the notion of paternity, which is central to the plot of *Les Faux-monnayeurs*: at the beginning of the novel, Bernard leaves his family home after discovering that he is illegitimate and that M. Profitendieu, the man he has hitherto called his father, is in fact a 'faux père'. As the text moves towards its conclusion, however, there is a sense that blood relations cease to matter as Bernard is reconciled with M. Profitendieu (who has, after all, played the paternal role much more successfully than many other 'legitimate' fathers in the novel). What this suggests is that the act of 'fathering' a child/work — the facts of provenance, pedigree, or 'parentage' — is ultimately of little importance. This of course plays into a broader reflection on signs and their substitutability (of which the false coin playing the role of the genuine coin is once again an emblem), but it also leads us, metaphorically, towards Gide's position on issues of artistic authenticity: while part of the 'masterpiece' status of the *Mona Lisa* is tied up with its relation to Leonardo da Vinci (the artist who 'fathered' it), Gide's novel ultimately suggests that a substitute father — a forger, another artist — would do just as well.

Duchamp and his Dada colleagues are of course not the only early twentieth-century artists to have engaged with these thorny problems of authenticity and aesthetic value, and Gide's novel is certainly not the only text to explore these problems and to relate them to the visual arts. These issues, and closely related ones, are taken up implicitly or explicitly in all of the texts considered in this study: across the broad spectrum of early twentieth-century fiction about art, we find authors reflecting on what (authentic) art is, what it is *for*, the kind of person who creates it, and how the spectator engages with it. In Chapter 1, I consider the treatment of art collecting and connoisseurship in Bourget's *La Dame qui a perdu son peintre* (1910) and Proust's *À la recherche du temps perdu* (1913–27), focusing on the figure of the connoisseur as an expert spectator, able to distinguish between genuine and fake, between art and non-art. The connoisseur is, as such, a privileged figure in a period anxious about authenticity, but at the same time, the existence of this figure begs the question: who or what is an authentic connoisseur, and what constitutes an authentic aesthetic experience? Bourget and Proust both reject the Morellian model of connoisseurship, which involves searching for marginal 'clues' to the artist's identity, in favour of a more sensuous and subjective mode of looking that privileges the impression above intellectual analysis. Chapter 2 considers issues of authenticity from a slightly different point of view, focusing on portraits of the artist in fiction. The cult status of the artist had increased, since the late nineteenth century, thanks to a biographical mode of art criticism which constantly linked *l'homme et l'œuvre* [the man and the work], and theories of art which read the work as an expression of the artist's unique personality or temperament: an authentic work of art, then, might simply be a product of a certain special kind of character. The popular understanding of the 'artistic' character was articulated through a certain number of myths which, as I wish to show in relation to Mauclair's *La Ville lumière* (1904) and Georges-Michel's *Les Montparnos* (1927), aim not only to position the artist as a heroic secular saint, but also to form his identity in relation to categories of gender and nationality.

The second part of the book examines texts that engage specifically with notions of 'modern' beauty. Just as the invention of photography in the mid-nineteenth century had led artists to query what art was for, and how it should adapt to a newly redefined cultural field, in the early twentieth century we find writers reflecting on the nature and function of the visual arts in an age of rapid scientific and industrial innovation. Painting and sculpture needed to innovate and adapt if they wanted to survive: traditional genres and visual tropes were seen as inauthentic precisely because they consisted of a facile rehashing of old, irrelevant models, and did not respond adequately to modernity. Equally, writing needed to adapt, and in Chapter 3 I consider the reflections of Apollinaire and Cendrars on the relationship between writing and the visual arts in the age of mechanical reproduction. Apollinaire initially appears to position painting as an ally to writing in its battle with utilitarian science and with a hostile cultural marketplace, but in his short story 'Le Poète assassiné' (1916) and novel *La Femme assise* (1920) the 'marriage' of text and image turns out to be an unfaithful one, and representatives of the visual arts to be constantly shifting, untrustworthy figures. In Cendrars's *Dan Yack*, meanwhile, the new media of the phonograph and the cinema are considered as potential models for a new, modern form of art, but both are seen to fail, embroiled as they are in the aesthetic ideals and the narrative tropes of the nineteenth century.

Chapter 4 moves on to the Surrealist treatment of art in fiction, and considers once again the rivalries and collaborations between writing and the visual arts. In Aragon's *Anicet* (1921), we find the writer dismissing painting, and more specifically Bleu/Picasso's postwar return to classicism, as a calculated, money-grabbing, and therefore inauthentic aesthetic stance. More convincing in its attempts to represent modern beauty is the cinema, to which Aragon responds by adopting 'cinematic' techniques in his writing. Having seen the art novel move beyond the traditional confines of painting and sculpture, I then go on to consider Breton's *Nadja* (1928), which exploits an even broader range of visual artifacts and suggests that 'real' or 'authentic' art need not be a product of the professional artist — and that aesthetic experience may just as easily be had on the streets of Paris as in a gallery or museum.

Cinema, it will be clear from the above, is one of the most important factors influencing the transformation of the art novel genre in the period 1900–30. From the unveiling of the Lumières' *cinématographe* in Paris in 1895, to the advent of the 'talkies' at the end of the 1920s, writers were inspired by the new technologies, effects, techniques, and perceptual dynamics of the cinema, but at the same time keenly felt the threat posed to literature by this new popular form of visual art, both in terms of its economic viability and its status within the field of cultural production. Equally important in terms of its impact on the art novel is a shift in gender roles, and especially a shift in women's roles in the art world, marked by the admission of women to the École des Beaux-Arts in 1897.[19] Marie Lathers has suggested that this shift may be another factor, alongside the decline in pictorial realism, accounting for the disappearance of the female model from fiction about art around the turn of the century: given that women now assumed a more important role as artists in their own right, they could no longer be considered simply as passive objects of the creative male gaze.[20] Correspondingly, we will not be surprised to find an acknowledgement and even a celebration of female creativity in the texts under consideration here: from Luce Elten in *La Ville lumière*, to Haricot-Rouge in *Les Montparnos*, to Tristouse and Elvire in 'Le Poète assassiné' and *La Femme assise* respectively, and finally to *Nadja*, female artists are often at the centre of the narrative and their work ostensibly placed on a par with that of their male counterparts. However, we will see over the course of my analysis that in spite of this willingness to attend to and represent female creativity, these texts (all of them by men) tend to marginalize that creativity and to position it as inferior to an avant-garde ideal which is almost universally identified with rugged masculinity.[21]

The final decisive influence on the trajectory of the art novel in the period 1900–30 is the public appetite for reality: for 'real', authentic stories about the lives of artists. Nathalie Heinich has suggested that this is one reason for the apparent death of the art novel after 1900: in the late nineteenth and early twentieth centuries, real artists such as Van Gogh seemed to be fulfilling the roles — especially that of *peintre maudit* — that nineteenth-century fiction had carved out for them:

> Alors, la fiction semblera désormais trop pauvre pour soutenir l'imaginaire, face à la fascinante richesse des vies réelles retravaillées par la biographie, telles que les construira au xxe siècle la légende dorée des artistes modernes. Les romans seront dès lors remplacés par les vraies vies d'artistes, les biographies des grands maudits: la réalité dépassera, comme on dit, la fiction, du moins en tant que le réel donne prise à une représentation légendaire, mythifiée.[22]

> [Fiction then appears to be too impoverished to support the imaginary, when compared with the fascinating richness of real lives reworked into biographies, constructed in the twentieth century as a kind of Golden Legend of modern artists. Novels will henceforth be replaced by the real lives of artists, by the life stories of the great and the damned: reality will overtake fiction, at least to the extent that the real gives rise to a legendary, mythologized representation]

This thirst for a mythologized 'real' explains the enormous popularity of biographies, memoirs, semi-fictional 'vies romancées', as well as art-historical monographs built on the model of 'life and work' in this period.[23] It also explains why, in novels that represent artists and their creative activity, authors often mingle fact and fiction, by inserting real-life figures into an otherwise purely fictional scenario (one might think of Rodin in *La Ville lumière*, or Cendrars and Kisling in *Les Montparnos*), or alternatively by cloaking real-life figures in a veneer of fictionality (and we will encounter a number of thinly-veiled portraits of Picasso over the course of this study). The result is often a complex conjunction of fiction and reality. This is also the case in those biographical texts that present themselves as fact and yet distort the truth considerably, and often quite self-consciously. 'Factual' accounts of the lives of painters such as Modigliani or Utrillo,[24] for instance, frequently borrow hagiographical tropes, contributing to a myth of the artist as saint or martyr just as much as Michel Georges-Michel's *Les Montparnos*, which more explicitly announces itself as a novel (but also, as we shall see, deliberately seeks to blur its generic status). A couple of key questions arise in relation to these practices: one is how we can put ourselves in a position to assess the relationship between myth and reality, given that both are known via the potentially distorting lens of text — and given that myth may, as Heinich and others have pointed out, become reality as artists step into the moulds defined for them by fiction.[25] Another is why authors might be motivated to create and sustain such myths — a problem that might once again be explained in terms of prevalent anxieties about art and authenticity: the myth of the artist as a pure, ascetic, saintly figure is attractive precisely because he is reassuringly aloof from the commercial realities that threaten to debase and corrupt art.

These varied concerns come to the surface in a heterogeneous corpus of texts, and the present study does not seek to reduce the complex textures of the art novel in the period 1900–30 to a unified, linear trajectory. The texts considered in the study were chosen, amongst a broader corpus of fictional works dealing with art and artists, primarily because they have something to say about art and its institutions — that is, they all articulate an art-critical position.[26] Moreover, all of the authors considered here also wrote art criticism alongside fiction (one might object that Bourget is something of a marginal case here, but he certainly does engage critically with art and its consumption in his non-fiction texts). This puts us in a position to compare across fiction and criticism, situating each fictional text in the context of the writer's critical thinking, and also within the broader context of art-critical discourse. It will also allow us to think through the relationship between fiction and criticism, considering what, if anything, art fiction can do that art criticism cannot — and why writers interested in art might turn to the novel form. Part of the reason, as indicated by Romy Golan, may be a fall in the stature of the art critic in the early twentieth century, and a concomitant sense that 'the *fortune critique* of recent art production was no longer primarily informed by critical texts but by dealers and the marketplace'.[27] Indeed, Malcolm Gee cites a 1927 survey by *Paris-Midi* in which respondents were asked about their attitudes to art criticism, and the mixed responses, including a fair number which 'denied that criticism was either useful or influential', seem to confirm that the public increasingly saw critics as either incompetent or as 'mere publicity agents for dealers'.[28] The art novel, then, might have appealed to writers as a less commercially-charged arena in which to debate aesthetic issues, removed from any perception of wheeling and dealing. It might also allow the writer implicitly to align himself with the literary *grands hommes* of the previous century — to take on the stature of a Balzac, a Zola, or a Goncourt. What I also hope to show, however, over the course of my analysis of these texts, is that the art novel might also be favoured over the critical text in that it provides a more expansive space to investigate art: a space in which the writer can not only get to grips with the work of art (and related issues such as its creation and reception), but reflect self-consciously on the relationship between text and image, and between his own creative activity and that of the artist. Ultimately, then, art novels are not just about visual art: they are also, as we will see, closely entangled with the writer's struggle to define and come to terms with his own medium.

Notes to the Introduction

1. Theodore Bowie, *The Painter in French Fiction* (Chapel Hill: University of North Carolina, 1950), p. 5; James Huneker, 'Literature and Art', in *Promenades of an Impressionist* (London: T. Werner Laurie, 1910), pp. 277–90 (pp. 285–90). On the critical devaluing of art fiction outside the 'big three', see Paul Smith, 'Literature and Art', in *The Nineteenth-Century Art Novel*, ed. by Paul Smith, *French Studies*, 61.1 (2007), 1–13 (p. 5).

2. Among the more useful critical surveys of the nineteenth-century French art novel are: Philippe Hamon, 'Le *Topos* de l'atelier', in *L'Artiste en représentation*, ed. by René Démoris (Paris: Éditions Desjonquères, 1993), pp. 125–44; Nathalie Heinich, 'Artistes dans la fiction: quatre générations', in *Images de l'artiste*, ed. by Pascal Griener and Peter J. Schneemann (Bern: Peter Lang, 1998), pp. 205–20; Marie-Françoise Melmoux-Montaubin, *Le Roman d'art dans la seconde moitié du XIXe siècle* (Paris: Klincksieck, 1999); Joy Newton, 'The Atelier Novel: Painters as Fictions', in *Impressions of French Modernity: Art and Literature in France 1850–1900*, ed. by Richard Hobbs (Manchester: Manchester University Press, 1998), pp. 173–89; Smith (ed.), *The Nineteenth-Century Art Novel*. For a comparative perspective, see Judith Labarthe-Postel, *Littérature et peinture dans le roman moderne: une rhétorique de la vision* (Paris: L'Harmattan, 2002). There are of course many critical studies dealing more generally with text-image interactions in the early twentieth century; particularly notable amongst these are Wendy Steiner, *The Colors of Rhetoric: Problems in the Relation between Modern Literature and Painting* (Chicago: Chicago University Press, 1982); Marjorie Perloff, *The Futurist Moment: Avant-Garde, Avant-Guerre, and the Language of Rupture*, 2nd edn (Chicago: Chicago University Press, 2003); Johanna Drucker, *The Visible Word: Experimental Typography and Modern Art, 1909–23* (Chicago: Chicago University Press, 1994); and, most recently, Linda Goddard, *Aesthetic Rivalries: Word and Image in France, 1880–1926* (Bern: Peter Lang, 2012).

3. The reading of Balzac's fictional painter Frenhofer as a quintessentially Romantic painter is, of course, somewhat anachronistic. Hans Belting's view of the tale as a foundational text in the history of modern art is typical of this (see *The Invisible Masterpiece*, trans. by Helen Atkins (London: Reaktion, 2001)); see also the critic François Fosca's point-by-point demonstration of the similarity between Frenhofer's aesthetic theories and those of Delacroix in *De Diderot à Valéry: les écrivains et les arts visuels* (Paris: Albin Michel, 1960), pp. 64–66.

4. Marie Lathers, *Bodies of Art: French Literary Realism and the Artist's Model* (Lincoln: University of Nebraska Press, 2001), p. 2.

5. Smith, 'Literature and Art', p. 3.

6. On the early twentieth-century Parisian art market, see Gérard Monnier, *L'Art et ses institutions en France: de la Révolution à nos jours* (Paris: Gallimard, 1995), pp. 276–87, and Malcolm Gee, *Dealers, Critics, and Collectors of Modern Painting: Aspects of the Parisian Art Market between 1910 and 1930* (New York: Garland, 1981); Gee cites the 1914 'vente de la Peau de l'ours' as one of the first major auction-room sales of modern art which confirmed that one could profitably speculate on the art market (pp. 23–24).

7. Emilie Sitzia, *L'Artiste entre mythe et réalité dans trois œuvres de Balzac, Goncourt et Zola* (Turku: Åbo Akademi University Press, 2004), p. 206; see also Bowie, *The Painter in French Fiction*, pp. 44–45, who notes that the last text to associate painterly genius with mental disequilibrium is Mauclair's *La Ville lumière* (1904).

8. Honoré de Balzac, *Le Chef-d'œuvre inconnu — Gambara — Massimilla Doni* (Paris: Garnier-Flammarion, 1981), p. 69.

9. On Balzac's reworking of the Pygmalion myth, see Diana Knight, *Balzac and the Model of Painting: Artist Stories in 'La Comédie humaine'* (Oxford: Legenda, 2007), pp. 11–29, and Alexandra Wettlaufer, *Pen vs. Paintbrush: Girodet, Balzac and the Myth of Pygmalion in Postrevolutionary France* (New York: Palgrave, 2001), pp. 1–30.

10. Belting, *The Invisible Masterpiece*, p. 126.

11. The classic analysis of this shift is of course Walter Benjamin, 'The Work of Art in the Age of Mechanical Reproduction', in *Illuminations*, trans. by Harry Zohn, ed. by Hannah Arendt (London: Pimlico, 1999), pp. 211–44.

12. Notable among these is the Tiare de Saïtaphernès, bought by the Louvre in 1896 but withdrawn from public view in 1903, having been discovered to be a fake: see Aviva Briefel, *The Deceivers: Art Forgery and Identity in the Nineteenth Century* (Ithaca, NY: Cornell University Press, 2006), pp. 6–7. This affair drew the attention of one of the writers included in this study, Guillaume Apollinaire: see 'Des faux', in *Œuvres en prose complètes*, ed. by Pierre Caizergues and Michel Décaudin, 3 vols (Paris: Gallimard, Bibliothèque de la Pléiade, 1977, 1991, & 1993), II, 74–77 (hereafter referred to as *Pr*). The Lemoine affair (in which a certain Lemoine duped the De Beers jewellery empire with a fake diamond-cooking procedure) also drew the attention of Marcel Proust: see Hannah Freed-Thall, ' "Prestige of a Momentary Diamond": Economies of Distinction in Proust', *New Literary History*, 43.1 (2012), 159–78.

13. See Patricia Mainardi, *The End of the Salon: Art and the State in the Early Third Republic* (Cambridge: Cambridge University Press, 1993). The official state Salon was abandoned in 1880, to be replaced by the artist-run *Salon des Artistes Français* from the next year; the latter, however, lacked authority as rival salons sprung up, private galleries and *cercles* became more popular, and the market assumed the role vacated by the state in determining artistic trends.

14. The Boronali hoax was revealed in [André Warnod], 'Un âne chef d'école', *Le Matin*, 28 March 1910, p. 4. For an overview of the affair, see Nicholas Hewitt, 'Images of Montmartre in French Writing, 1920–1960: "La Bohème réactionnaire" ', *French Cultural Studies*, 4 (1993), 129–43 (pp. 131–32). For a broader analysis of fears about the avant-garde's 'sincerity' in the pre-war period, see Jeffrey Weiss, *The Popular Culture of Modern Art: Picasso, Duchamp, and Avant-Gardism* (New Haven, CT: Yale University Press, 1994), pp. 89–102.

15. André Gide, *Les Faux-monnayeurs* (Paris: Gallimard, 1997), p. 221.

16. Jean-Joseph Goux, *Les Faux-monnayeurs du langage* (Paris: Galilée, 1984), p. 28.

17. Gide, *Les Faux-monnayeurs*, p. 421.

18. Jonathan Romney, 'Forgery and Economy in Gide's *Les Faux-monnayeurs*', *Neophilologus*, 71.2 (April 1987), 196–209 (p. 203).

19. Monnier, *L'Art et ses institutions en France*, p. 233.

20. Lathers, *Bodies of Art*, p. 3.

21. As Alexandra Wettlaufer has shown, female novelists from the early nineteenth century onwards created a counter-discourse which questioned the gendering of artistic vision and of the creative act as male, and sought to carve out a space for a specifically female artistic vision. See *Portraits of the Artist as a Young Woman: Painting and the Novel in France and Britain, 1800–1860* (Columbus: Ohio State University Press, 2011).

22. Heinich, 'Artistes dans la fiction: quatre générations', p. 220. See also Nathalie Heinich, *La Gloire de Van Gogh: essai anthropologique de l'admiration* (Paris: Minuit, 1991), pp. 211 and 221n.

23. Mary Shaw has also commented on the way in which the generic boundaries between fiction, art criticism, and documentary prose tend to dissolve in late nineteenth-century texts. See 'All or Nothing? The Literature of Montmartre', in *The Spirit of Montmartre: Cabarets, Humor, and the Avant-Garde, 1875–1905*, ed. by Phillip Dennis Cate and Mary Shaw (New Brunswick, NJ: Jane Voorhees Zimmerli Art Museum, 1996), pp. 111–57 (pp. 135–36).

24. See for instance André Salmon's *Modigliani: sa vie et son œuvre* (Paris: Éditions des Quatre

Chemins, 1926), and Francis Carco, *La Légende et la vie d'Utrillo* (Paris: Bernard Grasset, 1928).

25. See Smith, 'Literature and Art', p. 7.

26. This broader corpus includes novels whose major theme is bohemian life and in which artist characters feature, such as André Salmon, *La Négresse du Sacré-Cœur* (Paris: Nouvelle revue française, 1920), Francis Carco, *Scènes de la vie de Montmartre, roman* [1919] (Paris: J. Ferrenczi & Fils, 1939), André Warnod, *Lily, modèle: roman de Montmartre* (Paris: L'Édition française illustrée, 1919), and *Lina de Montparnasse* (Paris: Nouvelle revue critique, 1928). It also includes texts in which artist characters feature very prominently, but in which issues of artistic representation are nevertheless secondary, for example Joachim Gasquet, *Il y a une volupté dans la douleur...* (Paris: Bernard Grasset, 1921). It also includes novels about art by artists, such as Jacques-Émile Blanche's semi-autobiographical *Aymeris* (Paris: Éditions de la Sirène, 1922). For reasons of scope I have not been able to include the Swiss novelist C.-F. Ramuz's *Aimé Pache, peintre vaudois* [1911] (Lausanne: Plaisir de Lire, 1973), which links artistic temperament to *terroir* in a similar way to Mauclair's *La Ville lumière*; Victor Margueritte's *La Garçonne* [1922] (Paris: Flammarion, 1949); Georges de Lys and André Ibels's *L'Arantelle: roman d'art* (Paris: J. Bosc, 1908); or the critic François Fosca's art novel *Derechef* (Paris: Simon Kra, 1927). I hope to deal with some of these in future publications.

27. Romy Golan, 'From Fin de Siècle to Vichy: The Cultural Hygienics of Camille (Faust) Mauclair', in *The Jew in the Text: Modernity and the Construction of Identity*, ed. by Linda Nochlin and Tamar Garb (London: Thames and Hudson, 1996), pp. 156–86 (p. 161).

28. Gee, *Dealers, Critics, and Collectors of Modern Painting*, p. 101.

CHAPTER 1

Art and Connoisseurship in
Bourget and Proust

Although the best-known art narratives of the nineteenth century deal centrally with the artist, his creative struggles, and his failures, there is a parallel strand which concerns the reception of art: its purchase, display, and appreciation. From Balzac's *Cousin Pons* (1847) to the Des Esseintes of Huysmans's *À rebours* (1884), the collector provides a figure through which modes of art consumption may be represented and critiqued. As a number of recent scholarly accounts have demonstrated, the rise to prominence of the collector as a literary figure corresponds to the historical emergence of collecting as a pastime for the wealthy — and, with the advent of the department store and the mass-produced ornament or bibelot, for the less well-off too.[1] During the *Ancien Régime*, art collecting had been a more or less exclusively aristocratic activity, but in the wake of the Revolution a wealth of art objects belonging to the dispossessed nobility and clergy were suddenly released onto the market, alongside works of art imported from outside France (especially from Italy) as the Napoleonic empire expanded. This meant that art was suddenly put within reach of the bourgeoisie, readily available for purchase at relatively low prices. As Rémy Saisselin has shown, the growing popularity of collecting in the nineteenth century was a phenomenon typical of bourgeois culture, which saw the art object as just another product amongst so many others, blurring the lines between high art and *art industriel* — between the realm of aesthetics and that of the commodity.[2] The bourgeois spirit of investment and speculation in the art market persisted into the early twentieth century, which saw dramatic spikes in the price of contemporary art.[3] While some buyers clearly had one eye on potential returns — their thrill being, essentially, that of any other bargain hunter — there were many other possible motivations for collecting art. One might collect because art objects function as a marker of social 'distinction', as Pierre Bourdieu has claimed;[4] one might collect to leave something of oneself to posterity, passing the collection on to one's family, or to the state; in a world of uncertainty, one might find the practice of taxonomy, or imposing a stable classificatory system onto a series of heteroclite objects, particularly reassuring.[5] The collector might also seek a more intimate relationship with the objects in his collection, decorating his domestic interior with them as an expression not just of his social 'distinction', but of his innermost self. This is the collector as aesthete, the best-known literary incarnation of which is Des

Esseintes, whose creation of a richly adorned interior environment is itself a work of self-expression tantamount to a work of art. Indeed, by the end of the nineteenth century, the collector-aesthete was often seen as on a par with the artist (he simply lacked the technical skill of the latter),[6] while the terms 'artiste' and 'artistique' were frequently applied to collectors and their displayed collections, indicating a refined taste and 'artistic' sensibility that transferred to the collector something of the cachet and cult status of the artist himself.[7]

In the *fin de siècle*, then, appreciating and creating art were intimately linked. This is also the case in Proust's *À la recherche du temps perdu*, written in the early twentieth century but set in the *fin de siècle* period, and where the narrator's trajectory, the process by which he becomes a (literary) artist, is essentially a process whereby he learns to appreciate art, or whereby he learns to *look*. Thus, although this chapter will leave to one side many aspects of Proust's engagement with the visual arts in his fiction — his representation of artist figures such as the painter Elstir, his use of real and imaginary works of art in his narrative, and his techniques of visual writing, all of which have been skilfully unpacked by other scholars[8] — a focus on Proust's art of looking is absolutely vital in understanding his broader philosophy of artistic creation. But an examination of issues surrounding the reception of art in early twentieth-century fiction is also warranted because the act of looking at a painting or sculpture is an obvious locus for the anxieties about authenticity that were so prevalent in the period. The issue, in essence, is that of the spectator confronting the work of art: how does he or she tell that the art object is 'the real thing'? This question becomes increasingly pressing as art objects command ever higher prices in the early twentieth-century art booms, and also as it becomes a more popular activity, practised by everyone from the aristocratic *salonnière* down to the lowly functionary or petit bourgeois shopkeeper. In Proust's novel almost everyone collects art in some form, while in the other text to be examined in this chapter, Paul Bourget's *La Dame qui a perdu son peintre* (1910), the works of the Italian masters, which were once the exclusive preserve of the old nobility, are now bought up by nouveau riche collectors, including a particularly brash and uncultured American industrialist. The problem, for Bourget as for Proust, is therefore that of how to mark oneself out as an 'authentic' art lover, in contrast with those who consume it simply as a commodity, as an investment, or for the veneer of 'distinction' that it confers upon them. How, that is, does one go about having the kind of authentic aesthetic experience that is characteristic of the 'artistic' sensibility?

Precisely because of these anxieties around the authenticity of the art object and of the aesthetic experience that it elicits, the late nineteenth and early twentieth centuries see the rise to prominence of the connoisseur as both a real and literary figure. The connoisseur may be a collector himself, but often appears in the guise of an adviser or erudite authority who guides the collector in his purchases. In general terms, a connoisseur might be understood as a specially qualified kind of spectator, or an expert in judgements of taste. The discipline of connoisseurship in Europe goes back at least to the seventeenth century, but was given a formal theoretical framework in the late nineteenth century by Giovanni Morelli (1816–91), who laid the foundations of a 'science' of connoisseurship based on the identification of distinctive bodily traits in painted figures — apparently marginal and insignificant details that would give away the true identity of the artist. The Morellian connoisseur appears in both Proust's seven-volume novel and in Bourget's novella, allowing both authors to address questions of authenticity and aesthetic appreciation. These questions may be formulated roughly as follows: how can one tell that the work of art is 'authentic', (a) in the sense that it is correctly attributed to its creator, and (b) in the sense that it is really art, that it has real aesthetic value? These two senses in which an art object may be understood to be authentic may sometimes be at odds: a work of art may be misattributed, but this is not to say that it has no aesthetic value, or that it is not art. As we shall see over the course of this chapter, *À la recherche du temps perdu* and *La Dame qui a perdu son peintre* may both be read as art historiographies, tracing the tension between two broad models of connoisseurship operative in the *fin de siècle* period: the reassuringly stable analytic framework of the Morellian method versus a more subjective, properly aesthetic engagement with the work of art. Both Bourget and Proust test out Morellian theories of connoisseurship, querying the authority of the connoisseur's gaze. Both authors work to expose the contradiction between the two facets of the connoisseur's task — between attribution and appreciation — and tend to reject the importance of the former as a scientific, taxonomic endeavour in order to privilege instead a sensuous, imaginative, and above all subjective engagement with the work of art.

Artistic Fakes in Bourget's *La Dame qui a perdu son peintre*

Paul Bourget's 1910 novella *La Dame qui a perdu son peintre* provides an amusing, highly ironic investigation of Morellian connoisseurship which leaves the reader in doubt as to the authenticity not just of the various works of art represented, but of the various aesthetic approaches taken by the characters in relation to these. Although the novella is narrated by an artist, the tale focuses not on artistic creation but on the cultures of collecting, and of spectatorship, specific to the craze for Italian 'Primitives' in the early twentieth century. Bourget himself was an avid collector of Italian art,[9] and mined this subject-matter in his other short stories 'La Pia' (where the tensions between the art trade and disinterested aesthetic appreciation are explored, in a similar vein to *La Dame qui a perdu son peintre*), and 'La Seconde Mort de Broggi-Mezzastris', which interrogates practices of collecting, inheritance, and aesthetic taste.[10] Bourget's erudite knowledge of Renaissance art is apparent in these tales, as well as in his non-fiction writing on art; and yet he would certainly not have called himself an art critic or historian. In his *Sensations d'Italie*, a travel journal documenting his impressions of Italian art, Bourget specifically resists scholarly approaches, insisting that he is looking above all for 'ce petit frisson particulier qui ne se discute pas plus que l'amour. Ailleurs nous jugeons, nous critiquons, nous analysons; ici nous sentons' [that peculiar frisson which is not subject to discussion, any more than love is. Elsewhere we might judge, criticize, analyse; here, we feel].[11] Bourget self-consciously situates this text more as *chronique* than as criticism, proclaiming the revival of 'ce genre aujourd'hui démodé: la description d'un tableau ou d'une statue, toute littéraire et sans document sur le plus ou moins d'authenticité' [a genre that is now unfashionable: the description of paintings or statues, entirely literary and without documentation as to the object's authenticity, or lack of it].[12] As these statements imply — and as is borne out by an examination of *La Dame qui a perdu son peintre* — Bourget's connoisseurship is a sensuous one that privileges imaginative rather than intellectual engagement with the work of art and, as far as possible, leaves dry historical questions of attribution to one side.

La Dame qui a perdu son peintre is narrated by Monfrey, a fifty-something society portraitist who has gone to Milan following a tiff with his lover, to whom he relates the story. While there, he visits the nobleman Varegnana, an old friend and owner of a portrait of a 'Cassandra' formerly attributed to Leonardo, and which Monfrey admired in his youth. However, thanks to the burgeoning Morellian school of connoisseurship, enthusiastically represented by a pedantic young critic named Courmansel, Cassandra has lost her painter: the painting is now attributed not to Leonardo but to a certain Cristoforo, or 'Amico di Solario' — a clear reference to Bernard Berenson's notorious 'Amico di Sandro'. Of Morelli's various disciples, Berenson was the most famous popularizer of his method in France, having published his article on the 'Amico' in the *Gazette des beaux-arts* (the foremost art journal of the period).[13] The Morellian approach adopted by Berenson involved a kind of physiognomy of the painted figure, a reading of the body for minor details that would give clues to the identity of the painter. One worry for the collector was that a painter's distinctive style could easily be imitated, while convention might mean that painters of a given school or historical period could share many stylistic traits, making it difficult to attribute a work to an individual artist. Morelli proposed that, rather than having recourse to the vague notion of the 'general impression' created by a work, the connoisseur should take a more systematic approach, focusing his analytic gaze on apparently marginal details where the pressures of convention are relaxed, and where the artist's distinctive personal style would, without fail, find expression.[14] So, for example, Morelli might look at the way in which Botticelli paints ears, or the way in which Filippo Lippi paints hands (figure 1.1); the distinctive characteristics of these ears and hands could then be used to say whether or not a painting was an authentic Botticelli or Filippo. (This led to one contemporary critic's characterization of Morellian connoisseurship as the 'ear and toenail' school of criticism.)[15] This reading of the painted body was supplemented by Berenson with a reading of more general stylistic features — palette, modelling, *facture* and so on — which were held to be indexical signs of the painter's 'hand'. And Berenson used these features, these giveaway signs of the painter's identity, to devastating effect: undoing a host of earlier attributions of various Quattrocento paintings (to Botticelli, Lippi, and Ghiarlandaio), he attributed these instead to his 'Amico', a shadowy figure of his own creation, whom he held to be a close friend and disciple of Botticelli — but, crucially, not Botticelli himself, nor any other well-known or named artist.

This type of connoisseurial fiction — the 'Amico' being, essentially, a fictional persona with no historical substance — is the subject of Bourget's fictional tale.[16] Courmansel attributes the portrait of Cassandra to 'Cristoforo' on the grounds that it shares a number of features with another painting, which appears to be signed

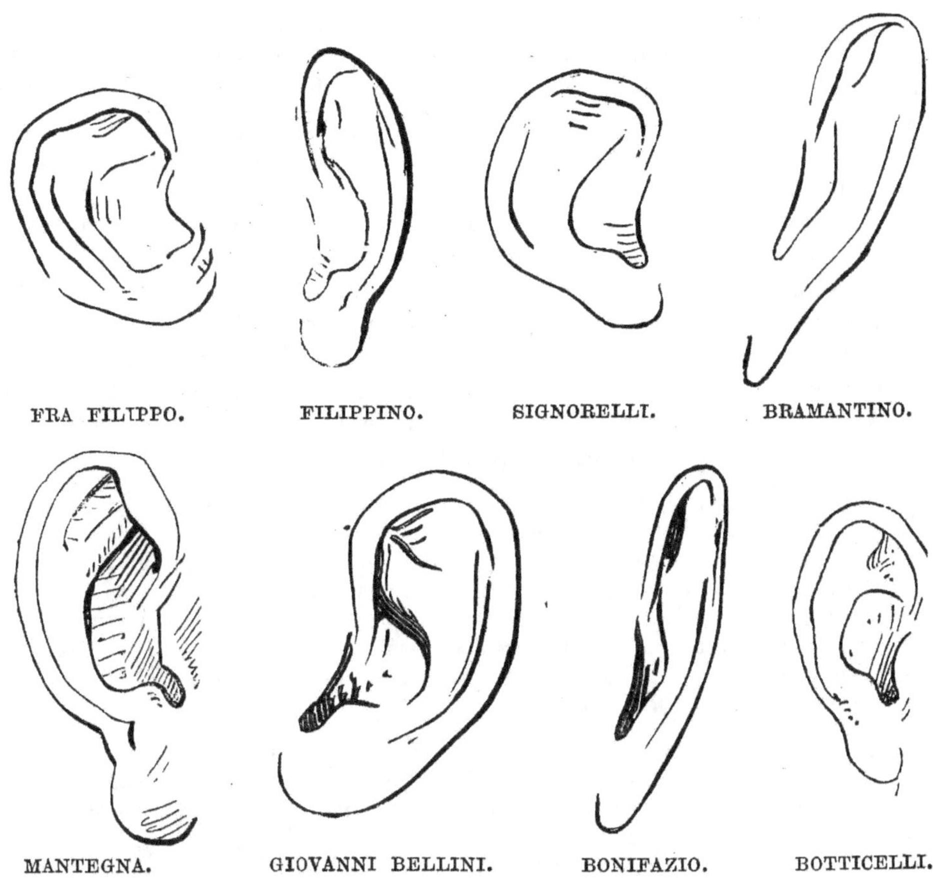

FIG. 1.1. 'Typical ears', from Giovanni Morelli, *Italian Painters: Critical Studies of their Works*, trans. by Constance Jocelyn Ffoulkes, 2 vols (London: J. Murray, 1892–93), I, 78.

with that name. But when Monfrey sees this second painting for himself, he realizes that it is a fake — a pastiche he created himself twenty-five years ago, on his first trip to Italy, in order to make a little money. The job done by the antiquarian who bought and treated it has been so convincing that this fake Quattrocento piece is read as genuine, and its similarities with the Cassandra portrait, which are easily explained by the fact that the young Monfrey had been inspired by the latter, only lend credence to its veneer of authenticity. Moreover, the 'signature' of Cristoforo is merely a partly effaced inscription into which Courmansel conveniently reads what he chooses, and which originally read 'P.X.T.F. RIUS M. PARISIENSIS', or '*Pinxit falsarius M... Parisiensis*', providing an ironic embedded confession of the painting's inauthenticity.[17] The most flagrant signs of inauthenticity are thus overlooked in order to read the fake as genuine, while the Cassandra portrait is a genuine Leonardo but is read as a fake. And like the mythical Cassandra, Monfrey himself is doomed forever to speak the truth and never be believed. Everyone around him has too much riding on the attribution of both paintings to Cristoforo — whether it be financial investment, scholarly reputation, or personal honour — to want to take his multiple confessions seriously. Courmansel in particular is quite simply blinded to the truth of the matter by his naive faith in the Morellian method, which Bourget represents as an absurd positivistic cult: 'Quand on a La Méthode [...] on est assuré de ne pas se tromper' [when one has The Method [...], one is sure not to be mistaken] (*D*, p. 38).

Bourget's plot turns on one of the most gaping holes in the Morellian system: one cannot attribute paintings to a given artist based on shared features unless one has, as a starting-point for these attributions, a work whose authorship is incontestable. If the starting-point is itself a fake, as Monfrey's painting is, then the whole series of attributions based around it will be incorrect. Bourget also takes issue, via Monfrey, with this approach on the grounds that it privileges the signifying detail over the global experience of the work of art, and an analytic, 'scientific', or erudite gaze over the engagement of the imagination and the pleasure of the senses:

> Critiquer une toile, au lieu d'en jouir, comme vous, comme moi, avec ses sens, son imagination, sa rêverie, tout son être intime enfin, c'est l'anatomiser, c'est la disséquer ligne par ligne, grain par grain. Puis commence, pour vérifier son origine et son histoire, un patient travail de bureaucrate, une vie de rat de bibliothèque, des semaines de fouilles dans des paperasses, des établissements de dossiers, des expertises d'écriture lettre par lettre, point à point, d'indéfinies comparaisons avec des photographies. Que sais-je? Le tout pour aboutir à une date incertaine et à un nom contestable! (*D*, pp. 36–37)

> [Critiquing a painting, instead of enjoying it as you and I do, with our senses, our imagination, our reverie, with all our intimate selves, amounts to anatomizing it, dissecting it line by line, mark by mark. Then, in order to verify its origin and history, one embarks on a patient labour of bureaucracy, the life of a bookworm, weeks of searching through papers, establishing files, getting expert opinions on handwriting, going through letter by letter, point by point, endlessly comparing with photographs. What do I know? All of this in order to arrive at an uncertain date and a questionable name!]

The connoisseur's gaze rips apart the cherished work of art, dismembering it in order to analyse its individual constituents, ignoring the global effect of the whole. The connoisseur's bureaucratic work is seen as alien to the genuine aesthetic experience of 'vous et moi' — Monfrey and his educated, art-loving partner, who stand here as the 'real' connoisseurs. The Morellian method is portrayed as reductive, arid, and pseudo-scientific, and is associated elsewhere in the text with Germanic pedantry and barbarism: Courmansel seems to Monfrey to represent 'le type accompli du Français germanisé' [the perfect example of a Germanized Frenchman] (*D*, p. 34), and he comments that he is 'digne d'enseigner l'esthétique à Kœnigsberg ou à Tubingue, chez les Barbares' [worthy of teaching aesthetics in Königsberg or Tübingen, in Barbarian country] (p. 45).[18] In this respect, *La Dame qui a perdu son peintre* is one example of a broader mapping of aesthetic issues onto national tensions in early twentieth-century art fiction, echoing both Mauclair's *La Ville lumière* and Georges-Michel's *Les Montparnos*, which will be examined in Chapter 2. Like these authors, Bourget implicitly identifies authentic art, and authentic ways of responding to art, with 'Latin' culture, and especially with Italy, while the art and the art-critical positions associated with Germany represent an aberration, an insult to real aesthetic experience.[19]

As Saisselin notes, Italy around the turn of the century stood as 'a refuge, an enchanting ivory tower, sheltered from the modern — New York and its vulgar multimillionaires, Paris and its fashions, and industrial, brutal, dynamic America'.[20] For Monfrey (as for the art collector Bourget himself), Italy represents precisely this kind of safe haven — a country in which an idealized past is still accessible, in which 'les habitants gardent un instinct de durer et de faire durer que l'exécrable manie d'être au courant, dont meurt l'Europe, ne détruira pas de sitôt' [the inhabitants retain an instinct for survival and preservation; the craze for being up-to-date, which is killing Europe, won't destroy this any time soon] (D, p. 78). And yet this safe haven is also coming under threat, the false portrait (which is held to be genuine) standing in parallel with a fake Italy designed to appeal to tourists. The connoisseur must therefore seek out the 'real' Italy, away from the tourist trail, and Monfrey does exactly this, explaining his decision to visit Milan by the fact that the average tourist passes it by: 'Et puis, quels trésors d'art, moins déflorés que ceux de Rome, de Florence et de Venise!' [And then, what treasures of art, unsullied compared to those of Rome, Florence and Venice!] (p. 10). Here Milan and its art are equated to a 'virgin' territory, untarnished by the gaze of the grubby masses. What this statement reveals is a conception of authenticity that is closely bound up with exclusivity. It is not enough for the connoisseur to have aesthetic experiences; rather, he must mark out his 'distinction' from the common herd of spectators by having aesthetic experiences to which others do not have access, which are reserved only for a select, enlightened few. Those experiences that are available to a wide audience — the purchase and contemplation of a mass-produced ornament, or a visit to a well-trodden tourist site — are, by virtue of their popularity, also vulgar, tainted by the stain of consumerism, and therefore less valuable. Given this emphasis on the appreciation of art as an elite activity, one further reason why Bourget objected to the Morellian method may have been its apparently democratic, open character: anyone, in principle (even a young upstart like Courmansel, of humble provincial origins) can learn Morelli's principles and thereby establish himself as an expert.[21]

We have seen, then, that authenticity is associated with Italy, and more specifically with a 'pure' Italy identified with the 'untouched' female body; it is also associated with the unassuming and undemanding artist's companion of the nineteenth-century art novel, 'une simple grisette logée en garni et trottant à pied, mais passionnée et naturelle' [a simple girl living in a rented room and getting about on foot, but passionate and natural] (D, p. 9). Like the 'real' Italy, however, the grisette is registered as a nostalgic figure, no longer at home in a world in which truth and falsehood have been lost as stable values. More representative of this modern world is the fake aristocrat Kennedy, an American industrialist, embodiment of the brave new capitalist order, who has adopted a title, and a crest, simply because it takes his fancy, as if these markers of aristocratic distinction were up for sale, like any other commodity. While this may be a caricature, and Kennedy's attempts at obtaining some of the cultural capital of the aristocrat via his consumption of high art may be laughable, this character does nevertheless bespeak a number of deep-seated anxieties. One of these concerns the foreign raid on Italian art at the turn of the century: the idea that a sacred 'Latin' artistic heritage may be pillaged by an unworthy foreign other. Another of these anxieties is about social order and readability: after all, if one can, in principle, buy the markers of socio-cultural distinction — if one can adopt the superficial trappings of the aristocrat — then to what extent is it possible to say with certainty who is 'real' and who is 'fake'?

While Kennedy is an obvious fake and as such does not truly undermine the principle of legibility, this issue resurfaces in a more insidious and worrying form with regard to various other characters in the novel, many of whom adopt a 'physionomie de poker' [poker face] (*D*, p. 92) which means that their outward appearance no longer functions as a transparent sign of their social or psychological identity. Just as the Morellian method attempts, and ultimately fails, to read paintings via bodily or physiognomical details that purport to reveal the truth of the artist's identity, Monfrey's own narrative readings of the people around him are constantly subject to doubt. He consistently identifies Varegnana, Kennedy, Courmansel, and others in terms of 'types', and justifies his confidence in these readings through the fact that he is a portraitist whose artistic currency is physiognomy, that distinctively nineteenth-century art of classifying people on the basis of their outward appearances: 'On ne devient pas un portraitiste professionnel, sans développer en soi un goût de la nature humaine qui doit être, j'imagine, celui des vrais romanciers' [One does not become a professional portrait painter without developing a taste for human nature which must, I imagine, be shared by true novelists] (p. 45). Here Bourget establishes a parallel between portraiture and the novel: both involve attention to the external details — the distinguishing mark, the unconscious gesture, the 'allure' — that betray character. But if Morelli's reading of the painted body is open to doubt, so is that of the portraitist and of the author or narrator: physiognomy is, at best, a broad clue to the identity of others, and at worst totally misleading — capable of being faked, or indeed of leading us off in the wrong interpretative direction, as is the case with the 'physionomie bien française' [truly French physiognomy] of the model in Monfrey/Cristoforo's portrait, whom we know to be Italian (p. 72).

The crisis of authenticity represented in *La Dame qui a perdu son peintre* thus extends well beyond the visual arts, and into the domain of narrative itself, ultimately leading us to question the very premises of the psychological novel, of which Bourget was the most famous proponent. Just as it is unclear whether anyone is able to say with any certainty who a painting is by, it is also unclear whether anyone is able to say who the people around them are — to get under their skin, to their true identity and character. Bourget adds further layers which place the reader in doubt as to the authenticity of his narrative: the novella's preamble queries whether the manuscript is really the work of Monfrey or of his lover, while the mixture of real and fictional details (the fictional portrait of Cassandra by Leonardo, versus a host of other verifiable art historical details) works to place us in an uncertain territory between fact and fiction. When truth and falsehood, fact and fiction, are so consistently confused, and authenticity vanishes as a stable epistemological concept, the reader (or spectator) can only respond by jettisoning these criteria and locating aesthetic value elsewhere. This is the position adopted in Bourget's novella by Boudron, a former painter who abandoned his art to become a successful fashion designer, and now, in his retirement, has become an art collector, guided by Courmansel, his future son-in-law. He tells Monfrey about his approach to painting:

> Je ne suis qu'un commerçant, mais j'aime les tableaux pour eux-mêmes, parce qu'ils sont beaux, comme on aime les fleurs, les femmes, la musique, le vin, tout ce qui exalte, tout ce qui grise. George [Courmansel] aime les tableaux comme un botaniste aime les plantes, pour les mettre dans ses herbiers et les étiqueter. Mon système est le bon. Qu'il soit de Léonard ou de Cristoforo, le portrait Varegnana n'en est ni plus admirable, ni moins. (*D*, pp. 51–52)

> [I am just a businessman, but I love paintings for themselves, because they are beautiful, as one loves flowers, women, music, wine — all that exalts, all that intoxicates. George [Courmansel] loves paintings like a botanist loves plants: he wants to put them in a herbarium and classify them. My system is the right one. Whether it's by Leonardo or Cristoforo, the Varegnana portrait is neither more or less admirable]

Boudron's stated view is that one must learn to appreciate the work of art for its own sake, disregarding the question of attribution completely, and reinstating the aesthetic experience itself as a criterion of authentic art. And yet this apparently disinterested, somewhat naive claim for pure sensuous enjoyment is undercut, a moment later, by Boudron jumping to defend the authenticity of a painting by Giovanni Bellini in his collection, and later hesitating to buy the Cristoforo due to doubts about its authorship. Despite his show of disinterested, pure connoisseurship, he is after all a 'commerçant', a bourgeois concerned to protect his investments.

Who or what, then, is the real connoisseur for Bourget? In his *Essais de psychologie contemporaine*, Bourget had reflected on the phenomenon of collecting, and the omnipresence of the bibelot in the nineteenth-century interior, as part of his examination of the life and writing of the Goncourt brothers. Amongst his key complaints about the bibelot, alongside the chaotically eclectic decors to which it gives rise and the way in which it seems to correspond to characteristically decadent mental pathologies, is its very popularity. The problem, for Bourget, is that everyone collects these mass-produced art objects, and that they may be found everywhere: in the doctor's waiting room, at the student bar, at the stationer's shop, at one's friends' houses. As such, the bibelot cannot function as a mark of distinction or of an artistic personality; indeed, the craze has spread even to 'ceux que l'œuvre d'art laisse indifférents et qui ne possèdent pas la fortune nécessaire à une acquisition de quelque valeur. La contrefaçon et le bon marché s'emparent de cette passion générale, pour l'exploiter' [those left indifferent by the work of art and who do not have the means necessary to acquire anything of value. Counterfeiting and cheap production seize on this general passion, in order to exploit it].[22] Particularly notable here is the way in which Bourget superimposes terms of aesthetics and of commerce: those who are indifferent to art are one and the same as those who cannot afford genuine art objects; fake or inauthentic art ('la contrefaçon') is, to Bourget's mind, as bad as cheap art ('le bon marché'). The implication is that authentic art, and authentic aesthetic experience, are the preserve of a select few — specifically, a wealthy social elite, able not only to afford to visit the 'real' Italy or to buy an original Old Master, but in possession of the cultural capital that valorizes these activities and enables one to set about pursuing them.

This takes us back to the insistence on exclusivity in *La Dame qui a perdu son peintre*, which gives rise to a similarly elitist vision of connoisseurship. Indeed, Dominique Pety has argued that this aesthetic elite, if not represented by the bourgeois 'parvenu' Boudron, may be represented instead by the nobleman Varegnana, 'l'aristocrate collectionneur, qui affirme sa supériorité en vertu d'une pratique plus ancienne et partant plus authentique, fondée sur d'autres valeurs que le savoir ou la mode. La collection est chez lui un héritage et une tradition, elle partage son cadre de vie, elle est chargée d'une histoire familiale' [the aristocratic collector, who affirms his superiority through a long-standing and thus more authentic practice, based on values other than erudition or fashion. Collecting is, for him, a heritage and a tradition, it is a part of his day-to-day life, and is laden with family history].[23] Varegnana is indeed a reassuring figure, a 'personnage d'ancien régime' [an old world character] (*D*, p. 126) removed from the pressures and uncertainties of the modern capitalist world, and living in close proximity to the works in his collection, inherited from earlier generations, rather than treating them as objects to be bought and sold. And yet, although Pety suggests that the aristocratic collector's expertise is guaranteed by his innate sense of 'le beau', Varegnana is in fact far from an ideal connoisseur.[24] At the end of the novella, Monfrey reflects on the fact that Varegnana was so easily taken in by Courmansel's theoretical postures, and that his artistic barometer has turned out to be so unreliable:

> Je me rends compte qu'au fond, tout au fond, ce possesseur de tant de merveilles n'est qu'un amateur. Il n'a jamais tenu le crayon et le pinceau. Devant une toile ou une statue, il n'a pas cette intuition de l'outil, qui ne s'apprend que par la pratique. Je vois distinctement, moi, un Titien et un Raphaël, un Mantegna et un Longhi travailler, broyer leurs couleurs sur leur palette, attaquer leur tableau. Pour employer une locution vulgaire, mais très juste, je sais comment c'est fait. (*D*, p. 128)

> [I have realized that deep down, this owner of so many miraculous works is just an amateur. He has never held a pencil or a paintbrush. Faced with a painting or a statue, he lacks an intuitive sense of the artist's tools, which can only be learned through practice. I, on the other hand, can distinctly see a Titian, a Raphael, a Mantegna or a Longhi working, mixing their colours on the palette, attacking the canvas. To use a vulgar but apt phrase, I know how it's made]

The ideal connoisseur, then, is not Varegnana, but Monfrey himself. As an artist, Monfrey is uniquely qualified to assess the work of art because of a certain bodily response to it: 'cette intuition de l'outil'. He is able to imagine himself into the bodily movements of the artist executing the work, an idea which echoes Bourget's discussion of aesthetic experience in the *Essais de psychologie contemporaine*, where he speaks of the spectator recreating 'l'état du cœur où vécut l'artiste' [the state of mind of the artist] and experiencing the work 'par le dedans, comme elle a été produite' [from the inside, as it was produced].[25] The physiognomy of the Morellian method, which reads painted bodily signs as indexes of the artist's identity, is replaced here by a different kind of bodily language, one in which the receptive spectator is able to feel himself into the artist's gestures, responding imaginatively and kinaesthetically to the art object.

The elite of genuine art lovers or connoisseurs which Bourget imagines does not, therefore, correspond exactly to a particular social class. High bourgeois or aristocrat, the connoisseur is marked out above all by his intimate acquaintance with artistic practice, which enables him to engage fully with the work of art.[26] This, for Bourget, is what makes the Goncourts genuine connoisseurs: having trained as artists, their writing on art attests to 'une entente pénétrante et quotidienne du métier, une fréquentation, non pas superficielle, mais profonde et de toutes les heures, avec l'objet d'art' [a penetrating daily grasp of the artist's task; a contact — not superficial, but profound and enduring — with the art object]. And as collectors, they avoid the superficiality of the bourgeois collector who adorns his interior with objects to amuse the eye, collecting 'non point par élégance, ou par mode, ou par intérêt, mais par un invincible et profond besoin de leur être' [not for the sake of elegance, fashion, or self-interest, but because of a profound, irresistible need inside them].[27] For Bourget, then, to appreciate art, to become a genuine connoisseur, one needs to be an artist — or at least to approach this, possessing an artistic sensibility. Proust's message seems to be the converse: in order to become an artist, one must first learn the rudiments of connoisseurship.

Proust's Art of Looking

Just as for Bourget art collecting is a fraught terrain which confronts the old aristocracy with the wealthy bourgeois elite, Proust's *À la recherche du temps perdu* represents the consumption of art as very much bound up with changing social conditions around the turn of the century. Proust's sweeping narrative is concerned partly with the demise of the aristocracy as a clearly delineated social category, and with the rise of the bourgeoisie within a capitalist order that not only blurs traditional class distinctions, but also (as we have already noted) turns art into a commodity. Where patronage of the arts had once been the preserve of the nobility, in the newly socially mobile *fin de siècle* world of Proust's novel, art is bought and sold often not for the sake of aesthetic pleasure, but as a convenient way of ensuring one's 'distinction'.[28] Bourgeois and aristocrat alike need art to cement their social standing: as Malcolm Bowie puts it, in Proust, 'art is a weapon in the salon wars'.[29] This instrumentalization of works of art leads us to question what genuine connoisseurship might consist in: how do we pick out the real connoisseurs, those who enjoy authentic aesthetic experiences, and who know how to look at the work of art, from those who merely maintain an appearance of 'taste' because they are skilled at following fashion, and at manipulating the outward signs of an 'artistic' sensibility? In considering these questions, this section aims to bring out the ways in which Proust's novel might formulate an art of looking, instructing us on how (and how not) to be connoisseurs.

Of course, these issues around spectatorship are only one aspect of a broader treatment of art in Proust's novel. In his representation of artistic creation, Proust seems to recommend — via the painter Elstir — a model that one might broadly define as Impressionism, although it is not to be tied down to a particular painterly school defined in terms of rough brushwork or *plein-air* subject matter. Rather, what interests Proust is the basic idea of an art that seeks to capture the artist's raw impressions, stripping away the intellectual and cultural overlay that distorts this primitive experience of the world: he evokes Elstir's efforts to 'ne pas exposer les choses telles qu'il savait qu'elles étaient, mais selon les illusions optiques dont notre vision première est faite' [not to represent things as he knew them to be, but according to the optical illusions of our primitive vision]; to 'se dépouiller en présence de la réalité de toutes les notions de son intelligence' [to strip himself, when face to face with reality, of every intellectual notion].[30] Elstir's art thus gives the spectator access to his personal vision, his unique way of seeing the world. Looking at Elstir's paintings, Proust's narrator ('Marcel') declares:

> J'avais devant moi les fragments de ce monde aux couleurs inconnues qui n'était que la projection de la manière de voir particulière à ce grand peintre et que ne traduisaient nullement ses paroles. Les parties du mur couvertes de peintures de lui, toutes homogènes les unes aux autres, étaient comme les images lumineuses d'une lanterne magique laquelle eût été, dans le cas présent, la tête de l'artiste. (*RTP*, II, 712)

> [I had before me fragments of that world of unknown colours which was nothing less than the projection of this great painter's particular way of seeing, and which his words did not express at all. The parts of the wall covered with paintings by him, all unified, were like projections from a magic lantern which in this instance was the mind of the artist]

This Impressionist account of the work of art applies to other art forms beyond painting: Mme de Sévigné's writing, for instance, is cited as a literary equivalent to Elstir's technique (*RTP*, II, 14).[31] As such, part of the purpose of Proust's novel is to allow the reader to enter into the narrator's experience of the world, to 'see' his impressions — quite literally so, employing what Mieke Bal has called 'subterfuges' through which the visual is allowed to be present in the textual domain.[32] The visuality of Proust's novel is not our principal concern here, however: what is of more importance for the present analysis is the fact that within this almost solipsistic text, in which the narrator experiences many of the other characters (especially Albertine) as profoundly unknowable, art provides the only surefire way of communicating, of getting inside someone else's head, as Proust puts it: all one has to do to get inside Elstir's head — to his very soul — is to *look* at his paintings.

But looking, as it turns out, is not as straightforward as all that. Many of Proust's characters fail to look at works of art, either because they do not know how, or because in an artistic economy that sees the art object primarily as status symbol, as an object of pseudo-intellectual chatter, the importance of looking — of consuming with the eyes rather than the wallet — has fallen by the wayside. The Verdurins, for instance, although they are known for their 'artistic' salon, seldom really look at their art: it is merely there in the background, like the view from the windows of their summer residence, which justifies its high price but is never directly contemplated. Not only art objects but also artists themselves are treated as commodities, 'le peintre qui avait alors leur faveur' [the painter who was then in favour] being an essential token presence at their gatherings, invited to shore up their idea of themselves as aesthetes (*RTP*, 1, 197). The aristocratic Guermantes scarcely fare any better: when the narrator asks M. de Guermantes whether he saw Vermeer's *View of Delft* on his visit to the museum at The Hague, his response is revealing:

> Le duc était moins instruit qu'orgueilleux. Aussi se contenta-t-il de me répondre d'un air de suffisance, comme chaque fois qu'on lui parlait d'une œuvre d'un musée, ou bien du Salon, et qu'il ne se rappelait pas: 'Si c'est à voir, je l'ai vu!' (*RTP*, 11, 813)

> [The Duke was less erudite than arrogant. He thus contented himself with replying in a complacent tone, as was his habit whenever anyone spoke to him of a picture in a gallery, or at the Salon, which he did not remember: 'If it's to be seen, I've seen it!']

This suggests not only that M. de Guermantes paid the paintings little attention, but also that the experience of seeing them is of less value to him than the ability to say that he has seen them, or to vaunt his cultural knowledge at the dinner table. This is borne out by his wife's injunction to the narrator:

> 'Comment! vous avez fait le voyage de Hollande et vous n'êtes pas allé jusqu'à Haarlem? s'écria la duchesse. Mais quand même vous n'auriez eu qu'un quart d'heure, c'est une chose extraordinaire à avoir vue, que les Hals. Je dirais volontiers que quelqu'un qui ne pourrait les voir que du haut d'une impériale de tramway sans s'arrêter, s'ils étaient exposés dehors, devrait ouvrir les yeux tout grands.' Cette parole me choqua comme méconnaissant la façon dont se forment en nous les impressions artistiques, et parce qu'elle semblait impliquer que notre œil est dans ce cas un simple appareil enregistreur qui prend des instantanés. (*RTP*, 11, 813)

> ['What! You've been to Holland and you didn't go to Harlem?', cried the Duchess. 'But even if you just had a quarter of an hour to spare, those Halses are an extraordinary thing to have seen. I don't mind saying that someone who glimpsed them from the top of a tram without stopping, supposing they were exhibited outside, should really open up his eyes.' This remark shocked me as revealing a misconception of the way in which our artistic impressions are formed in us, and because it seemed to imply that our eye is in that case a simple recording device which takes snapshots]

For Mme de Guermantes, art is 'une chose extraordinaire à *avoir vue*': the present-tense experience of the spectator confronted with the painting in all its material splendour is displaced here by the fact of having seen it, and by the snapshot-like memory of the painting that supports superficial knowledge of the kind one can show off in polite company. Art for the Guermantes is to be viewed at high speed, almost in passing: art for the narrator, in contrast, is the object of close, prolonged contemplation.

As Janell Watson has argued, alongside the breakdown of the remnants of an *Ancien Régime* social hierarchy, Proust depicts the breakdown of the cultural assumptions that supported that hierarchy: while Marcel expects the Guermantes to have the innate artistic sensibility that is supposed to go hand-in-hand with their aristocratic pedigree, it turns out to be the bourgeois characters who have superior taste. Watson cites as an example of this the encounter between the bourgeois Mme Verdurin and the aristocratic Mme de Cambremer: 'the former collects antiques and art objects which the latter misunderstands, preferring her own bourgeois decor. Madame Verdurin understands the "cultural capital" of artistic taste, effectively using it to proclaim her "distinction." These signs are lost on Madame de Cambremer'.[33] If art is indeed a weapon in the salon wars, then bourgeois consistently wins out over aristocrat. And yet it is not quite right to say that Mme Verdurin has better taste than Mme de Guermantes or Mme de Cambremer: she might, as Watson suggests, be skilled at manipulating the outward signs of an artistic sensibility, choosing the art objects that best convey a sense of her socio-cultural 'distinction'. But this does not necessarily imply that she appreciates the objects in question. There is in Proust an emptying-out of the notion of taste, which implies a bodily response or a sensuous engagement; this engagement with the work of art is replaced with a cynical manipulation of art objects as signs. As such, what is called 'taste' seems to amount to no more than fashion sense — as is seen in Mme de Guermantes's fluctuating attitudes towards the Empire style of decoration, or to Elstir's paintings, which she adores or detests according to whether their cultural stock is high at a given moment. Proust's narrator concludes that the aesthetic judgements of high society rest on '[un] néant de goût véritable' [a negation of true taste], and that the problem is that in all of their aesthetic pontifications one can find 'aucune impression vraiment sentie' [no genuinely felt impression] (*RTP*, ii, 571): Proust's consumers of art bypass the impression — the act of looking — as the basis of their aesthetic judgements.

In some cases, spectatorship never takes place because the spectator is simply not willing to look at the type of art in question. Mme de Cambremer, who is enthusiastically proclaimed to be 'si hartthhisstte!' [so harttissttick!] by her mother-in-law (*RTP*, iii, 218), is only interested in modern art, and dismisses as a matter of course anything she perceives to be old-fashioned — Poussin being singled out as 'le plus barbifiant des raseurs' [the deadliest of bores] (iii, 206). Mme de Villeparisis occupies the other end of the spectrum, being interested only in those paintings inherited through her own family and whose provenance can be traced: 'Elle ne voulait pas entendre parler des tableaux achetés on ne sait comment par un Crésus, elle était d'avance persuadée qu'ils étaient faux et n'avait aucun désir de les voir' [She would not hear a word about paintings bought, heaven knows in what circumstances, by a Croesus; she was convinced in advance that they were fakes, and had no desire to see them] (ii, 68–69). Faced with a new capitalist order in which any old rubbish may be passed off as art by unscrupulous dealers, and in which any 'parvenu' may buy it, Mme de Villeparisis responds by restricting her definition of the 'authentic' to the heirlooms that fill the domestic interiors of the aristocracy.

As Susan Stewart has argued, if the function of a souvenir is to serve as a trace of authentic experience, setting up a narrative of origins that connects the owner to this experience, then the purpose of an heirloom is to set up a narrative of family origins, or a genealogy.[34] An heirloom bears testament to a historical event (or figure), and to a family's connection to that event; Mme de Villeparisis's inherited paintings, depicting the duchesse de Montmorency, or the duchesse de la Rochefoucauld, speak of a long and noble lineage and a close relationship to the most prominent figures of French history. The baron de Charlus similarly revels in the privileged relationship between his art objects and history, pointing out to the narrator the 'jolies choses' [pretty things] in his apartment which include 'le portrait de mes oncles, le roi de Pologne et le roi d'Angleterre, par Mignard' [the portrait of my uncles, the King of Poland and the King of England, by Mignard], and his collection of hats worn by Marie-Antoinette, her sister and the princesse de Lamballe (*RTP*, II, 850). Like Mme de Villeparisis, Charlus particularly values 'ces tableaux anciens dont on sait l'histoire, depuis le Pape ou le Roi qui les commandèrent, en passant par tels personnages auprès de qui leur présence, par don, achat, prise ou héritage, nous rappelle quelque événement ou tout au moins quelque alliance d'un intérêt historique' [old paintings whose history is known, from the Pope or King who commissioned them, through the eminent figures whose acquisition of them, by gift, purchase, conquest or inheritance, reminds us of some event or at least some alliance of historic interest] (II, 117). What is at stake in this kind of relationship to the work of art is not just the authenticity of the work itself (which is guaranteed by the fact that it has been in the family for generations) but the authenticity, or pedigree, of the beleaguered aristocracy. The owner of the art object enters a reciprocal relationship with it whereby he or she confers a genealogy on the object, and it in turn confirms his or her family's genealogy, its connection to France's noble history. As such, the aristocratic treatment of art as heirloom is just as instrumentalizing as any bourgeois practice of art consumption: it is just another use of the art object as a sign guaranteeing 'distinction', and indeed is one of the few ways that the dying nobility can mark themselves out from their bourgeois contemporaries. Crucially, this is a practice in which spectatorship — the act of looking at the work of art — is less important than the simple fact of material possession.

Of course, while Proust's narrator may criticize the modes of art consumption adopted by his high society acquaintances, he does not speak from a position of authority: time and time again, his own spectatorship is revealed to be flawed. All too often his preconceptions distort his experience of the work of art, meaning he does not see it for what it is — as is the case when he sees the actress La Berma perform. The same is true of the church at Balbec, where the narrator's high expectations inevitably mean disappointment; his 'incapacité de savoir regarder' [inability to look properly] (*RTP*, II, 21) is only alleviated when Elstir furnishes him with an alternative approach which allows him a 'way in' to the sculpted facade, telling him that he must read it as a 'Bible historiée' [illustrated Bible] (II, 196). With failed or faulty spectatorship afflicting even the narrator — at least in the early stages of the novel, before his artistic education is complete — the character of Charles Swann appears to be the sole bastion of true connoisseurship in Proust's fictional world. A collector himself, 'ayant toujours eu une "toquade" d'objets anciens et de peinture' [having always been crazy about antiques and paintings]

(I, 16), he is also something of an authority, and his primary activity seems to be advising aristocratic ladies on what to buy for their collections. His advice is invaluable not just in matters of 'taste', but, crucially, in judgements of authenticity, for the savvy collector would not want to be taken in by a forgery: as Odette says of Swann, 's'il était là c'est lui qui saurait vous dire si c'est authentique ou non. Il n'y a personne comme lui pour ça' [if he were here he would be able to tell you if it's authentic or not. There's no one like him for that] (I, 369–70). His identity as connoisseur is also given away by his monocle, which allows him to scrutinize the work of art in detail, by his preference for Botticelli over Bouguereau, and by his penchant for Vermeer, who was only just being rediscovered in the late nineteenth century, and on whom Swann is writing a study.[35] He is convinced that 'une *Toilette de Diane* qui avait été achetée par le Mauritshuis à la vente Goldschmidt comme un Nicolas Maes, était en réalité de Ver Meer' [a *Diana and her Companions* which had been purchased by the Mauritshuis at the Goldschmidt sale as a Nicholas Maes was in reality a Vermeer] (I, 347–48). So it is clear that he is the kind of scholar interested in questions of attribution and authentification: exactly the kind of question the Morellian school of criticism sought to address through attention to the distinctive bodily signs — the rendering of the ear, the hand or the nose — that give away the identity of the artist.

Proust would certainly have been familiar with Morelli's theories via Berenson's publications in the *Gazette des beaux-arts*,[36] and although he does not mention either critic by name, Swann's identity as connoisseur in the Morellian mould is arguably given away by his careful attention to bodily signs, or to the physiognomical markers that his real-life acquaintances share with figures represented in artworks.[37] Constantly on the lookout for 'des analogies entre les êtres vivants et les portraits des musées' [analogies between real people and portraits in museums] (*RTP*, I, 317), Swann takes pleasure in identifying the kitchen girl at Combray with Giotto's Charity, or Marcel's friend Bloch with Gentile Bellini's portrait of Mehmed II: 'Oh! c'est frappant, il a les mêmes sourcils circonflexes, le même nez recourbé, les mêmes pommettes saillantes. Quand il aura une barbiche ce sera la même personne' [Oh, it's quite striking: he has the same arched eyebrows, the same hooked nose, the same prominent cheekbones. When he has a little beard he'll be the same person] (I, 96). Notable here and elsewhere is the fact that these analogies are based on bodily details which Swann singles out as distinctive markers: the eyebrows, the cheeks, the nose. And this way of looking is carried through to Swann's love for Odette, which is grounded in her resemblance to Botticelli's Zipporah. Having noticed this resemblance, Swann sees Odette in terms of the work of art, not as a body so much as a representation of a body, and this way of seeing her suddenly makes her legible to him — she becomes:

> Un écheveau de lignes subtiles et belles que ses regards dévidèrent, poursuivant la courbe de leur enroulement, rejoignant la cadence de la nuque à l'effusion des cheveux et à la flexion des paupières, comme en un portrait d'elle en lequel son type devenait intelligible et clair. (*RTP*, I, 220)

> [A skein of beautiful, delicate lines which his eyes unravelled, following their curves and convolutions, relating the rhythm of the neck to the effusion of the

hair and the droop of the eyelids, as though in a portrait of her in which her
type was made clearly intelligible]

Swann's connoisseurial gaze rests on each feature in turn: the neck, the hair, the
eyelids are considered in isolation and yet are inseparable from the unity of the
drawn or painted 'portrait'. In this moment of connoisseurial spectatorship, Swann's
search for analogies between life and art is pushed to an extreme as a living woman
is reduced to an image, an enigmatic and unknowable creature to an easily legible
physiognomical 'type'. Indeed, Swann's connoisseurial appreciation of Odette-as-
artwork is very much bound up with an attempt to know her, to expose her past
and the inner workings of her psychology, and especially to seek out any giveaway
signs of infidelity. As he becomes more and more obsessed with Odette, Swann
engages in detective work on her past life in Nice, and Proust directly likens these
investigations to the work of the art historian:

> Il eût mis à reconstituer les petits faits de la chronique de la Côte d'Azur d'alors,
> si elle avait pu l'aider à comprendre quelque chose du sourire ou des regards —
> pourtant si honnêtes et si simples — d'Odette, plus de passion que l'esthéticien
> qui interroge les documents subsistant de la Florence du xve siècle pour tâcher
> d'entrer plus avant dans l'âme de la Primavera, de la bella Vanna, ou de la
> Vénus, de Botticelli. (*RTP*, 1, 308)

> [He would have devoted to the reconstruction of the petty details of social life
> on the Côte d'Azur in those days, if it could have helped him to understand
> something of Odette's smile and the look in her eyes — candid and simple
> though they were — as much passion as the aesthetician who ransacks the
> extant documents of fifteenth-century Florence in order to penetrate further
> into the soul of the Primavera, the fair Vanna or the Venus of Botticelli]

Just as the scholar looks for the historical documentation that might allow him to
penetrate into the 'soul' of the painted woman, Swann looks for the facts about
Odette's past that might allow him to read her bodily gestures (her smile, her gaze),
and thereby to uncover her true self. What he wants, ultimately, is to be able to
read bodily signs: his is a Morellian way of looking that treats the surface of the
body (painted or flesh) as a venue for 'clues' to identity, a type of physiognomy that
not only classifies humans into 'types' based on their outward characteristics, but
singles out the bodily detail in support of such classifications. As such, Swann's way
of looking is very much part of an epistemological paradigm which according to
the historian Carlo Ginzburg came to prominence in the late nineteenth century.
Ginzburg characterizes this as a 'conjectural or semiotic' approach, 'a paradigm or
model based on the interpretation of clues' — or, more simply put, as 'detective
work'.[38] Examples of this epistemological model include medical diagnosis, which
involves the reading of bodily symptoms (and it is significant in this regard that
Morelli was himself a trained medic); we might also mention psychoanalysis,
thinking in particular of the visual taxonomies of hysteria proposed by Jean-Martin
Charcot's *Nouvelle iconographie de la Salpêtrière*, which often single out the face, hands,
or feet as zones in which the signs of mental pathology can be read by the clinician
(Figure 1.2). One might also think of Freud's reading of giveaway bodily signs in
his essay on Michelangelo's *Moses*, where he in fact acknowledges the similarities

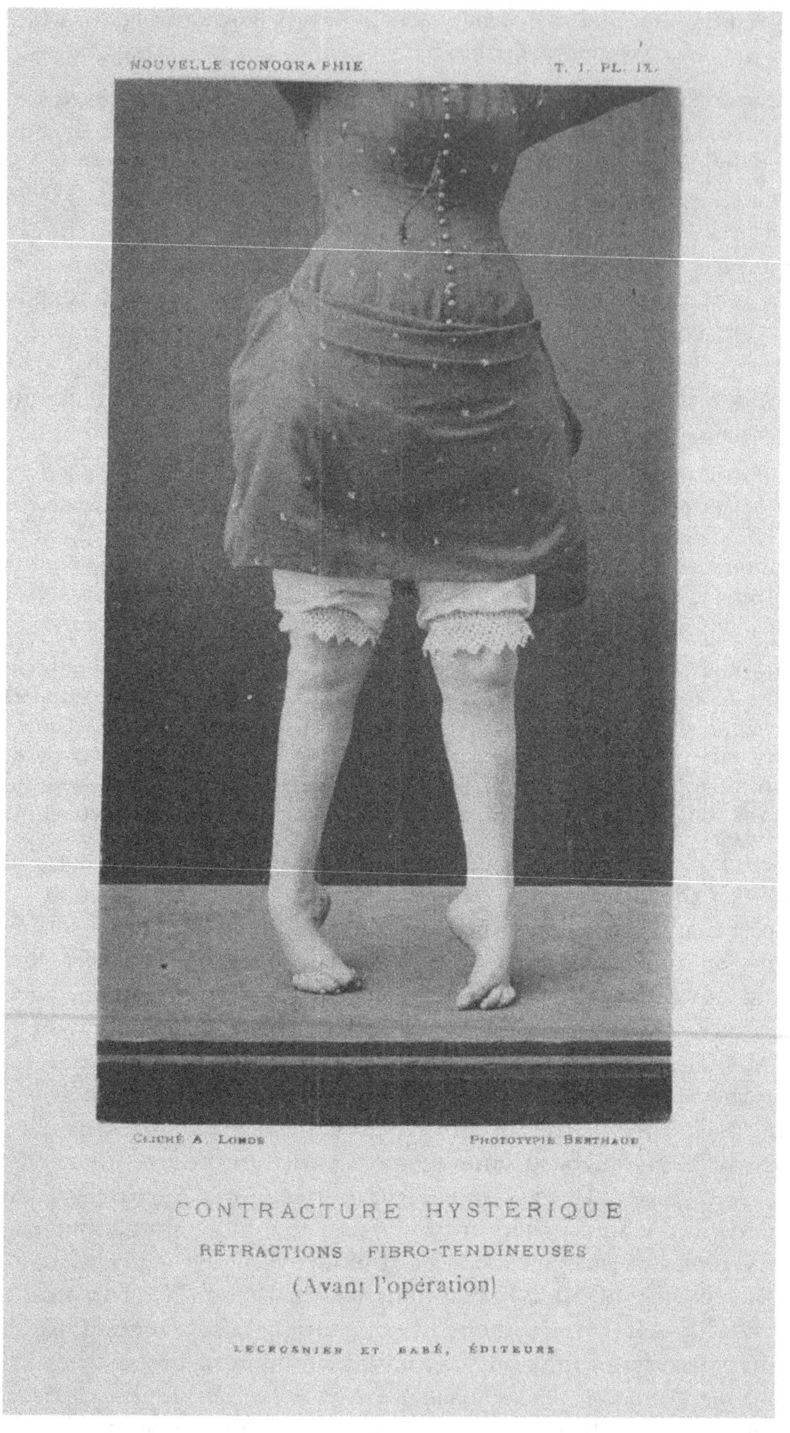

FIG. 1.2. 'Contractures hystériques', from J.-M. Charcot (ed.), *Nouvelle iconographie de la Salpêtrière*, 1 (1888). © The British Library Board, P.P.3137.E Vol. 1 Plate 9.

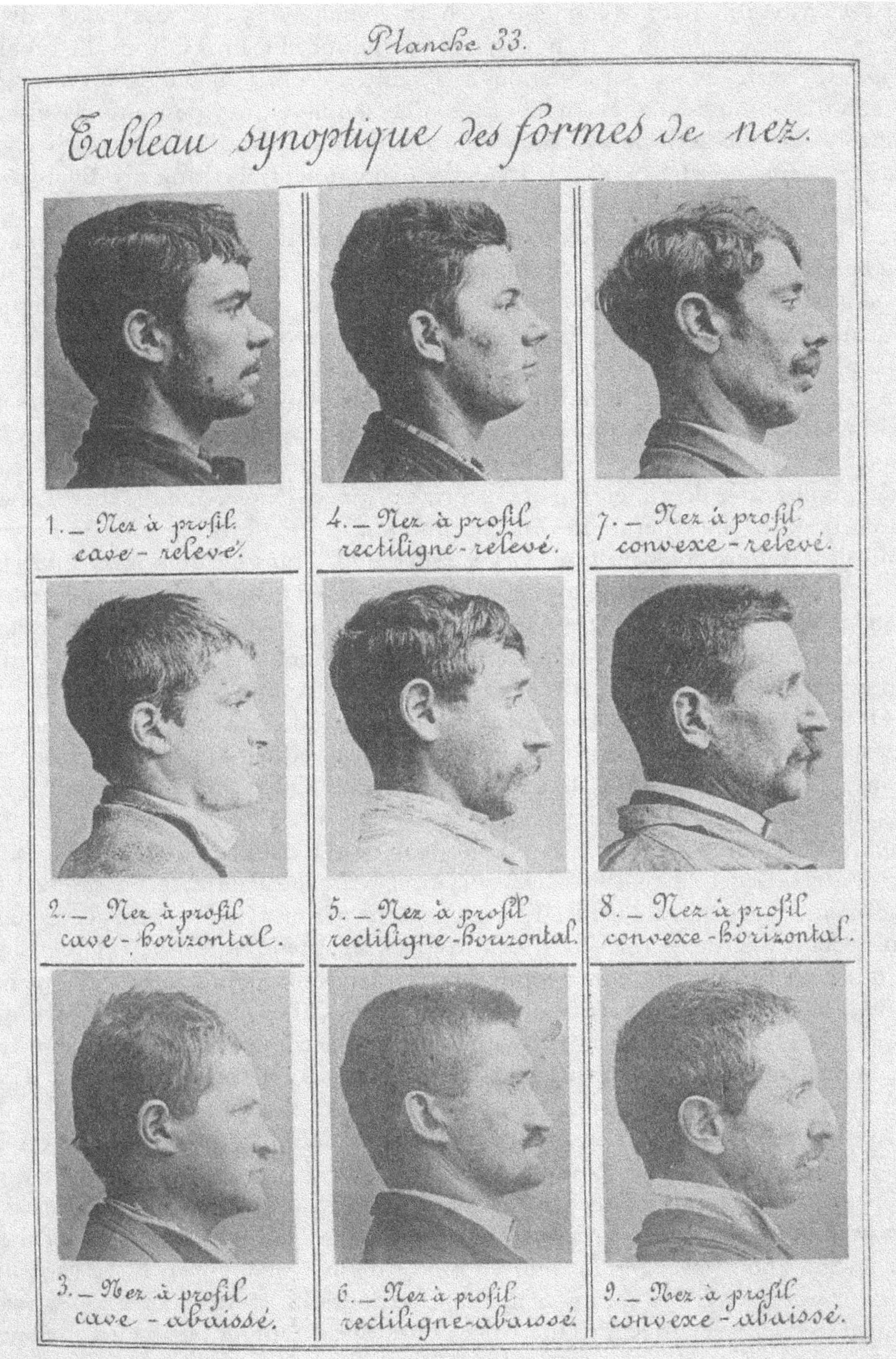

FIG. 1.3. From Alphonse Bertillon, *Identification anthropométrique: instructions signalétiques* (1893). © The British Library Board, 10008.ppp.31 Plate 33.

between Morelli's method and his own: both, Freud says, are 'accustomed to divine secret and concealed things from despised or unnoticed features, from the rubbish-heap, as it were, of our observations'.[39] Finally, one of Ginzburg's key examples — and the quintessential example of the nineteenth-century desire to classify and control — is the anthropometric system of Alphonse Bertillon, in which bodily features were measured and classified with the aim of allowing criminals to be identified (Figure 1.3).

Of course, the parallel between Bertillon's pages of body parts and Morelli's ears and hands is very clear, as Ginzburg notes. Moreover, for Ginzburg *À la recherche du temps perdu* is 'a rigorous example of the application of this conjectural paradigm'.[40] This mode of enquiry finds expression in Proust's novel not just in the figure of Swann, but also in the diagnostic gaze of his medical counterpart Cottard, who sees the outward signs of Albertine and Andrée's lesbianism where Marcel does not, and in Marcel himself, whose own connoisseurial gaze tends, like that of Swann, to pick out physiognomical 'analogies' between life and art, and often settles on the nose, his obsessive documenting of Gilberte's distinctive nose, and the 'bec d'oiseau' [bird's beak] of the Guermantes family, amongst others, forming a kind of textual equivalent to Bertillon's anthropometric crib sheets. This type of looking underpins Marcel's efforts to read those around him, to use their bodily features and gestures as indexes of their inner selves. His detective work on Albertine, as with Swann's detective work on Odette, is an attempt to read her body as a clue to her mind — and especially her sexual identity — and thereby to control her.

Over the course of *À la recherche,* however, we find this type of detective work repeatedly brought into question, as it turns out that bodily signs are not transparent: medical diagnosis fails, Marcel's gaydar is repeatedly shown to be deficient, and his protracted attempts to read, know, and thereby possess Albertine come to nothing. Moreover, Swann's authority as connoisseur is gradually eroded, his Morellian method revealed to be flawed by association with the failure of physiognomical reading more generally. That is, if Swann and the narrator cannot gain access to the inner identity of the people they seek to 'read' by attending to their bodily signs, then neither can the Morellian connoisseur's attention to the details of the painted body give access to the identity of the artist. If, as Gilles Deleuze has observed, *À la recherche* is primarily concerned with signs and learning to interpret them, then the bodily signifier — both in art and in reality — is one type of sign that Proust exposes as opaque, ambiguous, and impossible to 'read' with any certainty.[41]

As Richard Bales has noted, Swann's habit of looking for analogies between life and art is really little more than name-dropping: saying that the kitchen girl happens to share some bodily characteristics with Giotto's Charity shows that he has studied those characteristics closely, and that he has a clear memory of them, but it shows no further insight into Giotto or his art.[42] And even if the Morellian method were a reliable means of making attributions, it would remain a rather limited, reductive approach to the work of art. Swann might be able to attribute a painting to its author, to pick out the distinctive signs that guarantee a painting's attribution, but this can surely only get him so far, and for much of the novel it is unclear whether he is really able to enjoy or appreciate art. He seldom seems to make specifically aesthetic judgements: at Combray, when prompted by the narrator's great-aunts to express his own feelings about a painting, he is able to respond only with dry historical facts: 'il gardait un silence presque désobligeant et se rattrapait en revanche s'il pouvait fournir sur le musée où il se trouvait, sur la date où il avait été peint, un renseignement matériel' [he remained almost offensively silent and would then make amends by furnishing (if he could) some fact or other about the museum in which it was hung, or the date it had been painted] (*RTP*, I, 17). If he has any such thing as 'taste' (and we have already seen the extent to which Proust problematizes this notion), this is seen to fluctuate just as much as that of the most fashion-obsessed society hostess: one minute dismissing the restoration works of Viollet-le-Duc, he is keen to study them when he finds out that he may be able to see Odette at the same time (I, 288). Later on in the novel, his Dreyfusism is seen to cloud his literary judgement, becoming the sole criterion by which he judges works (II, 869–70), at the expense of their intrinsic aesthetic qualities. He never completes his monograph on Vermeer, perhaps because, aside from making and correcting attributions, he has little to say about his impressions of Vermeer's art or the qualities that make it great.

Of course, Proust's characters are mobile, their identities constantly shifting as they are glimpsed from different perspectives and at different points in their trajectories, and Swann is not always seen as an empty shell of a connoisseur. Elstir, in particular, views him as a privileged spectator of his work, along with M. Verdurin (whose capacities as art critic are only revealed at a very late stage in the novel): having received 'des leçons de goût de Whistler, des leçons de vérité de Monet, leur permettant de juger Elstir avec justice' [lessons in taste from Whistler, lessons in truth from Monet, allowing them to judge Elstir with justice], they are uniquely qualified to appreciate his art (*RTP*, IV, 349). Another intimation of Swann's true expertise comes when M. de Guermantes asks Swann for his opinion about a painting of one of his ancestors that he thinks may be attributed to Rigaud, Mignard, or even Velázquez: Swann responds by attributing it not to any of these 'grands pontifes' [great pontiffs], but 'À la malveillance!' [to malice] (II, 868). What this reveals is not only that Swann places the integrity of his judgement above flattery of the duke, but also, crucially, that he places aesthetic value above attribution: it matters little whether the painting is by Velázquez or anyone else, since it is quite simply awful. Here, then, we see Swann moving beyond the Morellian notion of authenticity, conceived as a relationship between a unique art object and its creator, towards a notion of authenticity grounded instead in aesthetic experience. This corresponds, furthermore, to Proust's own position in relation to issues of authenticity: as Gabrielle Townsend has observed, Proust habitually worked from reproductions of works of art, expressed a desire to buy copies of famous paintings, and was in general 'indifferent to the status of original works of art: reproductions and copies are just as desirable, because they fulfil the purpose of stimulating memory and imagination and are the starting point for reflections about memory, about beauty, about vision and representation'.[43] If a copy of a painting gives rise to a rich and authentic aesthetic experience, then it is, from this point of view, just as valuable as the original. Indeed, in 'Combray' Proust suggests that reproductions of works of art may be valuable in their own right since they present to the spectator 'plusieurs "épaisseurs" d'art' [several 'thicknesses' of art] (1, 40), the photograph or engraving of the original adding a supplementary layer of interpretation.

The many instances of flawed spectatorship in *À la recherche* work to build up an account of how *not* to look at the work of art, but it remains to be seen whether the novel also gives rise to a positive art of connoisseurship. Who or what is Proust's ideal connoisseur and how may we learn to look in an expert way at the work of art? As we have already seen (and at the risk of stating the obvious), the basis of real connoisseurship for Proust is the act of looking, and looking must be not only prolonged (as is the case when the narrator holds up dinner by his extended contemplation of the Guermantes' collection of Elstirs) but also solitary: like 'le travail solitaire de la création artistique' [the solitary labour of artistic creation] (*RTP*, II, 260), spectatorship is hindered by the distractions of conversation and social interaction, and Marcel comments that he only experienced pleasure at 'les belles choses [...] si j'étais seul, ou feignais de l'être et me taisais' [beautiful things [...] if I was alone, or pretended to be and remained silent] (III, 384). Moreover, as the foregoing discussion has demonstrated, the key tenet of Proust's art of looking is a reinstatement of the impression — the raw experience of seeing, liberated from preconceptions and expectations — as the basis of aesthetic experience. The impression is sensuous rather than intellectual; it involves an engagement with the materiality of the work of art that is self-sufficient, unlike the Morellian act of looking, which involves the application of a rigorous analytic framework. In this respect — and although it initially appears to be an example of overly naive, unintelligent spectatorship — the reaction of Elstir (or 'Biche', as he is known at the Verdurins' salon) to a contemporary's painting might be cited as a positive example of such engagement:

> 'Je me suis approché, dit-il, pour voir comment c'était fait, j'ai mis le nez dessus. Ah! bien ouiche! on ne pourrait pas dire si c'est fait avec de la colle, avec du rubis, avec du savon, avec du bronze, avec du soleil, avec du caca!
> [...]
> 'Ça sent bon, ça vous prend à la tête, ça vous coupe la respiration, ça vous fait des chatouilles, et pas mèche de savoir avec quoi c'est fait, c'en est sorcier, c'est de la rouerie, c'est du miracle (éclatant tout à fait de rire): c'en est malhonnête!' Et s'arrêtant, redressant gravement la tête, prenant une note de basse profonde qu'il tâcha de rendre harmonieuse, il ajouta: 'Et c'est si loyal!' (*RTP*, I, 250–51)

> ['I went up to one of them,' he began, 'just to see how it was done; I stuck my nose into it. Well, it's unbelievable! Impossible to say whether it was done with glue, with rubies, with soap, with bronze, with sunshine, with shit!
> [...]
> 'It smells good, it makes your head spin, it takes your breath away, you feel ticklish all over — and not the faintest clue as to how it's done. It's magic, a conjuring-trick, a miracle,' and bursting into outright laughter, 'it's almost dishonest!' And stopping, solemnly raising his head, pitching his voice on a *basso profundo* note which he struggled to bring into harmony, he added: 'And it's so sincere!']

Proust makes it clear that this is a performance, deliberately calculated to meet an audience's expectations: the painter is playing up to the role assigned to him within the salon gathering, and he is expected to get carried away, to respond to art in a naive, instinctive, and often crude fashion which corresponds to a vague Romantic notion of the artist as something of an outlaw in polite society. His response might also appear to make little sense: it is unclear how a work of art might be both 'malhonnête' and 'loyal'. And yet, the fact that Swann is the only one of the Verdurins' guests not to approve of this flight of fancy is revealing: Biche/Elstir's instinctive, sensuous experience of the work of art, his attention to its material *facture*, is something of which Swann (for the most part) seems utterly incapable. Elstir gets up close to the work of art, scrutinizes the very stuff it is made of, and this stuff prompts a primal, bodily response. Swann, in contrast, might get up close to the painting in order to focus on the detail, but the detail is read as signifying something beyond itself: for the Morellian connoisseur, it points beyond the work of art, to the identity of the artist.

The episode in which the writer Bergotte dies while viewing Vermeer's *View of Delft* is also instructive in connection with the more subjective, sensuous approach to the work of art that Proust's novel seems to recommend. Bergotte is alerted by a piece of art criticism to the presence, within Vermeer's painting, of an element he had previously overlooked: 'un petit pan de mur jaune [...] si bien peint qu'il était, si on le regardait seul, comme une précieuse œuvre d'art chinoise, d'une beauté qui se suffirait à elle-même' [a little patch of yellow wall [...], so well painted that it was, if one looked at it on its own, like a precious specimen of Chinese art, of a beauty that was sufficient in itself]. When he revisits the painting, his gaze is fixed on 'la précieuse matière du tout petit pan de mur jaune' [the precious material of the little patch of yellow wall]:

> Ses étourdissements augmentaient; il attachait son regard, comme un enfant à un papillon jaune qu'il veut saisir, au précieux petit pan de mur. 'C'est ainsi que j'aurais dû écrire, disait-il. Mes derniers livres sont trop secs, il aurait fallu passer plusieurs couches de couleur, rendre ma phrase en elle-même précieuse, comme ce petit pan de mur jaune.' (*RTP*, III, 692)

> [His dizziness increased; he fixed his gaze, like a child upon a yellow butterfly that it wants to catch, on the precious little patch of wall. 'That's how I ought to have written,' he said. 'My last books are too dry, I ought to have gone over them with several layers of colour, made my sentences precious in themselves, like this little patch of wall']

The central idea in this episode is that the very substance of the work of art — the written sentence, the painted 'pan' — may be aesthetically valuable, in and of itself. Spectatorship should therefore have at its centre a sustained focus on the material marks on the canvas. The way in which Proust's narrative gaze repeatedly returns to the 'pan', reiterating its yellow colour, and the key term 'précieux', throughout the passage, mimics this ideal act of spectatorship. As Georges Didi-Huberman has argued, the passage suggests that the 'petit pan de mur jaune' should be seen, first and foremost, as 'pan' and not as 'mur' — as a painted area of canvas rather than as a representation of something beyond itself.[44] Didi-Huberman frames this argument in terms of a broader objection to approaches to painting which either treat the work as a kind of *roman à clef* in which the significant detail offers up a solution to the work's meaning (as in Panofsky's iconography), or alternatively treat it simply as describing, quasi-photographically, a real-world referent (as Didi-Huberman accuses Svetlana Alpers of doing).[45] What these approaches have in common is that they read each element of the painting as a 'detail' that signifies something beyond itself — symbolic meaning or reference — and in doing so neglect to pay attention to the work's materiality. Proust, for his part, is certainly not arguing against figurative painting, and does not expect the spectator to ignore the fact that particular features of a painting are supposed to correspond to features of a represented scene; what he objects to is the kind of critical approach exemplified by the Morellian method, which reduces the painted detail to a 'clue' to be used in art-historical detective work, and in doing so fails to engage with it materially. This is a type of spectatorship that does not look *at* the painting but *past* it.

Of course, even if the raw impression of the material work of art is primordial within this account of spectatorship, Proust sets aside a role for the cultural knowledge that might inform our experience of the painting: after all, if he had not read any art criticism, Bergotte might not have seen the 'petit pan de mur jaune' at all; Swann and Verdurin would not have been able properly to appreciate Elstir's painting without the artistic education provided by Monet and Whistler, and the church at Balbec is incomprehensible to the narrator without the interpretative framework provided by Elstir. We do not come to the work of art free of all cultural baggage, and while Proust takes pains to emphasize that this baggage should not be allowed to get in the way of the impression itself, it might still play a role in a broader process of interpretation and understanding. This broader process also involves the spectator's analysis of his own impressions, as is made clear by a passage in *Le Temps retrouvé* in which Proust once again defines ideal spectatorship negatively, in opposition to that practised by what he calls 'les célibataires de l'art' [artistic celibates]: spectators whose experience of the work of art is ultimately sterile and unsatisfying because, while they have aesthetic impressions, they do not reflect on these:

> Aussi combien s'en tiennent là qui n'extraient rien de leur impression, vieillissent inutiles et insatisfaits, comme des célibataires de l'art! Ils ont les chagrins qu'ont les vierges et les paresseux, et que la fécondité ou le travail guérirait. Ils sont plus exaltés à propos des œuvres d'art que les véritables artistes, car leur exaltation n'étant pas pour eux l'objet d'un dur labeur d'approfondissement, elle se répand au dehors, échauffe leurs conversations, empourpre leur visage. Ils croient accomplir un acte en hurlant à se casser la voix: 'Bravo, bravo' après l'exécution d'une œuvre qu'ils aiment. Mais ces manifestations ne les forcent pas à éclaircir la nature de leur amour, ils ne la connaissent pas. (*RTP*, IV, 470)

> [And now many art lovers stop there, without extracting anything from their impression, and grow old useless and unsatisfied, like life-long artistic bachelors! They have the same sufferings as virgins and lazy people — sufferings which fecundity or work would cure. They get more excited about works of art than real artists do, because for them their excitement is not the object of a laborious and intimate study, but directs itself outwards, animates their conversations, makes them red in the face. They think they are doing their duty when at

the end of a concert they shout 'bravo, bravo' until they are hoarse. But these
demonstrations do not oblige them to clarify the nature of their admiration,
and of this they remain ignorant]

The genuine connoisseur, according to Proust, is rare because this type of looking
is hard work. It is not enough to look at the work of art, to have impressions, to feel
emotions; it is not enough to express these and to make the outward gestures that
denote aesthetic appreciation. Genuine appreciation involves delving into oneself
and seeking to uncover what it is about the work of art that touches one in that
particular way (as indeed Marcel does in those moments of felicity obtained not
just via the work of art, but in everyday life when his impressions seem to awaken
involuntary memory, to speak to something within him). It is about realizing that
great art does not only allow us to enter into the artist's vision of the world, and
thereby see the world differently: it also, crucially, tells us about ourselves.

In critiquing the detective work involved in Morellian art history, Proust also
provides an implicit critique of the kind of literary detective work to which,
somewhat ironically, his novel has been subjected. This is especially the case with
his treatment of the visual arts: scholars have been keen to find 'keys' or 'clues' to
the identity of the fictional painter Elstir (who might represent Monet or Whistler),
and possible models for the paintings Proust describes.[46] To focus on these factual
questions of reference is, we may surmise from Proust's art of looking, to miss the
point, to look past the work of art itself — beyond it, to its referents, its authors,
its contexts — rather than directly at it; or to stop short of it, as is the case with
Swann, who is said to remain 'en deça de l'art' [on this side of art] (*RTP*, II,
207). Connoisseurship or ideal spectatorship involves, for Proust, a direct sensual
engagement with the material work; at the same time, it also involves an inward
gaze, a reflection on one's own impressions. Confronted with a Morellian way of
looking that is scientific and analytic, that focuses on the signifying detail, and
that imposes a rigid framework on the act of looking, Proust, along with Bourget,
responds by recommending instead a way of looking that is impressionistic and
sensuous, that privileges instinct and the imagination over reason and intelligence.[47]
Neither text, however, presents a rigorous theory of spectatorship; nor are they
self-help manuals for the aspiring connoisseur. Bourget does not spell out how to
acquire artistic sensibility: it is simply something that artists, and some privileged
others, happen to have, a quality as mysterious as creative talent itself. (Indeed,
even if one could teach connoisseurship, one suspects that Bourget would be loath
to give away the secrets of his artistic elite.) Proust, similarly, stops short of telling
us how to set about examining our own aesthetic impressions. Indeed, one should
not be surprised to find that in a novel in which aesthetic experience is conceived
as profoundly and intimately personal, and 'le sens artistique' [the artistic sensibility]
is eventually defined as 'la soumission à la réalité intérieure' [submission to interior
reality] (IV, 461), the art of looking cannot be taught by numbers, and we are
ultimately left, as spectators, to the devices of our own subjectivity.

Notes to Chapter 1

1. See especially Janell Watson, *Literature and Material Culture from Balzac to Proust: The Collection and Consumption of Curiosities* (Cambridge: Cambridge University Press, 1999); Dominique Pety, 'Le Personnage du collectionneur au xixe siècle: de l'excentrique à l'amateur distingué', *Romantisme*, 112 (2001), 71–81; and Emma Bielecki, *The Collector in Nineteenth-Century French Literature: Representation, Identity, Knowledge* (Bern: Peter Lang, 2012).

2. Rémy G. Saisselin, *The Bourgeois and the Bibelot* (New Brunswick, NJ: Rutgers University Press, 1984).

3. Gee, *Dealers, Critics, and Collectors of Modern Painting*; for data on the price of contemporary art, see pp. 227–29.

4. Pierre Bourdieu, *La Distinction: critique sociale du jugement* (Paris: Minuit, 1979), pp. 309–21.

5. See Simone Francescato, *Collecting and Appreciating: Henry James and the Transformation of Aesthetics in the Age of Consumption* (Oxford: Peter Lang, 2010), p. 26.

6. See Saisselin, *The Bourgeois and the Bibelot*, p. 151.

7. Watson, *Literature and Material Culture*, pp. 58–65.

8. See especially Mieke Bal, *The Mottled Screen: Reading Proust Visually*, trans. by Anna-Louise Milne (Stanford, CA: Stanford University Press, 1997), and Thomas Baldwin, *The Material Object in the Work of Marcel Proust* (Bern: Peter Lang, 2005).

9. Bourget's collection is mentioned in Bernard Berenson's *Painters of the Italian Renaissance*, 3 vols (London: Phaidon, 1968), I, 505, as containing works by Beccafumi, Neroccio, and Sano di Pietro; it is also documented in Jean Aubert, 'À propos d'une acquisition du Musée de Chambéry: Paul Bourget, amateur d'art', in *Paul Bourget et l'Italie*, ed. by M.-G. Martin-Gistucci (Geneva: Slatkine, 1985), pp. 13–21.

10. Paul Bourget, 'La Pia' [1896] in *Voyageuses* (Paris: Nelson, n.d.), pp. 13–79; 'La Seconde Mort de Broggi-Mezzastris', in *La Dame qui a perdu son peintre* (Paris: Plon, 1910; fasc. repr. Elibron Classics, 2006), pp. 135–68.

11. Paul Bourget, *Sensations d'Italie (Toscane — Ombrie — Grande-Grèce)* (Paris: Lemerre, 1892), p. 38.

12. Bourget, *Sensations d'Italie*, p. 2.

13. Bernard Berenson, 'Amico di Sandro', *Gazette des beaux-arts*, 41 (1899), 459–71; 42 (1899), 21–36. Berenson published regularly in the *Gazette* between 1895 and 1902; see the bibliography in Ernest Samuels, *Bernard Berenson: The Making of a Connoisseur* (Cambridge, MA: Belknap Press, 1979), pp. 437–38. Saisselin argues that Bourget also represents Berenson in 'La Pia' in the figure of Bernard de la Nauve, a genteel wheeler-dealer who trades in art to supplement his dwindling fortune (*The Bourgeois and the Bibelot*, p. 135).

14. For a summary and discussion of Morelli's theory, see Richard Wollheim, 'Giovanni Morelli and the Origins of Scientific Connoisseurship', in *On Art and the Mind* (London: Allen Lane, 1973), pp. 177–201.

15. Cited in Samuels, *Bernard Berenson*, p. 213.

16. On Berenson's 'Amico' as fiction, see Jeremy Melius, 'Connoisseurship, Painting, and Personhood', in *Creative Writing and Art History*, ed. by Catherine Grant and Patricia Rubin, *Art History*, 34.2 (2011), 288–309.

17. Paul Bourget, *La Dame qui a perdu son peintre* (Paris: Plon, 1910; fasc. repr. Elibron Classics, 2006), p. 68. Subsequent references will be included in the main text, and hereafter referred to as *D*.

18. The association with Germany is no doubt based partly on the fact that Morelli had first published his treatise on Italian painters in German, as *Die Werke italienischer Meister* (1880), under the pseudonym Ivan Lermolieff; this was translated into English by Constance Jocelyn Ffoulkes as *Italian Painters: Critical Studies of their Works*, 2 vols (London: J. Murray, 1892–93). Bourget also associates pedantic art criticism with German culture at the end of 'La Seconde Mort de Broggi-Mezzastris', p. 168.

19. On Bourget's nationalist and conservative leanings, see Richard Hibbitt, 'Paul Bourget's Critique of *fin-de-siècle* Cosmopolitanism', in *The Cause of Cosmopolitanism*, ed. by Patrick O'Donovan and Laura Rascaroli (Bern: Peter Lang, 2011), pp. 173–87, and Yehoshua Mathias, 'Paul Bourget, écrivain engagé', *Vingtième siècle: revue d'histoire*, 45 (January–March 1995), 14–29.

20. Saisselin, *The Bourgeois and the Bibelot*, p. 99.

21. On the democratic character of Morelli's method, and elements of his conception of connoisseurship which undercut this, see Briefel, *The Deceivers*, pp. 55–64.

22. Paul Bourget, *Essais de psychologie contemporaine*, 2 vols (Paris: Plon, 1901), II, 138.

23. Pety, 'Le Personnage du collectionneur au XIXe siècle', p. 80.

24. The idea of innate aristocratic taste is also contested in Bourget's 'La Seconde mort de Broggi-Mezzastris', which features a philistine aristocratic collector.

25. Bourget, *Essais de psychologie contemporaine*, II, 136.

26. As Yehoshua Mathias argues ('Paul Bourget, écrivain engagé', p. 24) there is a distinction in Bourget's work between the 'bourgeoisie traditionnelle' and the bourgeois 'parvenu' or capitalist speculator: the latter, as in the case of Boudron, is unlikely to be a genuine connoisseur because his vision is clouded by his desire to cement his social position, and by his interest in financial gain.

27. Bourget, *Essais de psychologie contemporaine*, II, 134 & 139.

28. Edward J. Hughes has recently argued that Bourdieu's maxim 'Taste classifies, and it classifies the classifier' 'finds no more compelling literary instantiation than *Un amour de Swann*': *Proust, Class and Nation* (Oxford: Oxford University Press, 2011), p. 85.

29. Malcolm Bowie, *Proust Among the Stars* (London: Harper Collins, 1998), p. 70.

30. Marcel Proust, *À la recherche du temps perdu*, ed. by Jean-Yves Tadié, 4 vols (Paris: Gallimard, Bibliothèque de la Pléiade, 1987–89), II, 194 & 196. Hereafter referred to as *RTP*. Translations are adapted from *Remembrance of Things Past*, trans. by C. K. Scott Moncrieff and Terence Kilmartin, 3 vols (London: Chatto & Windus, 1981).

31. See on this point, and on Proust's treatment of visual art more generally, J. Theodore Johnson Jr., 'From Artistic Celibacy to Artistic Contemplation', *Yale French Studies*, 34 (1965), 81–90 (p. 86).

32. Bal, *The Mottled Screen*, p. 3.

33. Watson, *Literature and Material Culture from Balzac to Proust*, pp. 153–54.

34. Susan Stewart, *On Longing: Narratives of the Miniature, the Gigantic, the Souvenir, the Collection* (Durham, NC: Duke University Press, 1999), p. 137.

35. As E. H. Gombrich notes ('Psychoanalysis and the History of Art', in *Meditations on a Hobby-Horse*, 4th edn (London: Phaidon, 1985), pp. 30–44 (p. 37)), a taste for the Italian Primitives was, in the nineteenth century, far from standard and hence a mark of the aesthete. Cited by Gabrielle Townsend, *Proust's Imaginary Museum: Reproductions and Reproduction in 'À la recherche du temps perdu'* (Oxford: Peter Lang, 2008), p. 56.

36. Jean-Yves Tadié, *Marcel Proust* (Paris: Gallimard, 1996), p. 485, notes that Proust frequented the offices of the *Gazette des beaux-arts*, and its editor Charles Ephrussi, from 1900; indeed, he was contributing to the *Gazette* and its supplement, *La Chronique des arts et de la curiosité*, at the same time as Berenson (see for example his articles on Ruskin, published 1 April and 1 August 1900, in Marcel Proust, *Écrits sur l'art*, ed. by Jérôme Picon (Paris: Flammarion, 1999), pp. 105–30). On Proust's involvement with the *Gazette*, see also Philippe Kolb and Jean Adhémar, 'Charles Ephrussi (1849–1905); ses secrétaires: Laforgue, A. Renan, Proust; "sa" Gazette des beaux-arts', *Gazette des beaux-arts*, 6th period, 103.1380 (January 1984), 29–41 (pp. 36–38).

37. Swann's adherence to the Morellian way of looking does not necessarily exclude 'Ruskinian' characteristics; indeed, Swann's connoisseurship may also be flawed because he commits the Ruskinian sin of erudite 'idolatry', appreciating art, and indeed the people around him, not for themselves but for what they represent (in the case of Odette, for her associations with Botticelli). See Johnson, 'From Artistic Celibacy to Artistic Contemplation', pp. 82–83, and Proust's definition of aesthetic idolatry in the preface to his translation of Ruskin's *Bible of Amiens*, in *Écrits sur l'art*, pp. 166–80 (esp. pp. 173–75).

38. Carlo Ginzburg, 'Morelli, Freud and Sherlock Holmes: Clues and Scientific Method', trans. by Anna Davin, *History Workshop*, 9 (Spring 1980), 5–36 (p. 12).

39. Sigmund Freud, 'The Moses of Michelangelo', in *The Standard Edition of the Complete Psychological Works of Sigmund Freud*, 24 vols (London: Vintage, 2001), XIV, 211–36 (p. 222). Ginzburg ('Morelli, Freud and Sherlock Holmes', p. 10) suggests that Morelli's theories played a key role in the development of psychoanalysis; see also Richard Wollheim, 'Freud and the Understanding of Art', in *On Art and the Mind* (London: Allen Lane, 1973), pp. 202–19.

40. Ginzburg, 'Morelli, Freud and Sherlock Holmes', p. 28; Ginzburg promises to develop this observation further in a subsequent version of his article but it is unclear whether he ever did so. The connection between Swann and Morelli is also noted by Jean-Pierre Guillerm, 'L'Avènement du détail pictural: de Balzac à Proust', in *Écrire la peinture*, ed. by Philippe Delaveau (Paris: Éditions universitaires, 1991), pp. 97–106 (pp. 102–03).
41. Gilles Deleuze, *Proust et les signes*, 3rd edn (Paris: Presses universitaires de France, 2010), p. 10.
42. Richard Bales, 'Proust and the Fine Arts', in *The Cambridge Companion to Proust*, ed. by Richard Bales (Cambridge: Cambridge University Press, 2001), pp. 183–99 (pp. 187–88).
43. Townsend, *Proust's Imaginary Museum*, pp. 30–32 (p. 31).
44. Georges Didi-Huberman, 'Appendice: question de détail, question de pan', in *Devant l'image: question posée aux fins d'une histoire de l'art* (Paris: Minuit, 1990), pp. 273–318 (pp. 293–94). See also Townsend's summary of Didi-Huberman's argument in *Proust's Imaginary Museum*, pp. 82–85.
45. Didi-Huberman, 'Appendice', pp. 285–89.
46. For a discussion of such detective work, see Baldwin, *The Material Object in the Work of Marcel Proust*, pp. 22–23; for examples, see Raymond T. Riva, 'A Probable Model for Proust's Elstir', *MLN*, 78:3 (May 1963), 307–13; Juliette Monnin-Hornung, *Proust et la peinture* (Geneva: Droz, 1951), pp. 90–101, and (in places) J. M. Cocking, 'Proust and Painting', in *Proust: Collected Essays on the Writer and his Art* (Cambridge: Cambridge University Press, 1982), pp. 130–63. Eric Karpeles's recent *Paintings in Proust: A Visual Companion to Proust's 'In Search of Lost Time'* (London: Thames & Hudson, 2008), a compendium of works of art described or mentioned in the novel, is a corollary of this desire to penetrate through the novel to its referents.
47. See Adam Watt's discussion of the distinction in Proust's theory of art between instinct and 'esprit', on the one hand, and intelligence on the other, in *Reading in Proust's 'A la recherche': 'Le délire de la lecture'* (Oxford: Clarendon Press, 2009), pp. 143–45.

CHAPTER 2

Portraits of the Artist in
Mauclair and Georges-Michel

Bourget and Proust, as we have seen, are both grappling with the nature of aesthetic experience, locating artistic authenticity not in the correct attribution of a work to its author, but rather in the way in which the spectator engages with the work of art, subjectively and imaginatively. Of course, this interest in reception and in the activity of the spectator does not write the work's creator out of the picture: for Proust, after all, the work of art was an expression of the artist's unique vision, and spectatorship involved imaginative entry into the artist's 'world'. This conception of art corresponds, in fact, to a theory of artistic creation that was widespread in the late nineteenth and early twentieth centuries, from the 1870s onwards. For the Impressionists, the work of art captured the artist's unique experience of the world — his 'impression' or 'sensation'. This was echoed, around the turn of the century, in Maurice Denis's theory of 'déformation subjective', according to which the artist represented the natural world, but was free to 'deform' it, or transform it through his imagination.[1] Indeed, this kind of compromise position, which reconciled fidelity to 'nature', or objective reality, with the artist's right to subjective interpretation, underpinned mainstream art criticism as well as artistic practice throughout the period covered by this book. This tendency, which Kim Grant has called 'expressive naturalism', was figurative, and tended to stick to traditional subjects (the nude, landscapes, genre scenes), but it was also 'sensual', 'lyrical', or expressive of the artist's unique individual response.[2] One might think of a 1920s Derain, Matisse, or Segonzac as best representing the more conservative end of this expressive naturalist tendency, although work by Modigliani, Soutine, or Utrillo was equally subject to critical evaluation in terms of the way in which it reflected the artist's unique personality and vision.[3] While the biographical approach to art criticism has largely fallen from favour and has certainly been brought into question by Rosalind Krauss's critique of the 'art history of the proper name',[4] Maurice Berger and Griselda Pollock have demonstrated that it is actually still alive and well in recent art historical work which, in reading art in relation to the life of the artist, works to support myths of the artist as a 'special' sort of character.[5]

One corollary of this account of artistic creation in the early twentieth century was a renewed interest in the figure of the artist, in his or her life, and in the putative special qualities that characterized the artistic 'temperament'. If the aesthetic value, and the price, of a work of art was held to be related to the way in which it captured the artist's unique personal vision, then the artist's identity — his personality, or rather his persona — became the ultimate source and guarantee of this value. To judge a work of art, one might look to the artist himself, and decide whether or not he (or, rarely, she) fitted into the various preconceived identities that art criticism, artists' biographies, and of course art fiction had carved out: does this person correspond to what the popular imagination holds artists to be? The aim of this chapter is to examine two portraits of the artist, two elaborations of artistic identity, written at opposite ends of the period in question: Camille Mauclair's *La Ville lumière* (1904) and Michel Georges-Michel's *Les Montparnos* (1924). Both of these are relatively unknown and certainly non-canonical texts: Mauclair's novel is particularly difficult to obtain, and its tale of art retreating from the temptations of Paris is hardly the stuff of bestsellers. Georges-Michel's fiction of artists in Montparnasse, in contrast, is 'popular' in all senses of the word — trashy, often crude. My aim here is not to rehabilitate these texts, to argue for their rightful place in the canon or, indeed, for their literary value. But I do want to take them seriously as texts that engage with the visual arts, and with questions of authenticity as they pertain not just to works of art, but to artists themselves: both, that is, advance ideas about what the authentic artist is, or what he or she should be.

This chapter also aims to demonstrate that for both Mauclair and Georges-Michel, artistic identity is not self-contained, but is bound up with other identities: with gender, and with nationality. Try as Mauclair might to hold art aloof from everything that is not-art, his text implicitly maps artistic identity onto national identity. In doing so, it gives expression to nationalistic currents that were ever-present in the Third Republic, although they came to the fore especially at key moments such as the Dreyfus Affair, and of course the First World War and its aftermath. By the 1920s, nationalist discourses had invaded the aesthetic domain and pushed for a classicizing 'retour à l'ordre' [return to order] in the arts. Georges-Michel's text responds to this by emphasizing the avant-garde artist's allegiance to French, or more broadly 'Latin' traditions, adopting a conciliatory position opposed to the all-out xenophobia that Mauclair, in his later years, would eventually adopt. As we shall see, however, there is a self-consciousness about Georges-Michel's text: this is not simply a portrait of the artist, but a study of the way in which discourses, including fictional ones, contribute to the fashioning of his identity.

Artistic and National Identities in Camille Mauclair's *La Ville lumière*

Camille Mauclair is perhaps better known as a poet and critic, of visual art but also of music and literature, than as a novelist; within his vast output of over a hundred titles, his novels have all but slipped into obscurity.[6] A regular visitor at Mallarmé's Tuesday gatherings, and a key figure in the Symbolist circles of the 1890s, he was ideally positioned as a commentator on the contemporary arts scene, and he dealt with art and artists in a number of works of fiction, including *Les Mères sociales* (1902) and *Le Soleil des morts* (1898).[7] The latter is a *roman à clef* in which Mallarmé appears under the guise of the poet Calixte Armel, and Rodin seems to form the basis for the rustic sculptor Urbain Decize.[8] As in *Les Mères sociales*, where the representation of artistic creation gives way to questions of the role of women in society and the nature of motherhood, *Le Soleil des morts* mingles the aesthetic with the political, capturing the dilemma of the Symbolist generation caught between hermetic, ivory-tower aestheticism and anarchistic political engagement. *La Ville lumière* is constructed on the same fictional terrain as these earlier novels, featuring some of the same characters and considering how, in the wake of the failure of anarchism, a socially engaged art may still be possible. This is just one of the novel's multiple strands: Mauclair frequently moves away from the trajectory of his protagonist, the painter Julien Rochès, to focus on peripheral characters and through them to enter into digressions on the social function of art, the value of applied art, the relationship between the painter and his female companion, and the corrupting role of art critics and dealers, amongst other things. As such, while *La Ville lumière* is Mauclair's most focused and sustained examination of the visual arts and of the conditions of their production and consumption, it makes for a rather strange art novel, its many concerns never quite coalescing into a unified plot.

Critical responses to *La Ville lumière* are scarce, but notable amongst these is Marie Lathers's examination of the female protagonist, Luce Elten, in relation to the artist-model tropes that characterized nineteenth-century representations of art in fiction. Lathers demonstrates that Mauclair's Luce represents a new type of model, who avoids the passivity of the traditional model as object of the creative male gaze, and escapes being reduced to her corporeality, as she is a successful artist in her own right.[9] However, Luce's artistic activity is a relatively marginal element in the novel, and her role is increasingly subsumed by that of partner to the protagonist Rochès. That said, artistic creativity — whether that of Luce, of Rochès, or of any other artist — is not really Mauclair's focus here: there are no atelier scenes containing descriptions of painters engaged in the act of painting, and little in the way of ekphrasis. This may simply be because Mauclair approaches art from a literary point of view, and perhaps because he lacks the technical knowledge and precision to engage closely with a creative act in a foreign medium: indeed, even in his extensive art criticism, he tends to abstain from detailed description of artworks in favour of biographical portraits in the paradigm of *l'homme et l'œuvre*, justifying this perspective as follows: 'l'artiste est infiniment plus grand, plus complexe, plus passionnant que son œuvre. Elle n'est que le signe et l'exemple de ce qu'il est parvenu à faire de lui-même' [the artist is infinitely greater, more complex, more interesting than his work. The latter is only the sign and the example of what the artist has made of himself].[10] This focus on the figure of the artist, and the practice of reading works of art as 'signs' or expressions of the artist's unique personality, is highly characteristic of the period. It is unsurprising, then, that when Mauclair turns to art fiction his novel should be more about artists, and art theory, than art in its material *facture*. *La Ville lumière* is a novel focused on artistic identity, and on how artists 'make themselves' or constitute themselves as artists. Despite the obscurity into which the novel has fallen, it remains useful as a way into the complex terrain of art-critical debate at the turn of the century, and to the way in which notions of artistic authenticity and identity were being refashioned in a period where the legacies of Romanticism and Impressionism were subject to increasing pressure. As we shall see, Mauclair's examination of artistic identity is also politically inflected, quietly heralding the reactionary xenophobia for which his later art criticism is known.

La Ville lumière appears to set itself up as a kind of *Bildungsroman*, tracing the development of the painter Rochès as he arrives in Paris, gains success, and a year later leaves again for the South: at the end of the novel, Luce reminds him that his year in the City of Light 't'a fait toucher à une vérité plus haute et te l'a fait reconnaître en toi-même' [made you reach a higher truth and recognize it within yourself].[11] But Rochès does not really develop, or change in himself, over the course of the novel: if he has learned anything, it is the ability to distinguish authentic or 'sincere' art from that which is inauthentic or insincere, and to recognize the Parisian art world as an alluring but ultimately empty mirage. As such, the challenge in coming to Paris is not that of becoming an artist (he already is one), but that of *remaining* a true and authentic artist by resisting the pernicious 'faussetés corrosives' [corrosive falsities] (*VL*, p. 77) that inhabit the city and threaten his artistic integrity. Underlying the novel, then, is a conception of artistic authenticity that roots artistic creation in the artist's unique personal vision of the world, a conception that, as we have already seen, proceeds more or less directly from Impressionism, the school to which Rochès unconsciously subscribes. The Impressionist painter aims, first and foremost, to see 'innocently', to strip his vision of the external world of the distorting influences of culture and convention, and to translate this vision directly onto the canvas, paying no heed to academic convention.[12] Rochès's 'innocence', and the singularity of his artistic temperament, are therefore emphasized from the beginning of the novel:

> La peinture avait été pour lui l'exercice naturel d'un don spontané, une sorte de respiration heureuse de la vie. Sans éducation artistique, par la seule force de l'instinct et de la perception immédiate de la nature, il s'était trouvé être un magnifique Impressionniste avant de soupçonner Manet ou l'Académie. Regarder avec amour et prouver cet amour en respectant la vérité de ce qu'il regardait, c'était tout son credo artistique. (*VL*, p. 13)

> [Painting was for him the natural expression of an innate gift, a sort of breath of life. Without any artistic training, through the sheer force of his instinct and the immediate experience of nature, he had discovered himself to be a magnificent Impressionist, before even suspecting the existence of Manet or the Academy. Looking with love and proving this love by respecting the truth of what he saw: this was his artistic credo]

Rochès is an autodidact, a naturally gifted painter with little knowledge of schools or styles, and driven primarily by gut instinct rather than calculated or educated efforts. He is associated with nature above culture, with 'les rochers de Provence' [the rocks of Provence] (*VL*, p. 14), which his name evokes. Characterized as 'l'homme du Midi' [the man of the South] (p. 6), and associated with Mediterranean light and vivid colour, he is placed in opposition to his friend Morsanne, who represents the worldly, decadent Parisian, and whose painting is associated with an impoverished, sickly palette. As Simonetta Valenti has noted, Rochès's distinctive painterly vision is represented in instances of narrative focalization which transfer the qualities of his painting onto the world around him: seen through his eyes, the city is 'éclaboussée de couleurs violentes' [splashed with violent colour] (*VL*, p. 26).[13] With light and colour linked to a Southern *ailleurs*, Paris's title as City of Light is seen as highly ironic: there is only the odd beacon of artistic enlightenment in an otherwise sombre, decadent Northern climate.

Rochès's 'simplicité foncière' [fundamental simplicity] (*VL*, p. 13) extends to his relationship with art discourses, which are dismissed as 'des théories circulant comme des pièces fausses' [theories doing the rounds like fake coins] (p. 148) — inauthentic tokens irrelevant to real artistic practice. In fact, in a pattern which we shall see is shared by Georges-Michel's fictional painter Modrulleau, and which perhaps brings to mind the proverbial *bête comme un peintre*, Mauclair portrays Rochès as ill at ease in the domain of words more generally. Hostile to 'bavardage' [chitter-chatter] (p. 22) and to 'le bagout des journalistes' [journalists' jibber-jabbering] (p. 29) since it is alien to his own medium, Rochès frequently has difficulty expressing himself in words, admitting, 'Je ne sais pas bien parler, mais je crois que ce n'est pas indispensable. On se prouve par des œuvres, et surtout par l'effort qu'on y apporte' [I'm no great speaker, but I don't think that's indispensable. One proves oneself by one's works, and above all by the effort one brings to them] (p. 72). Art for Mauclair, and for Rochès, is a heroic effort, in contrast to 'l'art chic', which is easy, done by numbers, and propped up by discourses that are frivolous and ultimately irrelevant to art itself.

Mauclair's conception of the authentic artist also finds expression in other artist figures in the novel, beyond Rochès. Luce, for instance, is portrayed as outspoken and opinionated, following her own path both personally and professionally. She is 'toute naturelle' [totally natural] (*VL*, p. 64), and placed in opposition to the superficial Parisian 'facticité' [artificiality] (p. 42) of Morsanne's lover Irène Lénore. There is little description of Luce's work or its style, although we are told that she is an associate of the 'section d'objets d'art du salon' [the decorative arts section of the salon] (p. 43), so it is presumably mostly small-scale sculpture or decorative work. Her art does, however, gain validation from Rodin, who admires one of her sketches, and tells Rochès approvingly, 'Elle n'est pas appréciée, elle ne fait pas ce qu'il faut. Vous savez, Paris, ce parisianisme... Elle n'aime pas tout cela' [She isn't well-liked, because she doesn't behave as she is supposed to. You know, this Parisianness... She doesn't like all that] (p. 60). Rodin's cameo appearance in the novel, alongside a number of other contemporary figures such as Georges Rodenbach and Loïe Fuller, serves a number of possible functions. In representing a real artist, Mauclair anchors his fiction in the reality of the contemporary art world, on which he was, by the early years of the twentieth century, considered an expert; he also responds to the public's increasing thirst for information about the lives of real artists, seen in the growing popularity of biographies and *vies romancées*.[14] But Rodin also serves as a convenient, ready-made emblem of the ideal, authentic artist, which could be imported into the novel from Mauclair's critical writings. Mauclair's friendship with Rodin had been established over the course of the 1890s, and he had leapt to the sculptor's defence in his 1898 dispute with the *Société des gens de lettres*, who had commissioned a monument to Balzac and subsequently refused Rodin's finished work as too unconventional.[15] This was a key moment that established Rodin's public reputation as an artistic renegade, and Mauclair cemented this in a series of articles published both before and after *La Ville lumière*. (If Mauclair's vision of Rodin's work remains constant over a period of twenty years, this is partly because he tended to rework or even republish his texts with little modification.) In an article published in 1901 and subsequently incorporated into the 1904 *Idées vivantes*, Mauclair painted Rodin as 'un élément, une force de la nature' [a natural element, a force of nature][16] — terms which directly prefigure those used in the novel: 'Qu'il était loin du parisianisme et de l'art chic, ce Rodin élémental, force de nature!' [How estranged he was from Parisianness and fashionable art, this elemental Rodin, force of nature!] (*VL*, p. 58). Mauclair's critical depiction of Rodin has him happily cut off from the vagaries of the art world, and the 1901 article beckons the reader into the atelier ('Entrons donc chez lui' [Let's go into his studio]) as if into a sacred space, whose simplicity, even poverty is emphasized. Here we witness the sculptor's heroic struggle with the elements: Rodin appears to become one with his matter, his massive frame and rough-hewn features described as if they were carved in stone: 'Il est lui-même une sorte de rocher recélant des formes, il est le terrain rugueux étreignant dans ses replis d'immenses arborescences cristallisées' [He is himself a sort of rock hiding various forms within it; a rocky terrain concealing immense crystallized arboreal forms within its folds].[17] All of this brings to mind not just Rodin as he appears in *La Ville lumière*, but Rochès, the aptly named painterly double of the sculptor. The following passage on Rodin in particular recalls the description of Rochès cited earlier:

> Il n'a même pas d'esthétique. Là aussi il résume: aimer la vie des formes, c'est son credo. Il le répète sans cesse. 'On ne fera jamais aussi bien que la nature', dit-il en hochant la tête, et il s'en tient là. Il n'est ni réaliste ni intellectuel, on ne peut le savoir et il n'en a aucun souci. Mais il dégage un magnétisme de force effrayante. C'est un inspiré.[18]

> [He does not even have an aesthetic theory as such. He sums up his credo as follows: love natural forms. He repeats this credo endlessly. 'We will never do it better than nature', he says, nodding his head, and he stops there. He is neither a Realist nor an intellectual, he will not be tied down and he cares little about such labels. But he gives off a powerful, almost frightening magnetic energy. He is inspired]

The absence of theory; the limitation of artistic credo to the bare essentials; the love of nature; the insistence on instinct and inspiration: it is all there in Rochès. Of course, the latter is only starting out as an artist, and is hence less self-assured than the confirmed master, for whom Mauclair reserves his most bombastic language. But the basic characteristics are the same: prone to a certain stony intransigence in the face of criticism, both artists are seen as authentic because they are self-determining, bound only to their own unique creative visions.

This is, on the face of it, quite a radical aesthetic individualism, according to which all art is admissible provided that it is a direct, unadulterated expression of the artist's vision. But there are nevertheless limits: Mauclair is careful to insist, in his characterizations of both Rochès and Rodin, on the importance of fidelity to nature. If his aesthetic appears to recall Zola's dictum that the work of art represents 'un coin de la création vu à travers un tempérament' [a corner of creation seen through a temperament], he is not willing to sacrifice the faithful representation of nature to artistic temperaments that would bend or distort it beyond 'reasonable' limits.[19] This point of view is communicated via the figure of Brignon, an instinctive painter who recalls Monticelli and is Rochès's master before he comes to Paris.[20] More liberal than Rochès in his interpretation of nature, his downfall comes when he veers too far into his eccentric vision of the world, and his painting descends into nonsense, as we see when his final 'masterpiece' is unveiled:

> Religieusement, Brignon découvrit le tableau. Rochès fut épouvanté autant de ce qu'il vit que de l'éclat de rire que derrière lui brusquement Brignon acheva dans une sorte de râle haut et sinistre. C'était un amoncellement de taches qui ne représentait rien, sinon un chaos de végétaux et de chairs convulsé sous un ciel d'incendie, où ruisselaient des pétales et des éclairs, où les nuages fleurissaient sur des tiges invraisemblables. L'œuvre était toujours celle d'un incomparable magicien, traversée de frissons de nacre et d'or, pareille à des gemmes broyées, avec des rehauts superbes, des tons suaves et étranges, de délicieux ragoûts de couleur, le charme de la joaillerie et de l'émail, la volupté profonde des satins, la vibrante harmonie des soies: tout le génie coloriste de Brignon se concentrait là — mais l'œuvre était d'un fou! N'eût-elle été qu'un assemblage pur et simple de couleurs, Rochès se fût rassuré, croyant à une fantaisie de palette, à un projet de tapis, à une gamme... Mais il y avait des essais de formes qui prouvaient la démence, des femmes terminées en nuages, des rochers dans le ciel, des rivières verticales, toute une déroute des formes de la vie. (*VL*, pp. 181–82)

[Brignon uncovered the painting with religious care. Rochès was appalled as much as by what he saw as by the laughter that, behind him, escaped from Brignon in a sort of sinister groan. The painting was a piled-up assortment of marks which represented nothing other than a distorted chaos of plant-like and fleshy forms beneath a fiery sky, with streams of petals and lightning bolts, and where clouds sprouted on the end of incredible stems. The work was still that of a talented sorcerer, shot through with shivers of silver and gold, like crushed gemstones, with superb lighter tones, elegant and strange, delicious stews of colour, charming elements which recalled jewellery and enamel-work, the rich sensuousness of satin, the vibrant harmony of silk: all of Brignon's genius as a colourist was concentrated there, but the work was that of a madman! Had it been a simple assembly of colours, Rochès might have been reassured, believing it to be a mere exercise of the palette, a project for a carpet, perhaps a colour scheme... But the painter's attempts at representing forms proved his madness: women who turned into clouds, rocks in the sky, vertical rivers, a total collapse of natural forms]

This moment in the novel quite clearly references the unveiling of Frenhofer's painting in Balzac's *Le Chef-d'œuvre inconnu*, and in case this reference is not obvious enough, Mauclair goes on to tell us that Rochès sees in Brignon's downfall 'l'image de tout l'art romantique, disparu derrière l'horizon du dernier siècle' [the image of all Romantic art, lost beyond the horizon of the last century] (*VL*, p. 183). Frenhofer and Brignon's failures are essentially the same: in both cases, the painter has been unable to produce a faithful representation of a scene or motif from nature. However, whereas Frenhofer's Catherine Lescaut remains as a ghostly presence almost entirely hidden behind a non-representational 'muraille de peinture', Brignon's painting manages to represent something — but not according to coherent pictorial codes. Had he, like Frenhofer, produced a wall of paint, this could have been explained away in terms of a decorative project. But his scrambling of '[les] formes de la vie', of the language of nature, proves his 'madness', his estrangement from reality. This is not the kind of madness that can be recuperated as part of the artist's singular 'génie', or that simply signals his distance from the common, unartistic man; it is a madness that for Mauclair casts the painter out of the realm of art entirely, because it means breaching what he sees as one of art's central tenets: fidelity to the natural order of things.

Excessive individualism is just one of the dangers encountered by the painter. One can also veer too far in the other direction, absorbing the ideas of others to the extent that one's own unique 'tempérament' disintegrates. Mauclair provides us with a further cautionary tale in the figure of Alcime Weuille, another artist who falls prey to madness, but in this case because he overdoses on theory:

> Peintre dévoyé, intelligence supérieure et stérile, accueillant toutes les théories et ne sachant rien réaliser, Weuille s'était reculé hors de la vie, hors de soi-même, impersonnalité à force de compréhension, jusqu'à ne plus pouvoir comprendre l'immense différence de ses belles idées et de la piteuse transcription qu'il en faisait. (*VL*, p. 274)

> [A painter led astray, of superior intelligence and yet sterile, taking in all theories and yet not knowing how to create a thing, Weuille had retreated away from life, away from himself, losing himself in all this theory, to the point where he could no longer understand the massive difference between his grand ideas and the pitiful translation he gave them in his works]

Weuille becomes estranged from himself, and his art ceases to be based around his own distinctive vision, because he no longer has any sense of what that vision might be. Torn apart by competing discourses, he is just the shell of a personality. And this estrangement from oneself is echoed in a series of other failed, inauthentic artists. Alquier succumbs to the temptations of money, admitting, 'Oui, j'ai trafiqué du don de Dieu, j'ai surproduit, j'ai bâclé, j'ai fait de faux Alquier, j'ai déshonoré ma signature!' [Yes, I've trafficked God's gift, I've botched and bungled, I've produced false Alquiers, I've brought my own signature into disrepute!] (*VL*, p. 296). He has not only prostituted his art, submitting it to commercial imperatives, but in making 'de faux Alquier' he has also sold himself, constituted himself as false, as inauthentic. Morsanne does the same, but in his case his vice is Paris itself, and Irène, his *demi-mondaine* lover who embodies all of the city's vices, its superficial beauty, its changeability: 'Elle est si diverse! Jamais à soi pareil, c'est bien l'âme de Paris' [She is so diverse! Never the same, that's the Parisian soul] (p. 34). Morsanne is, correspondingly, a kind of Baudelairean *homme des foules*, his identity dissolving in the crowd, 'une personnalité entièrement composée d'une mosaïque d'idées parisiennes, incompréhensibles ailleurs' [a personality entirely made up of a mosaic of Parisian ideas which are absolutely incomprehensible anywhere else] (p. 177). His commitment to his art is sacrificed to his love of Paris, and he becomes nothing more than a feeble dilettante.

What, then, does *La Ville lumière* tell us about artistic identity? The picture that emerges is rather more complex than it would at first appear: while Mauclair seems to be making a straightforward statement to the effect that the authentic artist is simply one who remains true to himself (or herself), over the course of the novel, his definition turns out to be overwhelmingly negative. It is not enough just to 'be yourself': the authentic artist must also *not be* too Parisian, too in love, too wealthy, too fashionable, too abstract, too imaginative, too theoretical, too conventional. In the face of all of these qualifications, one cannot help but wonder whether Mauclair sets the artist a near impossible task. While his definition of the authentic artist appears to be inclusive, and in principle open to anyone (since all one has to do is represent one's own particular 'vision'), only a very rare personality will be able to run the gauntlet of obstacles and temptations to produce what Mauclair sees as authentic art. As such, *La Ville lumière* effectively sustains a myth of the artist as a special kind of personality: ascetic, pure, even saintly. Mauclair's language often takes on religious overtones as he speaks of artistic talent as 'le don de Dieu' [God's gift] (*VL*, p. 296), declares that art must be 'l'œuvre des mains pauvres et pures' [the work of poor, pure hands] (p. 280), and insists on Rochès's chastity as 'l'atelier [...] doit être pur pour le travail' [the studio [...] must remain pure for work to take place] (p. 127). In this respect, *La Ville lumière* anticipates some of the hagiographical tropes that are present, as we shall see shortly, in Michel Georges-Michel's portrait of the artist in *Les Montparnos*, and more generally in early twentieth-century discourses about art and artists.

This myth of the artist as a kind of saintly hermit figure, cut off from the superficial, debased world of commercial art, is a defensive posture which seeks rhetorically to rescue art from the many dangers it faces, to restore its authenticity by separating it off from extraneous influences that threaten to debase it. It is not difficult to see that this myth is politically inflected, and that the influences from which Mauclair seeks to protect art are, implicitly, foreign: foreign, that is, not just to art but to *French* art. That this kind of nationalistic discourse might underlie *La Ville lumière* is perhaps masked by a veneer of political progressivism: after all, it is difficult to square Mauclair's apparent defense of artistic individualism, his plea for a socially engaged art accessible to the masses, and his insistence that the artist should be active in a new social order, with the kind of reactionary chauvinism that one finds in his later criticism, particularly after the First World War. But as Romy Golan has shown, the seeds of this attitude — which would eventually see him become a key proponent of Vichy anti-Semitism — are in fact present much earlier.[21] Golan sees the 1906 critical text *Trois crises de l'art actuel* as the turning-point in Mauclair's attitude: here, in the final section entitled 'La Crise de la laideur en peinture', Mauclair lauches an eviscerating attack on the 'primitivist' works presented at the 1905 *Salon d'automne* and the 1906 *Salon des indépendants*, which he sees as willfully ugly, and, all-importantly, as flouting 'l'héritage traditionnel et les lois naturelles des arts' [the traditional heritage and natural laws of the arts].[22] These works (which, although Mauclair does not mention the movement by name, are clearly those of the Fauves) pose a problem for the critic because they represent an artistic individualism taken to extremes, pushed beyond the reasonable constraints imposed by pictorial traditions, and because in departing from these (French) traditions, they allow in what he clearly sees as barbaric, foreign influences: Mauclair can barely contain his disgust at 'les femmes équarries à coups de serpe et les barbouillages congolais' [women cut into pieces by machete, congolese scrawlings], at this atavistic return to 'l'état d'esprit de l'homme des cavernes gravant un os de renne' [the mindset of the caveman engraving a reindeer bone].[23]

Golan thinks that this reactionary turn in Mauclair's work occurs partly in response to a crisis in art criticism — to a sense of insecurity caused by a fall in stature of the critic, and an awareness of the increasingly important role of dealers in driving forward new art movements and determining public opinion. She also claims that his new obsession with savagery and the decadence of French art occurred partly in reaction to the 1905 separation of Church and State, which provoked a backlash of reactionary Catholic nationalism.[24] And yet these ideas are also very much present, just beneath the surface, in *La Ville lumière*, which predates the 1905 scission.[25] True, the kind of invective in which Mauclair engages in *Trois crises* is absent from the novel, and his brief portraits of foreign painters are no more than ambivalent. But in its simmering fears about Paris as 'creuset' (*VL*, p. 54), a confusing and disorientating melting-pot of aesthetic ideas and artistic identities, the novel is suggestive of fears about foreign influences on French art and on French identity more generally. Paris, or more specifically the sheer cosmopolitan diversity of artistic Paris, is seen to be responsible for Weuille's breakdown, as we are told that 'Le conflit passionnel des idées, *apportées de toutes parts*, avait brisé ce cerveau que la production en silence, dans le calme de quelque province, eût sauvé' [the passionate conflict of ideas, *imported from all over*, had broken a mind which silent production, in the calm of some province, would have saved] (p. 275, my emphasis). Only a retreat from cosmopolitan Paris into a culturally stable *France profonde* will save the artist from a crisis of identity. Hence why, just as Mauclair himself would by 1908 have left Paris and distanced himself from public life, Rochès must at the end of the novel return to the Midi, where he will renew contact with his coinciding artistic and national identities. Furthermore, the novel's plea for a socially engaged art is actually closely intertwined with this nationalist undercurrent: by and for 'les ouvriers', this new art responds not just to broadly socialist imperatives but also to a respect for 'le petit peuple', seen as the bastion of Frenchness in a period where elites were felt to be losing their identity to cosmopolitanism.[26] This art, Mauclair tells us, signifies 'le retour de la race française à son génie plébéien, du vieux temps des bons ouvriers de la pierre et du livre, de la peinture et du meuble' [the return of the French race to its plebeian genius, and of the old days of stone masons and book makers, of painters and furniture-makers] (p. 260), and he gives us a sense of its rootedness in *terroir* as he exhorts, 'que l'art revienne au sol qui l'engendra' [may art return to the land that conceived it] (p. 280).[27]

Golan is, of course, right to pick up on Mauclair's anxieties about the state of art criticism. In *Trois crises*, Mauclair notes that critical responses to the Fauve exhibitions have been excessively positive, and says that the only explanation for this is to be found 'dans la profonde démoralisation de la critique d'art, dans l'affolement de la boussole artistique que l'Ecole a cessé d'aimanter, et dont l'aiguille oscille au hasard' [in art criticism's profound demoralization, in the confusion of our aesthetic compass which the École has ceased to orientate, and whose needle is lurching around haphazardly].[28] As this metaphor implies, the problem is dually aesthetic and geographic: French art needs its compass resetting, to come back to a sense of itself as French, and ultimately to return to a stable set of values along the lines of those formerly provided by the École des Beaux-Arts. *La Ville lumière*'s investigation of artistic identity is, similarly, bound up in questions of national identity, and the battle between authentic and false or insincere art maps onto a cultural struggle between France and its non-French others. This struggle would of course intensify in the run-up to, and during, the First World War; it would remain important throughout the 1920s as foreign artists flooded into Paris and yet, at the same time, there was a broad movement towards an aesthetic 'retour à l'ordre', seen as a renewal of French and 'Latin' traditions and as an attempt to extricate French art from corrupting foreign influences. It is into this highly charged terrain that Michel Georges-Michel's novel *Les Montparnos* entered, in 1924.

Saints and Lovers: Myths of the Avant-Garde in Michel Georges-Michel's *Les Montparnos*

In the history of twentieth-century literature, Michel Georges-Michel (or, by his real name, Georges Dreyfus) is hardly a canonical figure, and is all but forgotten today. And yet, during a career spanning the first four decades of the century, Georges-Michel was a well-known and prolific *chroniqueur* and critic of art, theatre, and dance, and author of a number of novels, including his 1924 text *Les Montparnos: roman nouveau de la bohème cosmopolite*. The latter was an immense success: it went through a quick succession of new editions, was adapted for the theatre and staged at the Théâtre Antoine in 1927, was translated into English as *Left Bank* in 1931, and inspired Jacques Becker's 1958 film *Les Amants de Montparnasse*.[29] As such, Georges-Michel's text played a key role in propagating a myth of Montparnasse, and of the avant-garde artists who lived and worked there in the years following the First World War, which continues to haunt the popular imagination.[30] My aim here is to examine the representation of the artist in *Les Montparnos*, showing how this might correspond to ways in which artists in Paris in the 1920s fashioned their own identities — or indeed had their identities fashioned for them by critics. In particular, I wish to show firstly that Georges-Michel's novel reflects the attempt by many factions of the avant-garde to reinscribe themselves within aesthetic traditions they had once rejected, as part of a broad post-war 'retour à l'ordre'; and secondly that it reflects the gender politics of the avant-garde, whose cult of virility effectively devalued and marginalized female creativity. Alongside an exploration of these themes, I also wish to bring out the uses of myth in *Les Montparnos*, and in particular the ways in which myths of the avant-garde artist are generated, borrowed from other texts, and ultimately questioned in the novel. As we shall see, *Les Montparnos* is not simply a piece of myth-making, but also a self-conscious exploration of the processes by which cultural myths are created, and their function in relation to art.

In a review of the 1929 Fasquelle edition of *Les Montparnos*, François Fosca (a conservative art critic and editor of the highbrow magazine *L'Amour de l'art*) took issue with the novel's singular mix of fact and fiction:

> L'auteur n'a abouti qu'à un ouvrage boiteux, parce qu'il a fait se chevaucher deux plans différents, le plan du roman, c'est-à-dire celui de l'invention, et le plan du reportage, celui de la narration de l'exact. Ce n'est pas là, d'ailleurs, le seul défaut du livre. Écrit dans un style qui vise au pittoresque, et qui n'est que prétentieux, il dépeint la vie du Montparnasse selon l'esthétique du roman-feuilleton; et lorsqu'on y rencontre des personnages authentiques, ils sont tracés avec tant d'extravagance, qu'ils en sont méconnaissables.[31]

> [The author has produced a shaky piece of work, because he has superimposed two different frameworks: that of the novel, or of invention, and that of reportage, or the representation of the real. This is not, moreover, the book's only flaw. Written in a style which is intended to be picturesque and is really just pretentious, it describes Montparnasse life in the style of a serialized novel; when we do encounter authentic characters, they are depicted in such an extravagant way that they become unrecognizable]

The novel is, as Fosca notes, partly based in fact, and features a number of real Montparnasse personalities such as Cendrars, Léger, Kisling, Picasso, and the art dealer and poet Zborowski. The protagonist Modrulleau — a genial and original artist, who dares to flout Cubist orthodoxy, but whose talent is threatened by his alcoholism and goes unrecognized by the public, at least until after his tragic death — corresponds, at least in his broad outlines, to Amedeo Modigliani, who had died in 1920. The artist's companion, nicknamed Haricot-Rouge after the food she distributes to starving artists, corresponds roughly to Modigliani's partner Jeanne Hébuterne, who like her fictional avatar killed herself, and her unborn child with her, following her lover's death. What interests us here, however, is not the status of the novel as *roman à clef* or the question of how closely the story corresponds to the historical reality of Modigliani or Hébuterne's life.[32] What is crucial for our purposes, rather, and what escapes Fosca's grasp, is the fact that the obfuscation of the line between reality and fiction is absolutely central to Georges-Michel's procedure. In the preface to the novel, he tells the reader, 'Comme dans la plupart de mes autres livres, il n'y a pas une ligne, pas un mot de ce roman qui ne relate un fait, une parole qui n'aient été vus ou entendus' [As in most of my books, there is not a line, not a word of this novel that does not relate a fact or an utterance that I have seen or heard]. Having thus assured us of the text's authenticity, however, he goes on to maintain that, 'sauf ceux qui sont cités par leur nom, je n'ai dépeint personne particulièrement' [other than those who are cited by name, I have not depicted anyone in particular], and that Modrulleau and Haricot-Rouge in particular are 'des personnages synthétiques si l'on veut, chacun de plusieurs personnages du même milieu, du même esprit, mais fictifs' [synthetic characters, if you will, each one composed of several people of the same milieu and mindset, but fictional]. The preface quickly moves, then, from insisting that everything in the novel is true or authentic, to maintaining that its main characters are 'avant tout de purs héros de romans' [above all purely fictional heros] (*M*, p. 13). Thus, although one would usually expect such paratexts to clarify the text's relationship to historical reality,

Georges-Michel's preface actually works to obscure the matter further, by making it apparent that we have no means of ascertaining which elements are 'true', and which are not. Its function, then, is to draw attention to the narrative's ambiguous position in a realm between fact and fiction, between reality and the imagination: the realm of myth. And in doing so, the preface situates the novel itself as one example of many types of text or verbal discourse about art and artists which may or may not be 'true', but which Georges-Michel reveals nevertheless to play a fundamental role in the production and consumption of art.

Georges-Michel is extremely attentive to the various types of discourse circulating around 1920s avant-garde art, and which did the rounds of the Montparnasse café terraces, to the extent that some sections of *Les Montparnos* read as cut-and-paste collages of aesthetic musings:

> Le but de l'art...
> — L'art ne doit pas avoir de but...
> — Tous les grands déforment, voient autrement...
> — Les fous voient...
> — Les surhumains voient...
> — Un peintre fait toujours son portrait, quoi qu'il fasse...
> — La section d'or, si Raphaël l'a connue?...
> — On ne fait pas une cuisse de femme avec son cerveau...
> — Nous apportons à Paris la semence du Monde... (*M*, p. 215)

> [The aim of art...
> — Art should have no aim...
> — All great minds deform things, see things differently...
> — Madmen are seers...
> — Superhumans are seers...
> — A painter always paints his own portrait, whatever he does...
> — The Golden Ratio, was Raphael aware of it? ...
> — You don't paint a woman's thigh with your brain...
> — We're bringing the seed of the World to Paris...]

Of course, while part of the purpose of this kind of textual collage is to give the reader a sense of the energy and enthusiasm of contemporary aesthetic debate, the disconnectedness of these fragments gives one the impression of a group of painters and critics talking past one another, unable to arrive at a coherent position, and ultimately making little sense. This is in turn reflected in Modrulleau's own antipathy towards 'les froides gloses' [cold commentaries] of contemporary critics (*M*, p. 116), which he feels to be irrelevant to the practice of art itself, and his distaste for those painters who 'ne peuvent plus prendre un pinceau sans avoir rempli soixante pages d'algèbre' [cannot take up a brush without filling sixty pages with algebra] (p. 119). And yet this rejection of art-theoretical discourse is countered by the novel's insistence that various types of talk, or stories about art, are absolutely central to art's appeal, and to its purchase and consumption. Haricot-Rouge, for instance, is initially drawn to art through her reading of 'la vie des peintres, de Michel-Ange à Cézanne' [the lives of the painters, from Michelangelo to Cézanne] — hagiographical accounts that feed into her idea that 'leur vie devait être plus belle et certainement plus haute que ce qu'elle savait de l'existence' [their life must have been more beautiful and certainly more elevated than what she knew of existence] (p. 45). Her contact with art itself comes only later, and is of course mediated by the stories she has read.[33] The success of the art dealer Afthalien, meanwhile, is seen to be closely bound up with his skill in spinning yarns about art, often manipulating the art-historical narrative to suit his own purposes, and creating caricatured portraits of artists themselves, 'sans vergogne ouvrant leur vie privée, leur misère, l'exagérant souvent' [shamelessly exposing their private lives, their misery, often exaggerating it] (p. 60). Soutine, for instance, is portrayed by Afthalien as a naive, slightly deranged peasant who fits nicely into the mould of *peintre maudit* — a portrait that appeals to buyers and is used to justify the inflated price of his paintings. In a similar way, the newspaper accounts of Modrulleau's death, and the speeches at his graveside at the end of the novel, serve to consecrate the painter as a heroic avant-garde martyr, as in André Salmon's eulogy:

> C'était un grand seigneur... Il portait en lui des puissances d'épopée... toute la gloire de vivre en surhomme, si un destin forcené fit de ce prince l'hôte des lieux maudits ou des bouges... Dans son œuvre comme dans sa vie, le drame et l'idylle s'allièrent au-dessus de la mort. (*M*, p. 278)

> [He was a great master... He carried within him epic powers... the glory of living as a superman, even if a cruel destiny forced this prince into dives and hovels... In his work as in his life, the tragic and the ideal went hand in hand, beyond the reach of death]

But within this pairing of 'œuvre' and 'vie', it is the latter, or rather the mythologized version of the latter, that really counts. During the gold rush of dealers who swoop in to profit from Modrulleau's death, a 'monsieur Notaire, notaire' buys up Zborowski's stock of paintings without even viewing them, their commercial value guaranteed purely by their association with the artist whose story has been constructed in the tragic mode.

Clearly, there is an element of critique implicit in Georges-Michel's representation of such verbal portraits of the artist, which mediate the experience of art to the extent that the work is invaded, colonized, and even partially constituted by verbal discourse: a work of art is, at least in part, what is said about it, and what is said about it often serves solely commercial ends. This may be true, to some extent, of all art, but as Paul Mann has argued, avant-garde art is especially immersed in discourse, its movements driven forward by theory rather than practice, its experience necessarily mediated, and its value determined by the art-discourses that circulate around it.[34] Just as Mann's critical account of these discourses shows an awareness of its own inevitable contribution to the discursive economy governing the production and consumption of avant-garde art, *Les Montparnos* may be seen as just another portrait of the kind it critiques: a mythologized portrait of the artist which repackages the reality of the contemporary art world and 'sells' it back to the reader-consumer in a more tragic and glamorous form. What saves Georges-Michel's novel from total complicity in the kind of cynical, commercially-motivated myth-making it condemns is its self-consciousness — the way in which it draws attention to the role of stories about art in the appraisal of its value, both aesthetic and economic. This self-consciousness also operates via intertextual borrowings which point up the fact that *Les Montparnos* is in some respects simply a reiteration of an already well-established myth, and Modrulleau a modern incarnation of a more universal artistic 'type' deriving from Romanticism. As such, Georges-Michel's aim is not so much to persuade his reader to buy into the myth, or to swallow it wholesale, but to encourage a more critical awareness of the status of his text as a piece of myth-making — a verbal narrative which may transform or deform reality — amongst so many others.

Les Montparnos borrows extensively from the tropes of the nineteenth-century art novel, and in particular from Zola's *L'Œuvre*: Modrulleau's betrayal of Haricot-Rouge with the rich, elegant princesse de Laurence, and the metaphorical freight of this betrayal as a corruption of the ideal values of art, recalls Claude Lantier's betrayal of his partner Christine with the wealthy *cocotte* Irma Bécot.[35] Modrulleau's tragic demise is also very much reminiscent of Zola's novel. But the dominant model for Georges-Michel's text is perhaps the insouciant bohemia of Murger's *Scènes de la vie de bohème*. Indeed, when François Fosca witheringly referred to *Les Montparnos* as participating in 'l'esthétique du roman-feuilleton', he no doubt meant to liken it to trashy serialized fiction, but he may also have had Murger's text in mind, as one of the most famous examples of the *feuilleton* genre, which had recently been brought back into the public eye by the 1922 centenary of Murger's birth.[36] Georges-Michel's characters inhabit an artistic bohemia similar to that represented and popularized by Murger — a bohemia characterized by poverty coupled with youthful high jinks, and with a debauched atelier party as its central episode. The broad similarity between the two texts is also highlighted by Georges-Michel's preface, where the author's emphasis on the authenticity of his narrative (however much this may be undermined subsequently) recalls Murger's insistence on the documentary value of his text as a series of 'études de mœurs' [studies of manners].[37]

There are, however, some crucial differences between *Les Montparnos* and *Scènes de la vie de bohème*, differences through which Georges-Michel raises the status of the bohemian myth, and ultimately sets up the story of the artist as a kind of hagiography that moves beyond Murger's bohemian picturesque. In Georges-Michel's novel, the identification of the artistic avant-garde with bohemia is seen as a necessary one. The modern avant-garde artist is necessarily poor because society fails to understand his innovations, and it is only in posterity that his genius will be recognized: Modrulleau laments that 'ce siècle, ce temps, nous ont obligés à vivre comme des chiffonniers dans des quartiers lépreux' [this century, this time, has obliged us to live like ragpickers in crumbling slums] (*M*, p. 225). This stands in contrast to Murger's struggling artists, whose position in bohemia is only temporary: following Mimi's tragic death, they realize that 'on peut être un poète ou un artiste véritable en se tenant les pieds chauds et en faisant ses trois repas' [one can be a genuine poet or artist and all the while keep one's feet warm and eat three meals a day], and the end of the novel sees them sensibly rejoining the artistic mainstream in order to make a respectable bourgeois living.[38] Georges-Michel's artists thoroughly reject any such concerns, spurning commercial imperatives and sacrificing worldly glory and comforts for their art, which they treat as a mystical vocation: 'cette plus-que-religion qui nous donnait tout de suite le ciel' [a more-than-religion which gave us heaven on earth] (p. 113). This self-sacrifice is central to a conception of art as religion, according to which avant-garde painters are seen as prophets and martyrs, working towards a radically new form of art which will only be fully realized after their lifetime. As Modrulleau himself puts it, the avant-garde artists of his time are 'si désinteressés qu'ils ne travaillent même pas pour leur génération' [so disinterested that they do not even work for the sake of their own generation]:

> Ils savent qu'en recommençant toute la peinture, ce n'est pas en dix ans, ni même en vingt ans qu'ils aboutiront. Mais ils préparent la voie, pour QUELQU'UN qui viendra. Oui, comme au Moyen Age, tous les primitifs, et Giotto, et Masaccio, et Signorelli préparèrent inconsciemment, et en brûlant leur vie, cette flamme entre les flammes hautes: Raphaël! nous, consciemment, nous donnons la nôtre pour celui qui, ramassant tous nos efforts en un faisceau divin, en illuminera le monde. (*M*, p. 38)

> [They are aware that in starting painting anew, they won't achieve their ends in ten years or even in twenty. But they are preparing the way for SOMEONE who will come. Yes, just as in the Middle Ages, the primitives, and Giotto, Masaccio, Signorelli, all unconsciously prepared the way, burning up their own lives, for the flame among all flames — Raphael! — we consciously give our own flame for he who, combining all our efforts in one divine beacon, will illuminate the world]

Within the framework of this messianic narrative, Modrulleau, as 'le plus pur parmi les purs' [the purest of the pure] (*M*, pp. 44–45), 'un seigneur parmi les siens' [a lord amongst his own people] (p. 51), is the harbinger of this new artistic order, if not the messiah himself.

This metaphorical identification of art and religion is by no means original: it is present, as we have seen, in *La Ville lumière*, and indeed in Mauclair's earlier *Le Soleil des morts*, which more explicitly insists on the martyrdom suffered by contemporary artists, doomed only to attain glory after their deaths. Nathalie Heinich has also demonstrated that early twentieth-century biographies of Van Gogh (which proliferated in this period, as the cult of the artist grew) tended to borrow elements from hagiography, and to exclude any elements of his life — such as his interest in commercial success — that did not support this myth of the artist as saint and martyr.[39] Among the recurrent motifs of these biographical accounts, Heinich lists notions of the artistic calling or vocation; of the exceptional character of the artist/saint; of isolation, marginality, exclusion from everyday social and commercial life; of asceticism, poverty, detachment from the material world; of incomprehension or even hatred on the part of contemporaries; and of posthumous glory.[40] All of these hallmarks apply equally well to Georges-Michel's representation of Modrulleau-Modigliani. While this shows that *Les Montparnos* participates in a more general consecration of the artist as secular saint in the early twentieth century, and that Van Gogh is the paradigmatic case setting the tone for subsequent elaborations of this myth, Georges-Michel refers his hagiographical account not to such recent models, but rather to sources from the more distant past. If, as Ernst Kris and Otto Kurz affirm in their sweeping historical account of recurring patterns in literary representations of the artist, motifs such as poverty and divine vocation have been more or less a constant in accounts of artists' lives ever since the Cinquecento, it is above all the potential connection between the early twentieth-century avant-garde and the painters of the Renaissance that Georges-Michel wishes to privilege, as is evident from the passage cited above, where the new artistic messiah is likened to Raphael — his arrival, indeed, considered a second coming.[41]

Les Montparnos is peppered with references to Raphael, who is revered by Modrulleau: 'seul Raphaël est Dieu' [only Raphael is God], the painter proclaims (*M*, p. 145). Stylistically, Modrulleau's art is described as more primitive in form, and closer to earlier painters who prepared the way for Raphael, as is the case in Georges-Michel's critical writing on Modigliani, where the artist is situated as a 'descendant direct d'Andrea di Vanni, de Simone Martini et des peintres de l'École de Sienne' [a direct descendant of Andrea di Vanni, of Simone Martini and the painters of the Sienese School].[42] Yet Raphael remains the model to which Modrulleau aspires. This link between 1920s avant-garde painting and the Renaissance may seem unlikely, and the combination of a search for a radically new pictorial language with the idolization of a Renaissance master paradoxical. It is only by considering this aspect of Georges-Michel's novel within its historical context — that of the post-war 'retour à l'ordre' — that it may be fully understood. The years following 1914 saw not just a revitalization of French nationalism as a political current, but a transfer of nationalistic sensibilities onto the aesthetic domain. As Kenneth Silver and others have shown, in this period the French literary and artistic landscape was profoundly shaped by the idea that a new kind of art would replace the aesthetic chaos and excesses of the pre-war years.[43] This new art would establish a renewed connection with artistic tradition (particularly various forms of classicism), would restore a sense of measure and order, and above all would be French, freeing itself from the decadent influence of Germany that was thought to have blighted art before the war, and insisting on a renewed sense of national identity. Foreign painters in Paris during the war (particularly non-combatant painters such as Picasso) found themselves obliged to respond to this current of thought by integrating more traditional, classical elements into their painting. And for several years after the end of the war, art critics sympathetic to foreign painters — members of what André Warnod would baptize the 'École de Paris'[44] — accordingly tended to emphasize their profound allegiance to France and to French culture, if not their actual Frenchness.[45]

The 'retour à l'ordre' may go some way to explaining why Modigliani becomes a Frenchman in Georges-Michel's fictionalized portrayal (and the artist's Jewish origins are, of course, left out completely), and why the author felt the need to emphasize Cendrars's and Kisling's heroic wartime exploits in the opening chapter. It also helps to explain one of the novel's stranger episodes, in which Kisling travels to Berlin, where he enjoys a night on the town with a transsexual prostitute and ends up in the cellar of a nightclub. Here, drugged with a 'hyperesthésique' substance which heightens his senses, he witnesses the gruesome spectacle of his friend being tortured — his head cut open and his brain probed for the enjoyment of a crowd. Whether or not this episode is understood, within the frame of Georges-

Michel's fictional narrative, to have 'really' occurred (and since Kisling's friend appears shortly afterwards to be alive and well, we can only assume that it was a hallucination), this gory, immoral spectacle is taken as an indication of the current state of German aesthetic sensibilities, reflecting the wild, decadent painting of 'Kokoschka et sa bande d'expressionnistes' [Kokoschka and his Expressionist gang]. Kisling even goes so far as to suggest that if French avant-garde painters followed the lead of their German counterparts and abandoned the discipline of Cubism the ensuing chaos would be equivalent to 'la [...] cave où l'on triture les cervelles' [the cellar where brains are probed] (*M*, p. 168).

While Georges-Michel's novel suggests that German aesthetic influence is to be resisted, other foreign influences may be more welcome. Although he is French, Modrulleau's affinity with Italy is insisted upon through his trip to Rome, during which he discovers his artistic identity: he is to rebel against 'la religion du cube' [the cult of the cube] (*M*, p. 78) and find his own way, guided by the Italian masters. Again, this may be related to a historical context within which the dominant discourses on national identity privileged 'Latinity' (as opposed to barbaric German culture), and portrayed France not only as a natural ally to Italy but as the inheritor of the Italian Renaissance tradition.[46] Contemporary art-critical discourse in the post-war years often connected avant-garde artistic production to the Italian Renaissance, reading it, as Georges-Michel does, as a kind of 'Renaissance d'aujourd'hui' [contemporary Renaissance] (*M*, p. 71). Furthermore, Raphael seems to have been particularly singled out amongst Renaissance painters as a model for the 'retour à l'ordre'. In the January 1921 issue of the Purist organ *L'Esprit nouveau*, the critic Bissière wrote:

> Nous sommes à un moment de l'histoire de l'art où notre race ayant fourni un effort considérable, et ayant subi des convulsions incroyables, éprouve le désir de s'apaiser, de faire le total des trésors qu'elle a amassés. En un mot, nous aspirons à un Raphaël ou du moins à tout ce qu'il représente de certitude, d'ordre, de pureté, de spiritualité.[47]

> [We have arrived at a moment in the history of art where our race, having spent a considerable energy, and gone through incredible upheavals, now needs calm, and to take stock of the treasures it has built up. In a word, we aspire to a Raphael, or at least to all that he represents in terms of certainty, order, purity, and spirituality]

André Derain also declared, in a direct echo of Modrulleau's proclamation cited earlier, that 'Raphaël seul est divin!' [only Raphael is divine!][48] — as did Picasso, using almost exactly the same terms, according to Georges-Michel's numerous accounts of his conversations with the painter in Rome in 1917.[49] Now, Derain and Picasso may simply have been expressing a personal aesthetic preference for Raphael over other Renaissance artists, and it may be that in *Les Montparnos* Georges-Michel is merely following their lead, concerned as he is that his novel should be based around authentic aesthetic pronouncements of the avant-garde. On the other hand, the choice of Raphael as an emblematic figure for Modrulleau and his contemporaries — rather than, say, Michelangelo, whose reputation as a maverick would make him a much more likely hero for the avant-garde — is far from neutral.[50] As Bissière's article reveals, Raphael was synonymous with order and purity; that is, with stable qualities that were particularly valued after the chaos of the war. Furthermore, Carl Goldstein has shown that Raphael was strongly linked with the French academic tradition of painting, the emulation of his work having been a central part of training both at the Académie and later at the École des Beaux-Arts. Raphael was bound up with French artistic tradition, Goldstein claims, to the extent that he 'stood for French art as much as for Italian'.[51] It was precisely because of this association with academic traditions that Raphael's critical fortunes faded in France in the late nineteenth century, a period in which the state-sponsored Salon, as the bastion of academic art, finally came to an end; equally, it was for the same reason that he enjoyed a revival during the post-war 'retour à l'ordre'.[52] The fact that Georges-Michel chooses Raphael as an emblem of avant-garde production, then, testifies to the strength of his commitment to this post-war aesthetic agenda. The fictional artist Modrulleau is positioned as the inheritor of French academic traditions, his artistic identity, like that of the academically-sanctioned winners of the Prix de Rome, grounded in his return to Italian Renaissance sources, and especially to Raphael.

As we have seen, *Les Montparnos* may initially seem to be a celebration of cutting-edge artistic experimentation: Modrulleau and his colleagues aim to 'tout recommencer' [begin everything afresh], to overturn established pictorial conventions and invent a new kind of art so radically different from all that has gone before that it will require the work of several generations to bring it to fruition. And yet this insistence on the innovations of the avant-garde is undercut by a more conservative discourse emphasizing the value of aesthetic tradition. As the novel's subtitle implies, it is a celebration of 'la bohème cosmopolite' [cosmopolitan bohemia]; yet it simultaneously privileges a Latin, and specifically French, artistic heritage. And Georges-Michel makes it very clear that this is a direct response to the discursive climate of the period. This is pointed up by the inclusion, at the very beginning of the novel, of a lengthy excerpt from a newspaper article on Montparnasse, in which a fictional journalist characterizes the avant-garde art produced there as the work of foreigners, criminals, and sexual deviants. The quoted text echoes many real conservative voices of the post-war period: one might compare it to Mauclair's later attacks on cosmopolitan Montparnasse as 'souillure de Paris' [a stain on Paris], a dangerous breeding ground for foreign influence, criminality, and bad art.[53] Indeed, Georges-Michel was well-versed in this kind of chauvinistic discourse since he had himself attacked avant-garde art as the work of 'métèques' [dirty foreigners], in a 1916 article.[54] Neither this nor his subsequent turnaround in attitude is acknowledged in *Les Montparnos*, and the inclusion of the hostile journalist's voice functions to indicate what Georges-Michel, as defender of the 'Montparnos', is up against. Yet just as Modrulleau seeks to placate rather than to fight the journalist whose text has insulted his friends, Georges-Michel's novel takes on the conservative critics of Montparnasse and its art on their own terms: not by fighting or even by questioning their premises, but rather by emphasizing the avant-garde's hitherto unsuspected commitment to the values of tradition and national identity.

The references to Raphael that recur throughout *Les Montparnos* serve not only to connect Modrulleau-Modigliani's avant-garde art to the Italian Renaissance, newly revalorized in the context of the post-war 'retour à l'ordre', but also to relate Georges-Michel's narrative — and particularly the central coupling between Modrulleau and Haricot-Rouge — to the story of Raphael's love affair with his model, La Fornarina. The story in question originates in Vasari's biography of the artist, where a few short lines indicate the extent of Raphael's extraordinary sexual appetites. His needs were such, Vasari tells us, that he was unable to work without his mistress, and one of Raphael's patrons had to move La Fornarina into his palace, so that these needs could be fulfilled and his artistic production could proceed unhampered.[55] Vasari's account also attributes the artist's untimely death to his sexual appetites: having overindulged in sexual pleasures with his mistress, Raphael contracted a fever, and since he was too embarrassed to tell his doctors the real cause of the illness, they gave him an inappropriate treatment and he died as a result.[56] As Marie Lathers has shown, these details from Vasari were seized upon and reworked by nineteenth-century accounts of the painter's life, in which 'the myth of La Fornarina, the myth of the life-giving and death-provoking mistress-model' was a central component.[57] These nineteenth-century re-elaborations of the Raphael myth also worked to produce a reinforced identification of sexual and creative energies, according to which artistic creation was conceived as akin to procreation, and the artist as lover. This identification arguably finds its strongest expression in the avant-garde art of the early twentieth century, which often implies a conception of the artist as earthy, virile, and sexually prolific. Carol Duncan, for instance, has remarked on 'the vogue for virility in early twentieth-century art' and has argued that pre-war avant-garde painting tends to assimilate women to nature, while giving men an individuality that situates them on the other side of the nature-civilization dichotomy, thereby cementing the notion of artistic creation as an inherently male endeavour.[58] Furthermore, Duncan reads Fauve paintings of female nudes as denying the subjectivity of the female model, and effacing from her representation anything not relevant to the genital urge. As a result, Duncan asserts, such painting supports 'the notion that the wellsprings of authentic art are fed by the streams of male libidinous energy' and 'the expectation that significant and vital content in *all* art presupposes the presence of male erotic energy'.[59]

Duncan's seminal article, along with subsequent feminist criticism on avant-garde art,[60] is important in breaking the oft-assumed association between aesthetic and social progressivism: as the art-historical narrative tends to subsume avant-garde production into an inexorable march towards liberation, aspects of artistic practice that actually work to uphold entrenched social prejudices are swept to one side. Duncan's account is also supported by anecdotal evidence that painters themselves associated the creative act with male sexuality: Renoir, for instance, was cited as saying 'I paint with my prick', while Picasso conceived of painting in terms of lovemaking.[61] What is important for our purposes, however, is the way in which *Les Montparnos* reflects this conjunction of aesthetics and gender politics, and uses references to Raphael, as the archetypal painter-lover, to underpin a myth of art as an activity closely bound up with male sexuality — and, therefore, only open to men.

Georges-Michel's Modrulleau certainly fits into the mould of the vigorous and virile male painter. He is earthy — literally earthy, with ochre the dominant colour in his paintings — and his manly physicality, 'son beau corps musclé dont toute la poitrine haletait dans la large ouverture de la chemise' [his beautiful toned body, chest heaving in his wide-open shirt], is repeatedly exposed for the reader's admiration (*M*, p. 44). Modrulleau's muscular strength is such, indeed, that he is able single-handedly to haul a stone statue of Haricot-Rouge across Paris — a feat which, later in the novel, six men together are unable to repeat. His sexual magnetism, meanwhile, is exemplary of that of all painters: Georges-Michel tells us that women are 'invinciblement attirées par leur odeur toute-puissante de rut' [irresistibly attracted by their all-powerful aroma of animals in heat] (p. 174). And yet Modrulleau and Haricot-Rouge's relationship remains chaste until their trip to Rome, where it is consummated in the name of art. It is at this point in the novel that the broader cultural identification of sexual and creative energies finds its most direct expression, as Modrulleau and Haricot-Rouge make love in order to create the new artistic messiah, 'Celui que nous attendons tous' [He for whom we are waiting], metaphorically to give birth to a new art: 'elle s'ouvrait, douloureuse et désireuse, non de l'œuvre de chair, mais de création, de la création sublime du dieu de demain, elle!' [she opened herself up, suffering and yet full of desire, not for the work of the flesh, but for creation, for the sublime creation of tomorrow's god!] (p. 157). Sexual desire is thus sublimated as creative desire. This in turn allows Modrulleau's sexual profligacy to be squared with his supposed 'purity' (for he is, let us not forget, a saint-like figure as well as a lover): his affair with the princesse de Laurence is justified by his belief that she, and not the humble Haricot-Rouge, will bear 'Celui qui viendra'. Sex, once again, is seen as necessary to — indeed, identical with — the 'sacred' task of artistic creation.

The female body thus becomes the site and medium of male artistic creation: Haricot-Rouge is 'le moule et le modèle' [the mould and the model] into which Modrulleau's dual artistic and sexual energies are channelled (*M*, p. 139). And yet, Haricot-Rouge is not *merely* a model, a passive object of the active, creative male painter's gaze. Her humble origins as a grocer's daughter link her to Raphael's model, La Fornarina (a baker's daughter, as her name indicates), and in some respects she may be seen as a nostalgic throwback to the nineteenth-century *grisette* as she appears in Murger: an innocent and unassuming working-class girl whose role is to provide the artist with companionship and support. In other respects, however, she cuts a much more modern figure, for unlike Balzac's Gillette, the Goncourts' Manette, Zola's Christine, or Murger's Mimi, this painter's companion is also an artist in her own right. Moreover, Haricot-Rouge is presented as a genuinely gifted artist: since she is self-taught, her style is somewhat naive, but this quality is praised in Modrulleau's critique of her work, tinged with the primitivist emphasis on artistic instinct: 'Ah! c'est rude, c'est primitif: mais c'est juste, c'est courageux, c'est pensé, et pensé haut' [Ah! It's raw and primitive, but it's true, it's brave, it's intelligent, and high minded] (p. 31). Modrulleau values Haricot-Rouge's art to the extent that he insists that she must evade the gender roles occupied by the female partners of other painters, in order to pursue her artistic endeavours, telling Zborowski:

> Je ne veux pas qu'elle fasse rien d'autre que peindre, tu entends, même pas la
> cuisine chez toi. Elle ne sera pas une servante, ni une femme de boxon comme
> la plupart de celles qu'ils ont épousées, les autres, elle sera ma femme à moi.
> (*M*, p. 54)

> [I don't want her to do anything apart from painting, do you hear me, not even
> cooking for you. She won't be a servant, and she won't be a bordello girl like
> most of the women the other painters marry; she'll be my wife, mine]

Haricot-Rouge does continue to paint and draw throughout the novel, despite
her tragic trajectory into destitution. And yet her creative activity is progressively
sidelined and displaced by her role as mother-to-be and as companion to the 'real'
artist, Modrulleau: *Les Montparnos* is his hagiography, not hers. Haricot-Rouge may
not be subservient in the way that Modrulleau understands other artists' companions
to be — she may not be constrained by the domestic duties of a 'servante' or the
sexual duties of a 'femme de boxon' — but, as the last phrase in the above passage
indicates, her role as artist is nevertheless seen as very much secondary to her role
as Modrulleau's partner: 'ma femme à moi'.

More generally, women in *Les Montparnos* are defined and morally judged by
their service of, or the threat they pose to, the male artist's needs and ambitions.
Modrulleau's first companion keeps him under lock and key, in an echo of the con-
trolling Manette Salomon;[62] Haricot-Rouge ultimately disappoints since, despite
her loyalty to Modrulleau, her poverty and lack of conventional beauty make her
unworthy to carry 'Celui qui viendra'; the princesse de Laurence scuppers Modrulleau's ambitions by aborting the child in whom he had placed his hopes for the
future of art, and subsequently suffers a violent attack from the artist, an attack
which the author does not explicitly ask us to condemn. Indeed, although by the
end of the novel we may have little sympathy for Modrulleau, who has fallen into
a delirious alcoholism and has cruelly abandoned Haricot-Rouge, Georges-Michel
appears to solicit our approval for his violent revenge on the princesse by suggesting
that she has violated the religion of art: 'La madone était allée faire étrangler le
Jésus par le chirurgien louche' [the Madonna had gone and had Jesus smothered by
a dodgy surgeon], we are told (*M*, p. 198). Similarly, shortly before his premature
death, Modrulleau bemoans his downfall in the following terms: 'J'ai été la terre
pétrie et prodigue, et j'ai enfanté le ciel. Et les putains de la terre ont versé l'eau de la
chirurgie sur la flamme céleste que j'avais allumée' [I was a fertile, prodigious earth,
and I gave birth to heaven. And the whores of the earth poured surgical spirit on the
celestial flame that I had lit] (p. 269). The ghost of La Fornarina, whose sexuality,
according to the Raphael myth, simultaneouly aided and threatened artistic
creation, is arguably present here in Georges-Michel's multiple representations
of the artist and his women. Women are, on the one hand, essential to the male
artist's creation/procreation of the work of art, or to the metaphorical 'enfantement'
in terms of which Modrulleau imagines his creative act. But, as impure 'putains'
unequal to the sacred cause of art, they also stand to bring it back down to earth
from the lofty heights to which it aspires, and even to kill it.

The end of *Les Montparnos* sees an apparently optimistic celebration of avant-
garde art, and its mythologization in terms of a mystical vocation, give way to an

overriding sense of failure. After Modrulleau dies and as Haricot-Rouge throws herself from the window of their studio, we are witness to another gory spectacle, in which her child, the hoped-for artistic messiah, emerges from her mangled body as a limp pile of meat: 'Entre les jambes sanglantes, l'enfant divin sortait comme un immense saucisson nu, comme un immonde ver rouge de ce ventre écrasé' [Between her bloody legs, the divine child emerged like an immense naked sausage, like a foul red worm from her crushed belly] (*M*, p. 274). In an echo of the metaphorical identification of child and work of art in Zola's *L'Œuvre*, where the death of the sickly child, Jacques, is representative of Claude's failure to (pro)create artistically, Georges-Michel represents 'Celui qui viendra', the future of art, as stillborn. But this is only one aspect of a broader pessimism: if, as Modrulleau claims, art is brought down by 'les putains de la terre', its prostitution is not driven solely by women, but by the market. The religion of art is seen to die as speculation in Modrulleau's work commences in the wake of his death: indeed, in the final lines of the novel, we are told with precision for how much Modrulleau's statue of Haricot-Rouge has been bought and sold, and given details of the next auction where we, as readers and consumers, might hope to put in our bids, the narrator's matter-of-fact tone pointing up the reduction of rich aesthetic experience to monetary value. Commercial concerns are also seen to invade and compromise the integrity of Montparnasse as privileged artistic space:

> Montparnasse allait f... le camp, comme la Butte. Et ce nom, au lieu d'évoquer le rude travail de ceux qui 'venaient', n'allait plus signifier qu'un lieu d'amusements, à faux artistes, à vraies grues, à chansonniers retardataires. (*M*, p. 281)
>
> [Montparnasse was going to f... off, like Montmartre. And its name, instead of evoking the difficult labours of those on the rise, would henceforth refer to a place of amusements, of false artists, real whores, and nostalgic singers]

Just as artistic Montmartre has died and survives only as a myth, the death of Montparnasse as a hive of artistic creativity is seen to be imminent. Avant-garde artistic production will be replaced by mass entertainments and by peddlars of a myth — the myth of the old, authentic Montparnasse — that keep the consumers coming back for more. Once again, there is an irony in Michel Georges-Michel's position here: if Montparnasse is dead, surely his own myth-making discourse is no different from that of the 'chansonniers retardataires' whom he criticizes. And surely his own concern, ultimately, is to put that myth to commercial purposes, to use it to sell his own literary art. Indeed, as Georges-Michel's art criticism attests, he did not actually think that avant-garde art was doomed to fail: in texts such as *Les Grandes Époques de la peinture 'moderne'*, he does express the view that Cubism became too formulaic and stagnant (and this is reflected in *Les Montparnos*), but at no point does he reject avant-garde practice in general.[63] It is tempting, on the basis of this, to attribute the tragic conclusion of *Les Montparnos*, in which Modrulleau's death becomes emblematic of the death of avant-garde art, to an awareness that tales of artistic success, effortlessly achieved, hold little appeal for the reader. What the novel supplies, instead, is a re-elaboration of the Romantic myth of the flawed genius, doomed to fail through the internal logic of the messianic narrative which, marked by the conventions of artistic hagiography, makes the artist an inevitable martyr to the avant-garde cause. The fact that Georges-Michel chooses to exploit this myth in his fiction of the Montparnasse avant-garde shows an awareness that, however outmoded it may seem nearly a century on from Balzac's Frenhofer, and in a period often viewed as a golden age of avant-garde experimentation, it still exerts a powerful appeal, and, ultimately, *sells*.

★   ★   ★   ★   ★

Both *La Ville lumière* and *Les Montparnos* effectively sustain a myth of the artist as *à part*, as special. Both, that is, contribute to an early twentieth-century cult of the individual artist, and of his unique 'temperament' or talent, but they approach this cult in distinct ways. Georges-Michel, as we have seen, draws attention to the fact that his ideal, authentic artist is above all an attractive fiction, a figure borne of myth-making discourses of various kinds, and he is aware of the collusion of his own portrait of the artist in the kinds of commercial process that his text seems to criticize. There is little of this self-consciousness in Mauclair, who envisions not only a pure art and a pure artist — both being protected and insulated against the pernicious influences of various 'foreign' others — but concomitantly, a pure art writing. Although there is a brief mention, in *La Ville lumière*, of 'les livres à clefs' as a key feature of the Parisian art circus that Mauclair so derides (*VL*, p. 174), there is no hint of awareness that the novel itself — not quite a *roman à clef*, but close to it — may itself give rise to an idea of the artist that serves the market, and not purely aesthetic imperatives.

The cult of the individual artist also has limits. Mauclair is willing to accept individualism, but only within certain clearly defined boundaries. That is, his is not a cult of the individual artist per se, but rather a cult of the individual artist who fits into a very specific mould: the painter who balances subjective and objective tendencies, and remains true to his national identity. This is a pattern common in early twentieth-century art criticism, where the idea that the artist must express his personal vision but also remain faithful to nature appears to make room for individual style, but also allows the critic to lambast anything that strikes him as too eccentric, too estranged from reality. In an article on the 1927 *Salon des indépendants*, François Fosca criticized the imperative for modern painters to appear original at all costs, noting that,

> Il est vrai que le véritable artiste est toujours original; mais à condition que cette originalité s'exprime par les moyens propres de l'art, et corresponde à une personnalité authentique, ait une valeur propre. La vraie originalité est spontanée, involontaire.[64]

> [It is true that the genuine artist is always original; but only provided that this originality is expressed by means proper to art, and that it corresponds to an authentic personality and has its own value. Real originality is spontaneous and involuntary]

This position allows Fosca to establish himself as the arbiter of reason and defender of *le juste milieu*: he pays lip service to originality, but any work that seems too 'original' may simply be dismissed as inauthentic, a distortion of the artist's true temperament, or indeed a mere pose, artificially adopted so as to attract attention.

Mauclair's later art criticism adopts a similar stance, frequently insisting on avant-garde art's excessive individualism. In his *Les États de la peinture française* (1921), for instance, Mauclair is able simultaneously to praise Impressionism for teaching artists to 'considérer l'indépendance comme le seul dogme valable, et avant tout à être sincères, à s'éduquer eux-mêmes, à n'accepter aucune idée toute faite' [to consider independence as the only valid dogma, and above all to be sincere, to educate themselves, and to accept no preconceived ideas].[65] And yet subsequent avant-garde movements such as Fauvism are seen to go too far, 'la vision personnelle et incontrôlable du peintre' [the out-of-control personal vision of the painter] taking precedence over 'ses devoirs envers l'étude de la nature et la vision normale des autres hommes' [his duties towards the study of nature and the normal vision of other men].[66]

The contradictions of Mauclair's position are, of course, elided. It is, moreover, a politically motivated position, one from which, as we have seen, excessive individualism is easily cast as an aberrant distortion of the artist's 'Frenchness'. One might expect a more tolerant, inclusive view of avant-garde art from Georges-Michel's *Les Montparnos*, given the author's attack on Cubist orthodoxy, and indeed his apparent defence of cosmopolitanism. In reality, *Les Montparnos*, like *La Ville lumière*, champions a specific kind of art and a specific kind of artist, whose identity is not only overwhelmingly masculine, but is also firmly rooted in French and 'Latin' national identities and aesthetic traditions.[67] Artistic identity in the early twentieth century is therefore no longer just about the individual: while seeming to hark back to the Romantic idea of the artist as a renegade whose unique genius is never appreciated by his contemporaries, and to the core Impressionist notion of fidelity to one's individual temperament, the portraits of the artist examined in this chapter make it clear that it is also about mapping the artist onto preformed categories of nationality and gender. As we shall see in Chapters 3 and 4, these categories remain relevant even in the radical modernist rethinking of the nature of art.

Notes to Chapter 2

1. See for instance Maurice Denis, 'Paul Sérusier' (*L'Occident*, December 1908), repr. in *Du Symbolisme au classicisme: théories*. ed. by O. Revault d'Allonnes (Paris: Hermann, 1964), pp. 54–57.
2. Kim Grant, *Surrealism and the Visual Arts: Theory and Reception* (Cambridge: Cambridge University Press, 2005), p. 48.
3. See Gee, *Dealers, Critics, and Collectors of Modern Painting*, pp. 152–53; p. 257.
4. Rosalind E. Krauss, 'In the Name of Picasso', in *The Originality of the Avant-Garde and Other Modernist Myths* (Cambridge, MA: MIT Press, 1985), pp. 23–40 (p. 25).
5. Maurice Berger, 'Epilogue: The Modigliani Myth', in *Modigliani: Beyond the Myth*, ed. by Mason Klein, exhibition catalogue (New York: Jewish Museum/New Haven, CT: Yale University Press, 2004), pp. 75–85; Griselda Pollock, 'Artists, Mythologies and Media: Genius, Madness and Art History', *Screen*, 21 (Spring 1980), 57–96.
6. For an overview of Mauclair's work (excluding his art criticism), see Simonetta Valenti, *Camille Mauclair, homme de lettres fin-de-siècle: critique littéraire, œuvre narrative, création poétique et théâtrale* (Milan: Vita e Pensiero, 2003).
7. Camille Mauclair, *Les Mères sociales: romain contemporain* (Paris: Paul Ollendorff, 1902); *Le Soleil des morts* [1898] (Geneva: Slatkine, 1979).

8. See Susan Youens, '*Le Soleil des morts*: A *Fin-de-siècle* Portrait Gallery', *Nineteenth-Century Music*, 11.1 (Summer 1987), 43–58.

9. Lathers, *Bodies of Art*, pp. 209–11. As Lathers notes, in this respect *La Ville lumière* corresponds to the relatively progressive views expressed in Mauclair's article 'La Femme devant les peintres modernes', *La Nouvelle revue*, 2nd series, 1 (1899), 190–213.

10. Camille Mauclair, *Trois crises de l'art actuel* (Paris: Charpentier, 1906), p. viii.

11. Camille Mauclair, *La Ville lumière: roman contemporain* (Paris: Paul Ollendorff, 1904), p. 315. Hereafter referred to as *VL*.

12. For useful summaries of Impressionist theory, see Paul Smith, *Impressionism: Beneath the Surface* (London: Everyman Art Library, 1995), pp. 19–31, and Richard Shiff, *Cézanne and the End of Impressionism: A Study of the Theory, Technique, and Critical Evaluation of Modern Art* (Chicago: Chicago University Press, 1984), esp. pp. 3–38.

13. Valenti, *Camille Mauclair*, pp. 229–30.

14. Heinich, 'Artistes dans la fiction: quatre générations', p. 220.

15. Camille Mauclair, 'Les Deux Lions', *L'Aurore*, 16 May 1898, 1. For an account of Mauclair's relationship with Rodin, see Joy Newton, 'Camille Mauclair and Auguste Rodin', *Nottingham French Studies*, 30.1 (1991), 39–55.

16. Camille Mauclair, 'Auguste Rodin, son œuvre, son milieu, son influence', *La Revue universelle*, 1 (1901), 769–75 (p. 771); incorporated into 'Auguste Rodin', in *Idées vivantes* (Paris: Librairie de l'art ancien et moderne, 1904), pp. 7–60.

17. Mauclair, 'Auguste Rodin, son œuvre, son milieu, son influence', p. 772.

18. Ibid., p. 772.

19. Émile Zola, 'Proudhon et Courbet', in *Mes haines: causeries littéraires et artistiques* (Paris: Charpentier, 1879), pp. 21–40 (p. 25).

20. Brignon might also seem to recall Cézanne, but this seems unlikely given Mauclair's attitude to the latter's painting: see, for instance, Camille Mauclair, *L'Impressionnisme: son histoire, son esthétique, ses maîtres* (Paris: Librairie de l'art ancien et moderne, 1904), pp. 511–12, where he describes Cézanne almost as a simpleton, 'un peintre sans adresse'.

21. Golan, 'From Fin de Siècle to Vichy', pp. 159–60.

22. Mauclair, *Trois crises*, p. 295.

23. Ibid., pp. 314–15, & 306.

24. Golan, 'From Fin de Siècle to Vichy', pp. 159–61.

25. It is difficult to locate a precise turning-point in Mauclair's thought, or a point where, as Golan would have it, he moves from defending a progressive aesthetics to a more reactionary, nationalist position: while *La Ville lumière* is suggestive of fears regarding cosmopolitan influences polluting 'pure' French aesthetic traditions, in an article of the following year the writer provided something of a defence of aesthetic cosmopolitanism (although he also argued, somewhat paradoxically, in favour of native French traditions): see 'La Réaction nationaliste en art et l'ignorance de l'homme de lettres', *La Revue*, 54 (1905), 151–74. This allegiance to French tradition is also present in an article predating *La Ville lumière*, 'Le Classicisme et l'académisme', *La Revue bleue*, 4th series, 19.11 (14 March 1903), 335–40, in which he argues for a specifically French form of classicism, distinct from the unwelcome influence of Ancient Greece and Rome, and Renaissance Italy.

26. Charles Rearick, *The French in Love and War: Popular Culture in the Era of the World Wars* (New Haven, CT: Yale University Press, 1997), p. vii.

27. This idea of decorative or applied art as the expression of the genius of the French people 'qui maintint le don de perfection française aux heures d'invasion étrangère' [who maintained the gift of French perfection in the face of foreign invasions] is also expressed in Mauclair's 'Le Besoin d'art du peuple', *La Revue bleue*, 5th series, 4.10 (2 September 1905), 306–10 (p. 307).

28. Mauclair, *Trois crises*, p. 301.

29. Three editions were published by Fayard (1924 & 1933) and Fasquelle (1929). All citations refer to the most recent and widely available edition: Michel Georges-Michel, *Les Montparnos* (Paris: Livre de poche, 1976), hereafter referred to as *M*.

30. The popular myth of Montparnasse has been created and sustained not just by literary and artistic representations, but also, to a certain extent, by historical accounts. While some of these

accounts present a factual analysis of the development of Montparnasse as a centre of artistic activity (see for example Nicholas Hewitt, 'Shifting Cultural Centres in Twentieth-Century Paris', in *Parisian Fields*, ed. by Michael Sheringham (London: Reaktion, 1996), pp. 30–45 (pp. 36–43); and Simonetta Fraquelli, 'Montparnasse and the Right Bank: Myth and Reality', in *Paris Capital of the Arts, 1900–1968*, exhibition catalogue (London: Royal Academy of Arts, 2002), pp. 106–17), others exploit a wealth of sensational anecdotes about its inhabitants, giving currency (intentionally or not) to myths of 'les années folles': see for instance Dan Franck, *The Bohemians: The Birth of Modern Art, Paris 1900–1930*, trans. by Cynthia Hope Liebow (London: Phoenix, 2002), or W. Wiser, *The Crazy Years: Paris in the Twenties* (New York: Atheneum, 1983).

31. François Fosca, 'Les Montparnos', *La Quinzaine critique*, 1.3 (1929), 133–34 (p. 134)

32. There is no reliable biography to which Georges-Michel's fictionalized version might be compared, since, as Jeanne Modigliani has insisted, all narratives of Modigliani's life (even those provided by his own family) are infected with deformed, mythologized elements; see *Modigliani sans légende* (Paris: Gründ, 1961), p. 12. This is certainly true of many of the first-hand accounts of Modigliani's life that were published by friends after his death: see, for example, the tragic overtones of Salmon's early accounts, 'Modigliani', *L'Amour de l'art*, 3.1 (1922), 20–22, and *Modigliani: sa vie et son œuvre*, as well as the funeral-apotheosis in Francis Carco's 1927 memoir *De Montmartre au quartier latin* (Monaco: Éditions Sauret, 1993), pp. 214–15. Even Cendrars, in his 1948 *Bourlinguer*, cannot resist the hagiographical impulse, describing Modigliani as 'beau comme saint Jean-Baptiste'; see *Tout autour d'aujourd'hui*, ed. by Claude Leroy, 15 vols (Paris: Denoël, 2001–06), IX, 211 (hereafter referred to as *TADA*).

33. In an earlier novel, *La Bohème canaille*, Georges-Michel similarly depicted the heroine as being seduced by tales of 'La Vie de Bohème'. See Georges-Michel, *La Bohème canaille* (Paris: La Renaissance du Livre, 1922), pp. 5 and 8.

34. Paul Mann, *The Theory-Death of the Avant-Garde* (Bloomington: Indiana University Press, 1991), pp. 6–7.

35. Émile Zola, *L'Œuvre*, ed. by Marie-Ange Voisin-Fougère (Paris: Librairie Générale Française, 1996), pp. 356–58.

36. Jerrold Seigel, *Bohemian Paris: Culture, Politics, and the Boundaries of Bourgeois Life, 1830–1930* (Baltimore, MD: Johns Hopkins University Press, 1999), p. 367.

37. Henry Murger, *Scènes de la vie de bohème*, ed. by Loïc Chotard and Graham Robb (Paris: Gallimard, 1988), p. 82.

38. Ibid., p. 375.

39. Heinich, *La Gloire de Van Gogh*, pp. 59–92.

40. Ibid., pp. 63–64.

41. Ernst Kris and Otto Kurz, *Legend, Myth, and Magic in the Image of the Artist: A Historical Experiment* (New Haven, CT: Yale University Press, 1979), pp. 49 & 115.

42. Michel Georges-Michel, *Les Grandes Époques de la peinture 'moderne': de Delacroix à nos jours* (New York: Brentano's, 1945), p. 197; see also *Peintres et sculpteurs que j'ai connus, 1900–1942* (New York: Brentano's, 1942), p. 171.

43. Kenneth E. Silver, *Esprit de Corps: The Art of the Parisian Avant-Garde and the First World War, 1914–1925* (Princeton, NJ: Princeton University Press, 1989); Jean Laude, 'Retour et/ou rappel à l'ordre?', in *Retour au classicisme, 1917–1925*, exhibition catalogue (Saint-Tropez: Musée de l'Annonciade, 2002), pp. 17–56. There were, of course, some dissenting voices: many artists associated with Dada and Surrealism did not participate in the 'retour à l'ordre', and many writers treated it with far more scepticism than Georges-Michel. See, for example, Aragon's scathing treatment of Picasso's return to classical form in his 1921 novel *Anicet*, discussed in Chapter 4.

44. André Warnod, 'L'École de Paris', *Comoedia*, 27 January 1925, p. 1.

45. For instance, in 1923 Cocteau described Picasso as 'un Espagnol, pourvu des plus vieilles recettes françaises (Chardin, Poussin, Le Nain, Corot)' [a Spaniard, equipped with the oldest French formulae (Chardin, Poussin, Le Nain, Corot)] and insisted that 'Picasso est de chez nous. Il a mis toutes ses forces, toutes les ruses de sa race à l'école et au service de la France' [Picasso is from our country. He has put all his strength, all the guile of his race to the service of the School and of France]. Jean Cocteau, *Picasso* (Paris: L'École des lettres, 1996), pp. 26–27 & 27n. Apollinaire

had also taken pains to emphasize the Latin origins of Cubism: see 'L'Origine du cubisme', *Pr*, II, 1342–43, and my discussion of Apollinaire's adherence to the agenda of the 'retour à l'ordre' in Chapter 3.

46. Silver, *Esprit de Corps*, pp. 93–95.

47. Bissière, 'Notes sur Ingres', *L'Esprit nouveau*, 4 (January 1921), 388–400 (p. 390).

48. Cited in [Anon.], 'Revue esthétique des journaux et des revues', *L'Esprit nouveau*, 3 (December 1921), 310.

49. Michel Georges-Michel, *Ballets russes: histoire anecdotique, suivie d'un appendice et du poème de Shérérazade* (Paris: Éditions du monde nouveau, 1923), p. 33; *En Jardinant avec Bergson* (Paris: Albin Michel, 1926), p. 308; *Peintres et sculpteurs que j'ai connus*, pp. 20–21.

50. Apollinaire's 1912 article, 'De Michel-Ange à Picasso', *Pr*, II, 396–98, shows that Michelangelo was indeed a model for the pre-war avant-garde, before being displaced by Raphael in the post-war 'retour à l'ordre'.

51. Carl Goldstein, 'French Identity in the Realm of Raphael', in *The Cambridge Companion to Raphael*, ed. by Marcia B. Hall (Cambridge: Cambridge University Press, 2005), pp. 237–60 (p. 237); see also Jacques Thuillier, 'Raphaël et la France: présence d'un peintre', in *Raphaël et l'art français*, ed. by J. P. Cuzin, exhibition catalogue (Paris: Galeries Nationales du Grand Palais, 1984), pp. 11–36.

52. For an account of Raphael's critical fortunes, see André Chastel, *La Gloire de Raphaël, ou le triomphe d'Eros* (Paris: Réunion des musées nationaux, 1995), pp. 11–24.

53. Camille Mauclair, 'Montparno', in *Les Métèques contre l'art français: la farce de l'art vivant*, II (Paris: Nouvelle revue critique, 1930), pp. 39–44. On cosmopolitan Montparnasse as a frequent target for conservatives fearful of the foreign threat to traditional French culture, see Rearick, *The French in Love and War*, pp. 88–93.

54. *Excelsior*, 23 July 1916; cited in Gee, *Dealers, Critics, and Collectors of Modern Painting*, p. 222. Gee puts the shift in Georges-Michel's attitude down to the fact that in the post-war years, avant-garde art became fashionable with the aristocratic set (p. 183), but Georges-Michel's contact with Picasso and other artists via the Ballets Russes undoubtedly also affected his sympathies.

55. Giorgio Vasari, *Vies des artistes*, trans. by Léopold Leclanché and Charles Weiss, ed. by Véronique Gerard Powell (Paris: Grasset & Fasquelle, 2007), p. 245.

56. Ibid., p. 252.

57. Lathers, *Bodies of Art*, p. 71; see also Marie Lathers, ' "Tué par un excès d'amour": Raphael, Balzac, Ingres', *French Review*, 71.4 (1998), 550–64, and Thuillier, 'Raphaël et la France', pp. 25–26.

58. Carol Duncan, 'Virility and Domination in Early Twentieth-Century Vanguard Painting', in *The Aesthetics of Power: Essays in Critical Art History* (Cambridge: Cambridge University Press, 1993), pp. 81–108 (p. 90).

59. Ibid., p. 98.

60. Examples might include Lynda Nead, 'Seductive Canvases: Visual Mythologies of the Artist and Artistic Creativity', *Oxford Art Journal*, 18.2 (1995), 59–69, and Susan Rubin Suleiman, *Subversive Intent: Gender, Politics, and the Avant-Garde* (Cambridge, MA: Harvard University Press, 1990).

61. Elizabeth Wilson, *Bohemians: The Glamorous Outcasts* (London: Tauris Parke, 2000), p. 96.

62. Edmond and Jules de Goncourt, *Manette Salomon* (Paris: Gallimard, 1996), pp. 498–99, 507–09.

63. Georges-Michel, *Les Grandes Époques de la peinture 'moderne'*, pp. 168–70. This view of Cubism was a common one in the post-war period (see Gee, *Dealers, Critics and Collectors of Modern Painting*, p. 234). Indeed, its over-dependence on theoretical systems had already been highlighted by critics before the war: see Weiss, *The Popular Culture of Modern Art*, pp. 74–75.

64. François Fosca, 'Le Salon des indépendants', *L'Amour de l'art*, 8 (1927), 33–37 (p. 33).

65. Camille Mauclair, *Les États de la peinture française de 1850 à 1920* (Paris: Payot, 1921), pp. 110–11.

66. Ibid., p. 150.

67. Tradition itself is a key critical term in this period; as Malcolm Gee notes, even the most radical avant-garde art was constantly placed in relation to aesthetic tradition, and 'critical battles [...] were less for or against tradition than over which one', *Dealers, Critics, and Collectors of Modern Painting*, pp. 141–44 (p. 144).

CHAPTER 3

Art, Writing, and Modernity in Apollinaire and Cendrars

The early years of the twentieth century were a time of enormous scientific and technological progress. Dubbed the 'Futurist Moment' by Marjorie Perloff, the pre-war years in particular saw writers and artists opening their works up to modernity, and seeking to represent the perceptual and psychological changes brought about through technological innovations.[1] As poets, Guillaume Apollinaire and Blaise Cendrars both played a central role in this Futurist Moment. Thus Apollinaire's experiments in poetic simultaneity in his *poèmes-conversations* and calligrammes might be read as an attempt to respond to a new sense of the global brought about through high-speed travel (especially aeroplanes and automobiles), and, in the field of communications, the invention of the telephone and of wireless telegraphy. Cendrars's *poèmes élastiques*, meanwhile, pushed at stable notions of space and time, and experimented with 'telegraphic' languages.[2] Apollinaire outlined the importance of such experimentations in his November 1917 lecture, 'L'Esprit nouveau et les poètes', where he highlighted the gap between cutting-edge science and poetry. Scientific marvels, he wrote:

> nous imposent le devoir de ne pas laisser l'imagination et la subtilité poétique derrière celle des artisans qui améliorent une machine. Déjà, la langue scientifique est en désaccord profond avec celle des poètes. C'est un état des choses insupportable. Les mathématiciens ont le droit de dire que leurs rêves, leurs préoccupations dépassent souvent de cent coudées les imaginations rampantes des poètes. [...]
>
> Peut-on forcer la poésie à se cantonner hors de ce qui l'entoure, à méconnaître la magnifique exubérance de vie que les hommes par leur activité ajoutent à la nature et qui permet de machiner le monde de la façon la plus incroyable?[3]

> [impose upon us a duty not to let poetic imagination and subtlety lag behind that of artisans who tinker with machines. Scientific language is already at odds with poetry. This is an intolerable state of affairs. Mathematicians are justified in saying that their dreams, their preoccupations are a hundred miles ahead of the rampant imaginations of poets. [...]
>
> Can we force poetry to cloister itself away from that which surrounds it, and to ignore the magnificent exuberance of life that men, by their activity, add to nature and which allows them to manipulate the world in the most incredible ways?]

But Apollinaire's lecture, while it appeared to present an optimistic vision of an avant-garde poetry that was truly adapted to its time, also voiced a number of anxieties: what would poetry look like in the age of mechanical reproduction? Could it really remain relevant? How, in particular, might it compete with other art forms whose veneer of modernity might more easily capture the public's attention? In the early twentieth century, poetry was often held to be lagging behind in relation to other art forms, and was under particular pressure to reinvent itself: it seemed stuck in a time-warp, struggling to break free of the hermetic, ivory-tower aestheticism of the late nineteenth-century Symbolist movement. The novel did not suffer from the same complaint: with the prevailing trend towards literary realism, it seemed able to respond to readers' demands for material relevant to their own lives, and since the beginning of the nineteenth century had gained a wide readership. Poetry seemed particularly backward-looking when compared with the visual arts: by the First World War, avant-garde painting had already been through a number of dramatic and well-publicized shifts, from the first burst of Fauve activity in the mid-1900s, to the rise of Cubism. Painting enjoyed an increasing cultural prominence, and now seemed to be reversing traditional aesthetic hierarchies by exerting an influence over literature (in the form of 'cubisme littéraire').[4] But the perceived threat to poetry's position within an increasingly competitive cultural field came not just from painting or the novel but also from the new media of the cinema and the phonograph, whose challenges Apollinaire also acknowledged in 'L'Esprit nouveau et les poètes':

> Il eut été étrange qu'à une époque où l'art populaire par excellence, le cinéma, est un livre d'images, les poètes n'eussent pas essayé de composer des images pour les esprits méditatifs et plus raffinés qui ne se contentent point des imaginations grossières des fabricants de films. Ceux-ci se raffineront, et l'on peut prévoir le jour où le phonographe et le cinéma étant devenus les seules formes d'impression en usage, les poètes auront une liberté inconnue jusqu'à présent. (*Pr*, II, 944)

> [It would have been strange if, in a period where the popular art *par excellence*, the cinema, is a book of images, poets did not try to compose images for more refined and reflective minds who are not content with the vulgar imaginations of filmmakers. These will become more refined, and we can predict a time when the phonograph and the cinema will be the only forms of publication still in use, and poets will have a previously unknown freedom]

This is, once again, only an apparently optimistic statement. Apollinaire is staking a claim here for poetry's specificity, indeed its irreplaceability within the cultural field as it stands: cinema, since its birth at the end of the previous century, might have become the most popular art form, but at present it caters only for vulgar tastes, leaving room for poets to appeal to more 'refined' cultural consumers. At the same time, however, Apollinaire is also predicting a time when the printed book will be obsolete. As such, he makes it clear that poets cannot rest on their laurels or assume that their work will always retain the same prestige; they will need to learn to work with these new media, mastering them as part of an all-encompassing 'synthèse des arts' [synthesis of the arts] which will result in 'le livre vu et entendu de l'avenir' [the book of the future, which will be seen and heard] (*Pr*, II, 944–45).

As he advanced this vision of a new, multi-modal expressive medium, Apollinaire probably had in mind his own visual poetry, which he had begun to publish in 1914 but would be brought together in *Calligrammes* (1918), as a type of writing that might appeal to both eye and ear. He had also worked towards a synthesis of the arts through illustrated editions of his writing, and through his poetic art criticism, which we shall consider in more detail shortly.[5] As Anna Boschetti has noted, his desire to create new, multi-sensory languages is also frequently made evident in his fiction writing thanks to a profusion of invented art forms: tactile, cinematic, sonorous, and in one instance culinary or 'gastro-astronomic'.[6] While many of these invented languages and media are humorous and parodic, they nevertheless bespeak Apollinaire's conviction that poetic writing (broadly conceived not just as verse but as an experimental writing divorced from mass-market imperatives, a definition that may thus include Apollinaire's fiction)[7] needed to reinvent itself, to experiment with, borrow from, and join forces with other media in order to survive. In Boschetti's Bourdieusian analysis, Apollinaire is a writer whose aesthetic choices are always motivated, at least in part, by this struggle to survive, to win symbolic as well as financial capital within a very pressurized cultural field. What is particularly fruitful about such a perspective is that it allows us to register the full complexity of Apollinaire's strategies of collaboration and borrowing from the visual arts. Rather than reading these as a purely aesthetically motivated attempt to merge text and image into a more powerful multi-modal language, or indeed as an attempt to instill a chummy relationship between 'sister arts' that reflected Apollinaire's close real-life friendships with the most prominent artists of his period, this perspective might allow us to register the rivalry that is present within these strategies — the fact that Apollinaire is pushed, by the increasingly marginalized position of poetry and avant-garde literary writing more generally, to join forces with an art form that may itself be seen as partly responsible for that marginalization. This rivalry, this tension between the visual arts and poetic writing, is occluded in Apollinaire's art criticism, and is certainly not apparent in his poetry, but is allowed to emerge in his 1916 novella 'Le Poète assassiné'.[8] Here, what appears initially to be an insistence on the close relationship between art and poetry turns out, on further analysis, to reveal points of tension: the 'marriage' of text and image turns out to be a strained one, and representatives of the visual arts — painters and muses alike — to be perfidious bedfellows. These concerns about painting are taken up in the novel *La Femme assise* (first published in 1920, two years after the poet's death), where they are amplified through mounting intersecting anxieties about artistic creativity, sexuality, and gender. Like Tristouse Ballerinette in 'Le Poète assassiné', the woman painter Elvire Goulot in *La Femme assise* is an emasculating figure who stands to threaten male creativity, both poetic and painterly; here, however, Apollinaire responds not just to the pressure that poetry comes under from an increasingly prominent avant-garde painting, but to a broader crisis of masculinity which he relates to the First World War. As we shall see, both 'Le Poète assassiné' and *La Femme assise* are anxious texts, and Apollinaire a writer who, far from straightforwardly embracing the profound shifts associated with modernity, often registers them as traumatic, and expresses his fears about their impact on the arts.[9]

These anxieties are also present in Blaise Cendrars's 1929 novel *Dan Yack*. Up until the First World War, Cendrars moved within the same avant-garde circles as Apollinaire, and indeed sought to occupy a similar position within the cultural field, joining a generation of artists and writers who set out to reject *passéisme,* to renew and reinvigorate artistic forms, and to render in their work 'la beauté du monde moderne' [the beauty of the modern world].[10] Like Apollinaire, Cendrars forged alliances with key representatives of the visual arts, working towards a visual-verbal 'simultaneity' through his 1913 collaboration with Sonia Delaunay, *La Prose du Transsibérien et de la petite Jehanne de France.* He also envisioned new expressive languages, taking a particular interest in Léopold Survage's experiments in 'rythmes colorés' (an attempt at an abstract, coloured cinema); in his poetic, almost cinematographic writing on these experiments he sought not only to promote Survage's new art but also arguably to appropriate its resources for himself.[11] In the post-war period, however, Cendrars distanced himself from avant-garde painting (for reasons we shall consider later), and also from verse, gaining his first major success as a novelist with *L'Or* in 1925. Cendrars thus shifted from a position of avant-garde marginality (and financial penury) as a poet, to gaining a broader appeal as a novelist (even if his writing was never exactly mainstream or purely commercially motivated).[12] *Dan Yack*, then, is produced in rather different circumstances to 'Le Poète assassiné' and *La Femme assise,* and with a different sense of how the author might position himself within the literary marketplace. What is at stake in the narrative itself, however, is the aesthetic identity of literature — its essence as a medium of expression — which Cendrars seeks to define in relation to a number of art forms and media, both traditional (poetry, music, sculpture) and technologically advanced (the phonograph and the cinema). Like Apollinaire in 'L'Esprit nouveau et les poètes', Cendrars is asking how literary expression (or indeed art more generally) might reinvent itself for the age of mechanical reproduction: how it might adopt the model of new technologies, how it might manage to represent modern experience in a way that gives it meaning, what sort of position it might occupy within the cultural field and indeed what sort of role it might play in human life more generally. Just as Cendrars's career in the 1920s shows him moving towards the stance of a literary entrepreneur seeking to make his fortune, the novel ultimately suggests that there may be more artistry in the protagonist Dan Yack's own achievements as an industrialist than in the stale forms of traditional modes of expression, or indeed in art forms generated through mechanical technologies — forms which turn out to be threatening and indeed sterile. This insistence on sterility, as we shall see, emerges from an identification of artistic creation with male sexual energies and with procreation (an identification that also underlies both of Apollinaire's texts), with the failure of both the phonograph and the cinema finding an emblem in Dan Yack's barren marriage. Further connections with Apollinaire might be seen in the way in which Cendrars weighs up a number of competing models for artistic creation, recalling the inter-arts tensions and rivalries explored in 'Le Poète assassiné'. But the motif of the inter-arts competition also looks forward to Aragon's *Anicet*, where (as we shall see in Chapter 4) it once again features as a symptom of a literature whose encounter with modernity obliges it to redefine and reinvent itself.

'Le Poète assassiné' and the Marriage of Text and Image

'Et moi aussi je suis peintre' [I too am a painter], Apollinaire declared in the title of his 1914 collection of visual poems.[13] Borrowing the phrase purportedly uttered by Caravaggio upon seeing Raphael's painting for the first time, Apollinaire attributed to himself the same admiration, ambition, and desire to appropriate the tools of the painter's craft for his own poetic purposes. This strong sense of solidarity with the visual arts was also pursued through art criticism, in which Apollinaire, in defending Cubism and avant-garde art more generally, set out to align the interests of poetry and painting, insisting on his own close relationships with key figures such as Picasso, and implying that literary and artistic avant-gardes existed in a kind of creative symbiosis. In one article, he laid emphasis on the fact that Cubist painters surrounded themselves with poetry, and said of Picasso, 'Quant à Picasso, qui inventa la peinture nouvelle et qui, on ne peut plus en douter aujourd'hui, est la figure artistique la plus haute de ce temps, il n'a vécu que parmi des poètes dont je m'honore d'être' [As for Picasso, who invented the new painting and who, we can no longer have any doubt about it, is the most important artistic figure of our times, he has only ever lived amongst poets of whom I have the honour of being one].[14] Of course, this rhetorical strategy functions just as much to consolidate Apollinaire's own position as critical defender of and, by implication, poetic inspiration for Cubism as it does to legitimate Cubism by association with poetry.

But Apollinaire's art criticism is not merely a strategic tool or marketing ploy: it is also, very often, a highly allusive, properly poetic writing that seeks to translate the very difficult experience of looking at avant-garde art into words. Apollinaire tends to resist close ekphrastic descriptions of individual paintings, and this may simply be because he was aware of the limitations of such verbal descriptions, their incapacity to provide a true equivalent to the visual artifact: indeed, in a 1907 diary entry, Apollinaire had described Picasso's painting as an 'admirable langage que nulle littérature ne peut indiquer, car nos mots sont faits d'avance' [admirable language that no literature can indicate, for our words are made in advance], acknowledging the fact that pre-formed words may not be able to do justice to an innovative visual syntax.[15] Instead of describing paintings, Apollinaire's critical writing on Picasso employs techniques that are closer to prose poetry or indeed to imaginative fiction. In the passages from *Les Peintres cubistes* (1913) dealing with the 'blue' and 'rose' periods, we find Apollinaire mobilizing figures from Picasso's works and turning them into characters in a fictional world that is of his own making:

> Il y a des enfants qui ont erré sans apprendre le catéchisme. Ils s'arrêtent et la pluie cesse de tomber: 'Regarde! Des gens dans ces bâtisses et leurs vêtements sont pauvres.' Ces enfants qu'on n'embrasse pas comprennent tant! Maman, aime-moi bien! Ils savent sauter et les tours qu'ils réussissent sont des évolutions mentales.[16]

> [There are children who have wandered without learning their catechism. They stop and the rain stops falling: 'Look! There are people in those buildings and their clothes are poor.' These children whom no one cuddles understand so much! Mummy, love me! They know how to leap and their tricks are mental evolutions]

Picasso's Cubist works, as Jennifer Pap has argued, are much more resistant to this type of narrative entry: refusing to allow the viewer easy access to the world of the painting, they confront us instead with a flat material surface and a picture space that is difficult to make sense of.[17] As such, Apollinaire's attempts to gain some kind of hold on the image result in an even more elliptical writing: objects are mentioned but it is often unclear whether these are motifs from Picasso's paintings or collages, whether they are part of the writer's own imaginative response to the image, or indeed whether the narrative relates primarily to incidents from the painter's life. Pap cites the following passage:

> Et puis, il y a des pays. Une grotte dans une forêt où l'on faisait des cabrioles, un passage à dos de mule au bord d'un précipice et l'arrivée dans un village où tout sent l'huile chaude et le vin rance. C'est encore la promenade dans un cimetière et l'achat d'une couronne en faïence (couronne d'immortelles) et la mention *Mille regrets* qui est inimitable. On m'a aussi parlé de candélabres en terre glaise qu'il fallait appliquer sur une toile pour qu'ils en parussent sortir. Pendeloques de cristal, et ce fameux retour du Havre.[18]

> [And then, there are countries. A cave in a forest where they used to dance, a donkey ride beside a precipice and arriving in a village where everything smells of warm oil and rancid wine. Or a walk in a cemetery and buying an earthenware crown (crown of immortals) and the phrase *Mille regrets* which is inimitable. I've also heard of candelabras made of clay that had to be stuck to a canvas so that they would seem to protrude from it. Crystal pendants, and the infamous return from Le Havre]

What is clear from both these passages is that for Apollinaire, the boundaries between poetry, fiction, and criticism are extremely porous. While Apollinaire is engaged, in some parts of *Les Peintres cubistes*, in setting out aesthetic principles — much as one might expect him to do in a text subtitled 'Méditations esthétiques' — in passages such as these he crosses into a kind of writing that is much more generically problematic. Moreover, in these passages he blurs the boundaries not only between literary genres but also between painting and writing, to the extent that it is impossible to tell where exactly Picasso's painting stops and where Apollinaire's own writerly imagination takes over. As such, *Les Peintres cubistes* proposes a new kind of art criticism, but it also enacts a kind of marriage of text and image that foreshadows the way in which the relationship between poet and painter, and their respective arts, is represented in the central studio scene in 'Le Poète assassiné'.

'Le Poète assassiné' is, first and foremost, a tale about a poet, Croniamantal, whose story is loosely based on Apollinaire's own life. In a fractured narrative that mixes diverse literary styles and linguistic registers, Apollinaire recounts the birth, life, and death of the poet at the hands of a crowd turned against poetry by Horace Tograth, a demagogue and representative of utilitarian science. In doing so, he delivers a kind of parodic hagiography, insisting on the glory of the martyred poet but consistently undermining and mocking this through scabrous humour and farcical plotting, and alternating between lyricism and bathos. The theme of the persecution of poets, however, is much more than just a joke. Tograth and his acolytes not only find poets to be 'paresseux, inutiles, etc' [lazy, useless, etc] (*Pr*, I, 290), but are enraged by their enormous financial gains, and here Apollinaire's enumeration of the vast sums that they are awarded provides a bitterly ironic reflection of the lack of market for poetic writing in the early twentieth century.[19]

Also central to the novella's plot is the friendship between Croniamantal and the painter L'Oiseau du Bénin. The reference in the latter's name to African art, a key inspiration in the development of Cubism, signals that the character is a stand-in for Picasso, and a host of other 'clues' work to confirm this.[20] What is of most interest to us in considering 'Le Poète assassiné' (and indeed *La Femme assise*), however, is not the extent to which Apollinaire's texts correspond to the historical facts of his friendship with Picasso, or indeed with other artists represented here. While it might be tempting to read both texts in terms of Apollinaire's personal relationships (and one might want to argue that his portraits of Tristouse/Marie Laurencin and of Elvire/Irène Lagut as fickle backstabbers might be motivated by romantic rejections suffered by the writer),[21] these *romans à clef* were clearly written with a purpose beyond that of communicating in-jokes and coded messages to a small circle of initiates: as Caroline Levitt has argued, they have 'more to do than simply veil or reveal identity', and are not just a 'mystery' to be unlocked.[22] One of the main purposes of these texts, rather — and this is what interests us here — is to say something about art, to articulate certain art-critical positions through the fictional text.

The scene in which Croniamantal visits L'Oiseau du Bénin at his studio is critical in this regard. At the beginning of Chapter x, entitled 'Poésie' as if to signal that the painting described here is on a par with, indeed an alternate form of, poetic creation, Croniamantal makes his way through a hostile city:

> Les clameurs et les tonnerres de Paris éclataient au loin et autour du jeune homme qui s'arrêta tout essouflé, tel un cambrioleur trop longtemps poursuivi et prêt à se rendre. Ces clameurs, ce bruit indiquaient bien que des ennemis étaient sur le point de le traquer, comme un voleur. (*Pr*, I, 254)

> [The clamours and thunderous noises of Paris could be heard in the distance and all around the young man who stopped, out of breath, like a burglar tired of the chase and willing to give himself up. These clamours, this noise signalled the presence of enemies who were about to track him down, like a thief]

Although the persecution of poets is not threatened until much further on in the tale, Apollinaire makes it clear that already the modern city is a dangerous environment for poets, and for poetic creation. When Croniamantal arrives at the painter's studio, however, there is an immediate sense of solace, not only in the space of the studio itself, which is closed off from the hostile world of the city, but also in the friendship and support of L'Oiseau du Bénin:

> Il toquait à la porte et criait:
> 'C'est moi, Croniamantal.'
> Et derrière la porte les pas lourds d'un homme fatigué, ou qui porte un faix très pesant, vinrent avec lenteur et quand la porte s'ouvrit ce fut dans la brusque lumière la création de deux êtres et leur mariage immédiat.
> Dans l'atelier, semblable à une étable, un innombrable troupeau gisait

> éparpillé, c'étaient les tableaux endormis et le pâtre qui les gardait souriait à son ami. (*Pr*, I, 255)

> [He knocked on the door and cried:
> 'It's me, Croniamantal.'
> And behind the door he could hear the heavy footsteps of a man who was tired, or bearing a heavy load, and when the door opened there was in the sudden light the creation of two beings and their immediate marriage.
> In the stable-like studio an innumerable flock was scattered around; the paintings were sleeping and the shepherd who watched over them smiled at his friend]

Outside the studio it is cold and dark, but when Croniamantal goes inside there is an intense light, connoting creative enlightenment and joy. Poet and painter come together in a meeting of minds, and there is a sense here that they and their respective media are intimately linked, 'wedded' together, and that they create and constitute each other. In the comparison to a 'pâtre', or shepherd, watching over his flock, and the studio to a biblical stable, the painter is not only associated with the pastoral — distancing him, once again, from the harsh realities of the modern city — but becomes something of a Christ-like figure. Along with later mentions of the painter's simple clothes and 'pieds nus' [bare feet] (*Pr*, I, 256), this description works to represent L'Oiseau du Bénin as a kind of hermit or saint, and painting as a divine act of creation, or indeed a quasi-religious duty which the poet must bear as a heavy burden ('faix'). All of this is very much consonant with Apollinaire's 'critical' writing: in *Les Peintres cubistes*, for instance, we are told that the painter must 'se donner le spectacle de sa propre divinité' [give himself the spectacle of his own divinity] (*Pr*, II, 7); moreover, Apollinaire goes on to place Picasso amongst those authentic artists for whom this 'divine' act of creation is never easy, but is a constant struggle, with little respite: 'Hommes créés à l'image de Dieu, ils se reposeront un jour pour admirer leur ouvrage' [Men created in the image of God, they will one day stop to rest and admire their work] (*Pr*, II, 23).[23]

The description of the studio continues as follows:

> Sur une étagère, des livres jaunes empilés simulaient des mottes de beurre. Et repoussant la porte mal jointe, le vent amenait là des êtres inconnus qui se plaignaient à tout petits cris, au nom de toutes les douleurs. Toutes les louves de la détresse hurlaient alors derrière la porte, prêtes à dévorer le pâtre et son ami, pour préparer à la même place la fondation de la Ville nouvelle. Mais dans l'atelier il y avait des joies de toutes les couleurs.

> [On a shelf, piles of yellow books resembled pats of butter. And pushing in the wonky door, the wind brought with it unknown beings who let out plaintive little cries of suffering. All the she-wolves of distress howled behind the door, ready to devour the shepherd and his friend, to clear the way for the foundation of the New City. But in the studio there were joys of every colour]

Once again, the artist's studio is presented as a refuge, a reassuring space in which painter and poet can be safe from the threatening forces that characterize the modern world. Daniel Delbreil has read the 'Ville nouvelle' in this passage somewhat more positively, as a reference to Rome, and indeed, the mention of 'louves' [she-wolves] does call to mind the myth of Romulus and Remus, whose role Croniamantal and L'Oiseau du Bénin might take on as founders of a new city of the arts.[24] Yet the 'louves' here are howling in distress, and the poet and painter stand to be 'devoured' or eaten up by the forces that wish to establish the new city; as such, the latter seems not so much an emblem of artistic vibrancy and enlightenment, as of a rationalized, mechanized civilization that has no place for art, poetry, or their practitioners, who must unite to protect themselves. (Here one sees that the imperative to respond to modernity, expressed in 'L'Esprit nouveau et les poètes', is not a requirement to embrace it in all its aspects.)

A threat to art is also present within the space of the studio itself:

> Il y avait encore dans l'atelier une chose fatale, ce grand morceau de miroir brisé, retenu au mur par des clous à crochet. C'était une insondable mer morte, verticale et au fond de laquelle une fausse vie animait ce qui n'existe pas. Ainsi, en face de l'Art, il y a son apparence, dont les hommes ne se défient point et qui les abaisse lorsque l'Art les avait élevés. (*Pr*, i, 256)

> [In the studio there was also a fatal object: a large piece of broken mirror, held onto the wall with hooked nails. It was an unfathomable dead sea suspended vertically, and within which a false life animated non-existent things. Facing Art, then, was its appearance, of which men are not sufficiently wary and which debases them, whereas Art had elevated them]

The mirror, as a number of critics have pointed out, clearly represents artistic mimetism, or a superficial type of pictorial realism.[25] This is not Art — not, that is, *authentic* art as Apollinaire understands it — but merely its appearance. As Delbreil has noted, however, the mirror is also implicitly associated in this studio scene with Croniamantal's doomed pursuit of his love interest Tristouse Ballerinette, who is introduced immediately after this. As such, Delbreil argues that the mirror is linked to the feminine, with Tristouse and other female characters in the novella becoming closely bound up in notions of superficiality, false appearances, and inauthenticity.[26]

Tristouse is not herself a painter, but her dark colouring and characterization as a *femme-enfant* bring her close to Marie Laurencin, the painter with whom Apollinaire had had an intense and ultimately failed love affair.[27] L'Oiseau du Bénin's initial description of her also links her to avant-garde aesthetics, as he states, 'Elle est la laideur et la beauté; elle est comme tout ce que nous aimons aujourd'hui' [She is ugliness and beauty: she is like everything we love today] (*Pr*, I, 256). Her unconventional, *jolie-laide* looks thus associate her with modern art's break with traditional notions of beauty. Tristouse's status as a figure or muse for modern art is also confirmed later in the text, where she delivers a long monologue on the latest fashions. In this strange parody of fashion journalism, she describes ever more fantastical creations, including coats made of book covers, hats decorated with fish bones, bags made of glass eyes, and a scarf made of live birds. This use of diverse, highly unusual materials irresistibly calls to mind Cubist collage (which had employed some of the materials mentioned in this passage, including mirrors, as well as others such as gingerbread, sand, and nails).[28] While such references to Cubism work to confirm Tristouse's association with avant-garde experimentalism and, more generally, with the type of non-mimetic art of which Apollinaire clearly approves, the language in which her monologue is delivered works against this, allying her instead with the superficial, or with the deceptive 'appearance' of Art. Beginning by affirming, 'Cette année [...] la mode est bizarre et familière, elle est simple et pleine de fantaisie' [this year [...] fashion is strange and familiar, it is simple and full of fantasy] (a statement whose contradictions surely render it meaningless), the speech ends with an insistence that, 'La mode devient pratique et ne méprise plus rien, elle ennoblit tout. Elle fait pour les matières ce que les romantiques avaient fait pour les mots' [Fashion is becoming practical and does not look down on anything: it elevates it all. It is doing for materials what the Romantics did for words] (*Pr*, 1, 275–76). This again reflects the Cubists' collage aesthetic, and in particular the idea of elevating certain everyday materials by incorporating them into the work of art. But this closing statement is also pure platitude, one of a number of a set formulae included for the sake of form. Tristouse's fashion discourse remains superficial, but then fashion is an art of appearances, and the clothes she describes might themselves be seen as an attempt to appropriate a genuinely disruptive, non-mimetic art and submit it to the demands of pure appearance. This is not Cubism, but rather an attempt to ape the most superficial characteristics of Cubism; it is Cubism for fashion's sake.

Just as Tristouse's monologue situates her ambiguously in relation to the two competing currents of art identified in the studio scene — non-mimetic and mimetic, Art and its 'appearance' — elsewhere in the text she is seen as fickle, characterized by constantly shifting sympathies. This not only makes her impossible to classify, it also means that she eludes possession. Her resistance to the poet's desires is predicted from the outset, as L'Oiseau du Bénin describes her 'mains qui se redressent pour repousser' [hands that rise up to push you away] (*Pr*, 1, 256). Initially rejecting Croniamantal, her feelings then change and they enter into an affair, only for her to leave him after all of eight days as she has got what she wanted: Croniamantal has glorified her through his poetry, and her beauty is now lauded by all. She then runs away with a 'fopoîte' (the false poet Paponat, another figure for the superficial imitation of art), while Croniamantal continues to pursue her. Finally, she is instrumental in Croniamantal's death: as the crowd, led by Tograth, turns against the poet, she goes into a frenzy and, with the tip of her umbrella, stabs Croniamantal in the eye as he declares his love for her. There is, following this, yet another apparent reversal of feeling as Tristouse mourns for the poet, but her 'crise de nerfs dans les règles' [obligatory crisis of nerves] (*Pr*, 1, 300) is once again pure performance, a superficial enactment of conventional behaviour.

Within the allegorical schema of the novella, then, we find poetry being (almost literally) stabbed in the back by a figure closely associated with the visual arts — a figure whose dalliance with poetry is entirely self-serving, and who appears to be entirely empty of genuine feeling beneath her superficial exterior. Towards the end of the tale, L'Oiseau du Bénin, as the only artist in the text, and as Croniamantal's sole ally, is also revealed to be a somewhat ambivalent figure. In the final chapter, entitled 'Apothéose', L'Oiseau du Bénin sculpts Croniamantal a monument, as a way of ensuring the poet's enduring glory; he refuses marble and bronze as too old-fashioned, and vows to make Croniamantal a decidedly modern sculpture, which he erects in the Bois de Meudon, and which takes the form of 'une profonde statue en rien, comme la poésie et comme la gloire' [a profound statue of nothing, like poetry and like glory] (*Pr*, 1, 301).[29] This idealized statue, made of 'nothing', might initially seem to be a chimera, recalling Frenhofer's invisible masterpiece and its legacy in nineteenth-century art narratives; one initially wonders how such a sculpture can exist as anything more than an idea. Apollinaire makes it clear, however, that the work does have a material form, albeit a highly unconventional one:

> Dans la clairière, l'oiseau du Bénin se mit à l'ouvrage. En quelques heures, il creusa un trou ayant environ un demi-mètre de largeur et deux mètres de profondeur.
> Ensuite, on déjeuna sur l'herbe.
> L'après-midi fut consacré par l'oiseau du Bénin à sculpter l'intérieur du monument à la semblance de Croniamantal.
> Le lendemain, le sculpteur revint avec des ouvriers qui habillèrent le puits d'un mur en ciment armé large de huit centimètres, sauf le fond qui eut trente-huit centimètres, si bien que le vide avait la forme de Croniamantal, que le trou était plein de son fantôme. (*Pr*, 1, 301)

> [In the clearing, L'Oiseau du Bénin set to work. In a few hours, he dug a hole around half a metre wide and two metres deep.
> Next, they had a picnic on the grass.
> L'Oiseau du Bénin devoted the afternoon to sculpting the inside of the monument in Croniamantal's likeness.
> The next day, the sculptor returned with some workmen who equipped the well with a wall of reinforced concrete eight centimetres thick, except at the bottom where it was thirty-eight centimetres thick, so that the empty space had Croniamantal's form, and the hole was full of his ghost]

The empty shell of the poet's form is then filled in with earth and a laurel tree planted on top, the only visible trace of the monument. This lack of visibility is key to understanding the meaning of the statue — as, indeed, is its emptiness, which as Daniel Oster has suggested, bespeaks the emptiness of the poet's glory, and of the language that constitutes him.[30] Commemorative monuments usually work to keep the memory of a person, or people, visible; they function to reinsert them into the present, into everyday life, so that they are not entirely lost to history. That the sculpted monument might even work metaphorically to bring its subject back to life is pointed up by Apollinaire earlier on in 'Le Poète assassiné', in an episode where the conventional bronze statue of the poet François Coppée is animated and converses humorously with Croniamantal. No such resurrection seems possible for Croniamantal himself, whose supposed apotheosis — the moment at which the poet should transcend the world of the living and move upwards, towards the heavens — is in fact a movement down into the ground: a burial. Instead of commemorating the poet, L'Oiseau du Bénin's statue obliterates his memory and renders his glory invisible, arguably completing the work of those who had persecuted him. As a personal tribute, it is also far from heartfelt: the fact that the artist waits until after a 'dîner avec l'élite montmartroise' [dinner with the elite of Montmartre] to commence the project, and punctuates his work with a frivolous *déjeuner sur l'herbe*, trivializes the whole undertaking. To add insult to injury, L'Oiseau du Bénin betrays Croniamantal by seducing Tristouse, which he does easily and without compunction.

The end of the text thus translates a feeling that while painting might appear to be a close ally of poetry, the latter is ultimately on its own, betrayed and cuckolded. In this respect, the ending also brings to the fore certain anxieties about masculinity and sexual/creative potency that circulate throughout Apollinaire's text. From the outset, we are invited to consider Croniamantal's masculinity (or lack of it): discussing the etymology of Croniamantal's name, the narrator says that it refers in some languages to the male genitals, and then mentions the poet's autopsy report which records the exceptionally small size of his appendage (*Pr*, I, 227). The poet's birth in 1889, the year of the Exposition universelle, is placed under the phallic sign of the Eiffel Tower, which salutes Croniamantal 'd'une belle érection' [with a fine erection] (*Pr*, I, 242). And yet there is a constant insistence in the text on Croniamantal's lack of sexual prowess: unlucky in love, as he is rejected once again by Tristouse, he laments, 'je suis moins puissant que tout autre homme, je n'ai plus rien et je ne sais rien' [I am less potent than all other men, I have nothing and know nothing] (*Pr*, I, 269). Unable to get Tristouse to submit to his desires, the poet is seen as — indeed sees himself as — impotent and emasculated. This may be reflected further in L'Oiseau du Bénin's inverted statue, particularly if, as Peter Read suggests, we compare it with another of Apollinaire's fictional statues, the monument to Mony Vibescu erected at the end of the erotic novel *Les Onze Mille Verges*. Here, Read argues, the 'proud and virile verticality' of the latter reflects the sexual prowesses of its dedicatee, 'making it the symmetrical male opposite of Croniamantal's inwardly shaped, female monument, sculpted as a hole in the ground'.[31] The 'profonde statue en rien' thus works to confirm our sense of the poet's beleaguered masculinity, and, following on from this, his beleagueredness in other domains: his lack of cultural capital, lack of social status, and ultimately his lack of creative power. For although Croniamantal declares himself 'le plus grand des poètes vivants' [the greatest of living poets] (*Pr*, I, 298), within the framework of Apollinaire's sardonic, mock hagiography, it is difficult not to read this as empty bluster.

While 'Le Poète assassiné' initially appears to echo the emphasis placed elsewhere in Apollinaire's work on the close relationship between poetry and painting, over the course of the text it becomes apparent that the poet (and, by extension, the genre of poetic writing, broadly conceived) is very much isolated within the cultural field, and that the solidarity and support that the poet might gain from collaborations with the visual arts is at best short-lived, and at worst entirely illusory. The muse who is linked throughout the text with the visual arts is fickle and seems to side with an art of *trompe-l'œil* deception; the painter to whom he had creatively married himself provides him with a highly ambiguous monument that obscures his legacy and points up the fact that throughout the text Croniamantal is shut out of the kind of sexual/creative mastery that the painter himself enjoys. All of this is of course closely linked to anxieties relating to the cultural marginalization of poetic writing, contrasting with the increasing prominence of avant-garde painting. While Apollinaire did briefly acknowledge this disparity, in an article of 1917 where he talks of 'l'injustice de la situation de l'écrivain vis-à-vis de celle qui est faite au peintre dans la société actuelle' [the injustice of the writer's position compared to that given to the painter in today's society], this is a mere blip in a defensive strategy that consists primarily in allying poetry with painting, and insisting on the solidarity and common ground between the two.[32] 'Le Poète assassiné', however, seems to provide a fictional space in which his suppressed grievances can be vented.

In the figure of Tristouse, 'Le Poète assassiné' circles around certain fears about creativity, sexuality, and gender, and specifically the threat posed by women to a model of artistic creation that is identified as essentially male: it may be that only the poet is to blame for his lack of virility, but Tristouse's refusal to submit to the poet's desires forms yet another obstacle in his quest for mastery. More generally, the text casts feminine forces in a negative light, with a succession of women seen as deceitful and resistant to male desires, and with a Jewish prophet encountered by Croniamantal predicting the demise of poets at the hands of female demons including Lilith (Adam's first wife, cursed as a result of demanding to be her husband's equal).[33] As we shall see over the course of our discussion of *La Femme assise*, these fears are taken up and amplified further as the First World War brings about profound shifts in the cultural field and in gender roles, and triggers a crisis of masculinity which bears directly on cultural assumptions about the fundamentally masculine nature of artistic creation.

La Femme assise: False Women, Authentic Art?

The gendered conception of artistic creation that is present beneath the surface of 'Le Poète assassiné' is by no means unique to Apollinaire: it is, as we saw in Chapter 2, a commonplace assumption in early twentieth-century art writing. Just as in Michel Georges-Michel's *Les Montparnos* women are defined and judged in terms of their ability to service or hinder male sexual and creative energies, so Apollinaire presents Tristouse as a fickle muse, one whose resistance to Croniamantal's desires stands in the way of his creative trajectory. *La Femme assise*, meanwhile, presents a rather more complex treatment of such issues because its protagonist, Elvire Goulot, is not a mere muse, model, or artist's companion, but an artist in her own right. In order to understand fully the way in which Apollinaire treats the challenge she poses to a male-centred model of artistic creation, the novel needs to be considered in the historical context of the First World War, during which women often took on traditionally male work in factories and munitions plants, and also took action to demand fair pay and working conditions as well as universal suffrage.[34] This upset to traditional gender roles was countered by propaganda imagery of women as dutiful mothers and loving wives, supporting their departed men and serving France's interests, as well as by a growing pronatalist agenda to which Apollinaire himself subscribed, arguing in an article of 1917 that 'Il faut avoir beaucoup d'enfants pour le bonheur du foyer et de la nation' [We must have lots of children for the sake of the family and the nation], and writing a play, *Les Mamelles de Tirésias*, which addresses France's low birth rate as well as marriage and women's rights.[35] The play is certainly not a simple piece of conservative propaganda, however, and its playful reversals of gender roles in fact give rise to a highly ambiguous moral universe. Nevertheless, its engagement with the pronatalist cause may be seen to reflect Apollinaire's move towards a more conservative political (and, as we shall see, aesthetic) position in the context of the war and of the *union sacrée*. *La Femme assise* corresponds to certain aspects of this position, presenting a critique of the female artist who profits from the war to usurp male power and fails to submit to her patriotic duty to produce children. And yet the novel's treatment of the intersection between gender and creativity is a little less straightforward, ultimately suggesting that women are not necessarily excluded from authentic artistic creation, but that in order to succeed as artists they must take on certain 'male' characteristics.

La Femme assise has attracted little in the way of critical commentary, and has often been considered a second-rate work, no doubt because it brings together two apparently separate texts and positions their stories in a somewhat awkward parallel, and also because of the various sections that have been cut and pasted in from earlier texts (a technique common across Apollinaire's work, but all the more evident here because the novel remained unfinished at his death).[36] The recycling of articles from Apollinaire's column *La Vie anecdotique* and other non-fiction sources distances the text from the novel genre, and the apparently close relationship between fictional and real worlds is also pointed up by its subtitle ('Chronique de France et d'Amérique'), and by its use of thinly disguised portraits of real-life figures: thus Elvire corresponds to the painter Irène Lagut,[37] the poet Anatole de Saintariste to Apollinaire himself, and the painters Nicolas Varinoff and Pablo Canouris to Serge Férat and Picasso respectively. The latter is given a rather more mocking treatment than in 'Le Poète assassiné': while his fictional avatar's name once again links him with a bird (*Canouris* plays on *canari*), and the divine associations of this are brought out by repeated descriptions of him as 'le peintre aux mains bleu céleste' [the painter with hands of celestial blue] (*Pr*, I, 422), Picasso is also a figure of fun here, his heavy accent caricatured and ridiculed. His foreignness is hence accentuated, but the narrator is also at pains to emphasize his culturally sympathetic and non-threatening Latinity. In doing this, the text quickly shifts from a discussion of the origins of this fictional character to a critical defence of real avant-garde painters:

> Aucune école depuis le Romantisme n'a autant remué le monde que la nouvelle école de peinture où seuls ont joué un rôle des artistes resortissant à la civilisation méditerranéenne, des artistes appartenant à une race latine. Ce succès est cause de la résistance que l'on oppose dans certains milieux officiels à l'art d'un Canouris, d'un Picasso, d'un Braque, d'un Derain et qui va devenir plus violente encore qu'elle ne le fut jamais. Les philosophes ont rempli, paraît-il, en vue de combattre l'art moderne, tout un 'arsenal de sophismes' [...]. Mais que peuvent les philosophes contre les formes et la matière qui sont les objets et les sujets des meilleurs d'entre les peintres d'aujourd'hui? Que la peinture nouvelle soit différente de celle d'hier, c'est évident; qu'elle ne s'accorde pas avec la tradition du grand art, c'est une chose que je défie à quiconque de démontrer. (*Pr*, I, 423–24)

> [No school since Romanticism has stirred things up like the new school of painting, in which only artists originating from Mediterranean civilization, or belonging to a Latin race, have played a role. This success is one cause of the

resistance with which the art of a Canouris, a Picasso, a Braque, or a Derain meets in certain official milieux, and which is about to become more violent than ever. It seems that philosophers have built up a whole 'arsenal of sophisms' with which to fight modern art. But how can the philosophers resist the forms and matter which are the objects and subjects of the best of the contemporary painters? It is clear that the new painting is different from the painting of yesterday; but I challenge anyone to demonstrate that it is not aligned with the traditions of great art]

Rather than merely emphasizing the close relationship between fiction and reality, the fact that Canouris rubs shoulders here with the painter whom we easily recognize as his model and real-life 'referent' causes a friction, a momentary fracture in the illusion of fiction, and this generic slippage is reinforced by the shift in this passage from the fictional plot into the terrain of art criticism. The fact that Apollinaire emphasizes Pablo Canouris's Latin origins, as well as those of the real avant-garde painters, is of course fully in line with the aesthetic 'retour à l'ordre' that had commenced during the war and would continue into the 1920s, and which demanded a move away from 'decadent' Germanic influences and a renewal of classical French, or Latin, aesthetic values; likewise, the narrator-critic's insistence that avant-garde art is in fact closely linked to artistic traditions also stems from this classicizing agenda. All of this echoes Apollinaire's critical writing during the war, in which he seeks to align the interests and values of artistic modernity with those of the French nation, in a rhetorical strategy that was, at least in part, intended to protect his own position as an avant-garde writer of foreign origins, but also no doubt reflected a deeply-felt patriotism and a genuine attachment, as expressed in 'L'Esprit nouveau et les poètes', to 'l'ordre et [le] devoir qui sont les grandes qualités classiques par quoi se manifeste le plus hautement l'esprit français' [order and duty which are the great classical qualities through which the French spirit manifests itself most nobly] (Pr, II, 946).[38]

Despite the inclusion of such critical-theoretical passages, there is little direct representation of the act of painting in *La Femme assise*, and certainly the art of Canouris and Varinoff is scarcely discussed. The focus here is very much on the female artist Elvire, whose work is situated within the distinctly 'feminine' aesthetic realm of the frivolous, light-hearted, and decorative. She draws 'des fleurs, des petits cochons, des chevaux qu'elle enluminait ensuite et qui lui servaient de papier à lettres' [flowers, little pigs, horses which she then illuminated and used as writing paper] (Pr, I, 414). Initially this serves as a distraction from her stormy love life, and later becomes a more serious endeavour:

> Elvire peignait avec une fantaisie délicate et non sans force, des bouquets éclatants où paraissaient des marguerites aux pétales noirs et cette vie qu'animaient l'art, l'amour, la danse à Bullier et le cinéma, continue jusqu'au moment de la déclaration de guerre. (Pr, I, 414–15)

> [With a fantasy that was delicate and yet not lacking strength, Elvire painted blooming bouquets of flowers where one could see daisies with black petals, and a life animated by art, love, dances at Bullier and the cinema, which continued until the declaration of war]

Her painting is once again floral and 'delicate', but these feminine qualities are balanced out by the more masculine 'force', by her representations of modern urban life (a key concern for the predominantly male painters of the Parisian avant-garde), and also by the black daisy petals (a subversive image which anticipates the more threatening, deviant aspects of Elvire's femininity as developed later in the novel).

   This characterization of the fictional painter in terms of gendered qualities is very much in keeping with Apollinaire's treatment of female painters in his art criticism, itself part of a broader tendency by early twentieth-century art critics to assimilate women artists into what Gill Perry calls a 'vocabulary of difference', appraising them in terms of their adherence to conventional notions of femininity in art.[39] While in *Les Peintres cubistes* Apollinaire insists on feminine art as an entirely distinct aesthetic domain rooted primarily in the decorative and applied arts of embroidery and lacework (*Pr*, II, 34–39), elsewhere his emphasis on Marie Laurencin's 'feminine' qualities ('grâce', 'allégresse', 'charme', and 'délicatesse') is countered with an appreciation of her more 'masculine' aspects: in one article, Apollinaire notes that Laurencin's art is 'plus mâle que celui des autres femmes qui s'adonnent aux arts plastiques. Et cette virilité idéale s'allie à une grâce, un charme qu'on ne trouverait pas ailleurs' [more male than that of other women who have taken to the visual arts. And this ideal virility is combined with a grace, a charm that one could not find elsewhere].[40] On the one hand, this allows Apollinaire, in a cultural context where artistic creation is seen implicitly as a virile endeavour, to argue that Laurencin's work should be taken seriously, setting her on a level playing field with her male counterparts; on the other, his constant policing of gender categories makes it clear that a woman's art should never be *too* masculine, lest it become threatening. He applauds Laurencin for not committing 'la plus grande erreur de la plupart des femmes artistes: elles veulent surpasser l'homme et perdent dans cet effort leur goût et leur grâce' [the greatest error of the majority of female artists: wanting to surpass men, and losing in the process their taste and their grace] and for being aware of '[les] différences profondes qui existent entre l'homme et la femme: différence d'origine, différence idéale' [the profound differences that exist between men and women: original differences, ideal differences].[41] Laurencin and other female artists such as Alice Marval are thus praised for remaining within the boundaries of a conventional and familiar femininity, and yet within Apollinaire's critical texts there are also moments where this distinctly feminine creativity itself takes on a somewhat threatening, subversive character. This is allowed to emerge in *Les Peintres cubistes* when Apollinaire says that Laurencin's work 'danse comme Salomé' [dances like Salomé], and later compares it to the 'serpentine' dance of Loïe Fuller (*Pr*, II, 35 & 38–39); elsewhere, she is characterized as 'le démon de l'arabesque' [the demon of the arabesque].[42] Similarly, in his preface to the catalogue for an exhibition of paintings by Férat and Lagut, Apollinaire calls the latter 'une de ces singulières Satanes de l'Art qui a fait jaillir la magnifique incertitude de notre âge' [one of those singular she-devils of art who has brought forth the magnificent uncertainties of our age].[43] Feminine art, then, is for Apollinaire beguiling but demonic, a seductive figure of serpentine temptation — and intrinsically linked with the uncertainties of a modern age in which everything, including traditional gender roles, is seen to be open to question.[44]

Returning to *La Femme assise*, we find this imagery taken up in the representation of Elvire's sexuality, which is seen as deviant and therefore threatening to hetero-normative order. This, as Daniel Delbreil has noted, is reflected in her name, with 'Goulot' suggesting 'goule', meaning a lesbian or a ghoulish female demon; it also suggests 'goulue', implying insatiable appetites.[45] Her lesbianism and cross-dressing disturb conventional gender categories, and in fact recall the perfidious Tristouse, who disguises herself as a man and possesses a 'démarche virile et saccadée' [a virile, jerky gait] (*Pr*, 1, 227). Towards the beginning of *La Femme assise*, this behaviour is treated with indulgence, as Apollinaire compares Elvire to the androgynous nineteenth-century 'débardeur' figure immortalized by Gavarni, and indicates that within the carnavalesque atmosphere of pre-war Montparnasse pretty much anything goes. But the war puts an end to this carnival, and the author's position gradually shifts towards a more moralizing one as Elvire's breaches of sexual convention come to pose a direct challenge to male power, itself under threat from the war machine which makes man 'l'esclave de la nation' [the slave of the nation] (*Pr*, 1, 487). Elvire flits back and forth between Pablo Canouris and Nicolas Varinoff, cynically casting each aside without a thought, and ultimately sets up a personal harem of both men and women. Reflecting back on the story of her grandmother's dalliance with Mormonism, Elvire decides that polyandry will be the best way to take advantage of the new-found freedom and power that women have obtained thanks to the war. She thus comes to practise a 'mormonisme à rebours' [a topsy-turvy Mormonism], which is presented as unnatural and morally objectionable on a number of levels, not only because it departs from the model of the monogamous heterosexual couple, but also because Elvire ensures that she remains childless 'en un temps où la défense et l'honneur social eussent exigé des femmes une fécondité particulière' [at a time when national defence and social honour would have demanded a particular fecundity from women] (*Pr*, 1, 488).

As a woman, then, Elvire meets with unequivocal moral condemnation; what is more complex, however, is the relationship between her sexual behaviour and her artistic practice. Surrounded by her harem, her painting suddenly takes off:

> Elle travailla avec une ardeur inimaginable, ayant à cœur de ne pas être à charge à un homme, et le succès aidant elle gagnait bien sa vie.
> Elle jouait en reine de la puissance que la guerre lui avait donnée. (*Pr*, 1, 487)

> [She worked with an unimaginable passion, having made up her mind not to be dependent on a man, and with the help of a few successes, she earned a good living.
> Like a queen, she played with the power that the war had bestowed on her]

Once again, there is a clear sense of authorial disapproval here: Elvire has unjustly profited from the war to wrest power from suffering men. At the same time, however, she has also attained a position of sexual mastery, with multiple partners readily available to her, and as such she is realizing a male fantasy. This fantasy is closely bound up with the Apollinairean conception of (male) artistic creation as linked with sex and procreation, which we have seen to be present in 'Le Poète assassiné', and which also finds expression in *Les Mamelles de Tirésias* in the figure of the husband who adopts a female role and gives birth to 40,050 children.[46] In *La Femme assise*, this identification of creation with procreation perhaps explains Apollinaire's lengthy, fascinated treatment of the Mormon practice of polygamy, which is justified by a fictionalized Brigham Young in the following terms: 'C'est la joie immense de l'homme de pouvoir procréer comme la divinité. Et l'on voudrait limiter le pouvoir créateur de l'homme au ventre d'une seule femme? N'est-ce pas insulter la génération?' [It is man's immense joy to be able to procreate like a god. And some would wish to limit man's creative power to the belly of a single woman? Isn't this insulting the act of creation?] (*Pr*, I, 454). By assuming a 'male' role at the head of the harem, Elvire gains metaphorical access to this 'divine' creative power.

This implicit approval of Elvire's ascendancy as an artist is once more brought into question in the closing passages of the novel, however, as she is viewed through eyes of Nicolas, her one-time lover:

> Elvire siégeait devant son chevalet et Nicolas pensa involontairement à la Femme Assise, cette pièce de monnaie helvétique que dans son enfance il fallait prendre garde de ne pas accepter.
> 'Elvire se dit-il en lui souriant, existera toujours. Elle est, à un haut degré, comme sont toutes les femmes. Ainsi que la femme assise de l'écu suisse de cinq francs, elles sont fausses et ne passent pas.'
> Et 'femme assise' au temps des 'hommes debout', Elvire pensait alternativement aux agréments durables de la faiblesse et aux avantages de la fausseté. (*Pr*, I, 493–94)

> [Elvire was sat before her easel and Nicolas's mind wandered to the Seated Woman, the Helvetic coin that during his childhood one had to make sure not to accept.
> 'Elvire,' he said to himself, smiling, 'will always exist. She is, to a great extent, like all women. Just like the seated woman of the Swiss five franc coin, they are false and can't pass as genuine.'
> And, 'seated woman' in an era of 'men on their feet', Elvire thought of the enduring charms of being weak and the advantages of being false]

Nicolas relates Elvire here to a false coin known as 'la femme assise', as an emblem of inauthenticity, which of course looks forward to Gide's use of the false coin as a symbol of a crisis of values of various kinds in *Les Faux-monnayeurs*. Elvire is seen here as playing on her female 'weakness' and using false appearances to her own advantage (recalling, once again, Tristouse's superficiality and slipperiness). The figure of the seated woman also appears earlier in *La Femme assise*, in the passages on Mormon Utah, where she takes the form of a huge automated statue representing American democracy, a 'simulacre' [simulacrum] (*Pr*, I, 463), and hence another symbol of deceptive appearances that is in turn linked to the 'unnatural' or 'false' order of polygamy. Like the false coin, like the deceptive statue, Elvire comes to stand for an era in which everything is false, in which values — moral, social, monetary, and aesthetic — are no longer guaranteed or stable.

As a woman, then, Elvire is morally condemned, but as an artist, perhaps less so. Of course, as Apollinaire ties Elvire herself up so closely with images of superficiality and deception, we might surmise that anything she creates can only ever be superficial, a mere going-through-the-motions, or indeed the sort of facile, mimetic art of appearances of which the mirror stood as the emblem in 'Le Poète assassiné'. And yet the end of the novel certainly does not say as much, leaving us only with the impression that Elvire is at the peak of her creative powers and that these surpass those of her male counterparts. Indeed, if we look across once again at *Les Peintres cubistes* it becomes apparent that an art associated with falseness may actually be held in esteem within an aesthetic schema in which 'vérité' [truth] in art is not identical with 'vraisemblance' [credibility, or literally, the semblance of truth] (*Pr*, ii, 8): that is, in which art does not mimetically copy the superficial appearances of the real world, but moves beyond these to a deeper reality. In his response to a 1914 literary 'enquête' Apollinaire defined truth as follows: 'Vérité: authentiques faussetés, fantômes véritables' [Truth: authentic falsehoods, genuine ghosts].[47] Within this apparently paradoxical formulation, 'falseness' is framed as a key value in Apollinaire's aesthetics, and may in fact give rise, in his view, to a more 'authentic' art.[48]

It is thus perfectly possible, within the fictional schema of *La Femme assise*, for authentic (non-mimetic, avant-garde) art to be created by a woman who emblematizes falseness. But in presenting things in this way, the novel also gives rise to a problem, as it seems effectively to decouple art from the personality of the artist, and in doing so signals a break with the cult of the artist and attempts by other twentieth-century writers to define art as an expression of the artist's unique temperament or personality. Within the art-critical schemas created in Mauclair's *La Ville lumière* or Georges-Michel's *Les Montparnos*, authentic art is always the direct expression of a distinctive, 'pure', and unsullied personality, and in much of Apollinaire's criticism, we find a similar emphasis on the unique 'personnalité' of the artist, who is often perceived as saintly and as striving to keep art pure of exterior influences. Mondrian's personality, we are told, 'reste entière' [remains intact] despite the influence of Picasso;[49] Rousseau, meanwhile, has 'une personnalité trop forte pour ressembler à quelqu'un' [too strong a personality to resemble anyone else];[50] while Braque is painted as an angelic figure: 'Plus pur que les autres hommes, il ne se préoccupe point de ce qui étant étranger à son art le ferait soudain déchoir du paradis qu'il habite' [Purer than other men, he cares little about that which, being foreign to his art, would bring it down from the heaven it inhabits].[51] Elvire simply does not fit into this critical framework: her personality is characterized by its very instability, by flightiness and inconstancy; her art cannot be read as the expression of a morally unimpeachable or 'pure' personality that remains true to itself. *La Femme assise* thus witnesses Apollinaire moving away from the commonplace emphasis on the relationship between art and its creator's personality, towards an art-critical stance that locates aesthetic value within the work of art itself. This move is arguably anticipated as early as the 1903 critical text 'Des faux', in which Apollinaire argues that it matters little who created a work or in what historical circumstances, as long as it is beautiful.[52] But if Apollinaire's novel divorces the work from the personality who created it, and as such heralds an end to the cult of the artist, this may also be because the (male) artist no longer seemed to cut a particularly heroic or indeed potent figure.

Elvire's role at the end of the novel leaves men disenfranchised and emasculated, little more than slaves to the female artist, but any moral judgement is not reserved for her alone. Elvire as *femme assise* may be a sign of the times but she is not personally responsible for the ineptitude and inaction of her male counterparts. Nicolas Varinoff is 'cocu' [cuckolded] (*Pr*, I, 481), and his lacklustre performance as Elvire's often indifferent lover is equally damning. Pablo Canouris, meanwhile, is presented as a somewhat ridiculous embodiment of machismo: when we first encounter him, we find him declaring, 'Por aboir braiment une femme, il faut l'aboir enlébée, l'enfermer à clef et l'occuper tout lé temps' [To reeeelly ab a woman, you ab to grab err, keep err locked up and keep err beethy] (*Pr*, I, 423), and this is followed by a long episode in which the narrator recounts how Canouris had kidnapped a young girl, who is 'fascinée par la prestance mâle de son ravisseur [...], ravie dans tous les sens du terme' [fascinated by the male presence of her kidnapper [...], ravished in all senses of the word] (*Pr*, I, 426). And yet given Canouris's inability to keep a hold of the capricious Elvire (who at one point locks him out of her apartment/studio, leaving him crying 'Elbirre, écoute-moi oubrre-moi, jé te aime' [Elbirre, leeesten to me, open up, I looove you], *Pr*, I, 478), this episode appears increasingly as a desperate fantasy of dominance, an attempt to impose male desires onto an increasingly recalcitrant womankind. Neither Varinoff nor Canouris is ever seen in the act of painting; nor are their paintings ever described, and their apparent creative inactivity is of a piece with their sexual impotence. The soldier-poet Anatole de Saintariste, meanwhile, traumatized by his experiences of war and rejected by his lover Corail (who leaves him for Elvire), is unable to win her back via poetic language, and indeed the battle seems lost in advance as he tells her, 'Je voudrais vous conquérir. Les captives aiment les conquérants, mais j'ai trop longtemps fait la guerre pour croire à la réalité des conquêtes qui, je le crois, sont impossibles' [I would like to conquer you. Captive women love their conquerors, but I've been at war for too long to believe in conquests, which I think are impossible] (*Pr*, I, 492). Creative and sexual mastery are both out of reach for the beleaguered poet, who consoles himself with nostalgic fantasies of wartime prowess and a 'religion of honour'.

The weakness of the male characters in the novel, its lack of a true hero, betrays what Philippe Renaud calls Apollinaire's 'hantise de l'impuissance masculine' [obsession with male impotence]: a deep-seated anxiety for a writer for whom creation, as we have seen, is identified with procreation, and artistic failure with sexual impotence.[53] While all of this is suggestive of the demise of the myth of the potent male painter (or poet), it also bespeaks broader cultural anxieties about masculinity and male power in a time of war: the male characters in the novel may be read as symptomatic of what Elaine Showalter has called a 'crisis of masculinity' brought about by the First World War, during which not only were traditional gender roles challenged and the male body came under physical attack in the trenches, but the male psyche — indeed the very notion of 'manliness' — was brought under pressure by the condition branded 'shell shock' in part so as to obscure the fact that its symptoms were embarrassingly close to the 'female' nervous disorder of hysteria (its sufferers were widely thought to be weak, effeminate, or unmanly).[54] The crisis of male creativity that finds expression in *La Femme assise* may thus relate to the war's revelation that codes of masculinity were fragile and liable to collapse under pressure, and that the heroic fighter of the recruiting posters was not all he was cracked up to be.

In 'Le Poète assassiné', poetry is betrayed and cuckolded by a female figure closely associated with painting; in *La Femme assise*, the stakes are somewhat different as it is not just poetry but male creativity more generally that comes under threat from Elvire as a disruptive figure of feminization and emasculation. The anxieties around gender and creativity expressed in the novel are deep-seated and genuine, and Apollinaire's critique of the female artist cannot simply be explained away as a mere rhetorical stratagem or posture adopted to shore up his cultural capital in an increasingly conservative political climate. If this seems troubling, it is perhaps because it is difficult to square Apollinaire's commitment to a genuinely progressive aesthetics (albeit one that he takes care to link, in the context of the 'retour à l'ordre', with traditional aesthetic values) with a more reactionary position that warns of the dangers of women supplanting male creative supremacy. And yet *La Femme assise*, while it might reflect a more austere, restrictive moral universe associated with wartime, is not quite as clear-cut as all that: Apollinaire may subscribe to the idea that artistic creation is fundamentally masculine in character, but this theoretical schema nevertheless allows a female painter to attain the heights of creative mastery and to outdo her male counterparts in the process. Moreover, in reflecting on our own response to Apollinaire's treatment of gender and creativity, we should perhaps remind ourselves that modernism does not have to be 'progressive' in all respects, and that in wanting it to be so we often risk eliding and obscuring its more disruptive, but nevertheless productive, aspects. Thus Apollinaire's modernism sets out to respond to the present, to provide an apt creative response to its shifting forms, but it does not set out to embrace it wholeheartedly — or indeed to jettison artistic traditions in favour of an aesthetics of speed and machinery as in Italian Futurism.[55] Instead, it freely registers the fears, traumas, and anxieties engendered by shifts in the economic, social, and cultural spheres. *La Femme assise* is a text which captures the traumas and uncertainties of war, and its impact on notions of masculinity and male artistic creation; 'Le Poète assassiné' deals with the precarious position of poetry and its lack of power relative to painting in a pressurized cultural field. This anxious response to modernity, and anxious querying of the possibility of an authentically 'modern' art, is one that is taken up and explored further by Blaise Cendrars in his novel *Dan Yack*.

An Art Novel for the Age of Mechanical Reproduction: Blaise Cendrars's *Dan Yack*

Blaise Cendrars's *Dan Yack*, published in two parts in 1929 and re-issued as a single volume in 1946, is certainly not a conventional novel: lacking consistent, linear plot development and narrative continuity, its peripatetic structure and shifts in narrative perspective give rise to a somewhat disjointed, fragmented text. Neither, like many of the other texts examined in this study, is *Dan Yack* an art novel in any very conventional sense: in contrast to the best-known nineteenth-century examples of the genre, Cendrars's protagonist is not an artist, and the novel does not present itself explicitly as a vehicle for the discussion of aesthetic theory. Nevertheless, while *Dan Yack* may be read as a story about modern man's quest for identity, inseparable from that quest is an engagement with the nature and function of art, or with the question of how to express oneself in the age of mechanical reproduction. Close examination of the novel also reveals a wealth of embedded references to a tradition of stories about artistic creation stretching from Ovid to Poe and beyond, which provide points of departure for Cendrars's enquiry. This section will consider the ways in which the author appropriates and adapts these stories in his representations of sculpture and the new technologies of cinema and sound recording, and in so doing queries the status of the latter as privileged instruments of expression for the modern age.

From his collaborations with Sonia Delaunay and Fernand Léger (on *La Prose du Transsibérien*, and the 1919 illustrated book *La Fin du monde filmée par l'ange N.-D.* respectively), to his *Dix-neuf poèmes élastiques*, Cendrars's early works display a recurrent concern with the visual arts and their relationship to writing. In the post-war period, however, a series of articles published in *La Rose rouge* reveal a steady disillusionment with painting, and with Cubism in particular, which Cendrars found to be fatally constrained by its own rules, and drained of life by its limited palette.[56] This series culminated in the 1926 article 'Pour prendre congé des peintres' [To take leave of painters], in which Cendrars bluntly stated his disillusionment with modern painting, blaming the art market for corrupting aesthetic values and arguing, by way of a lengthy quotation from Kipling's *Letters of Travel* ('Half a dozen pictures'), that artistic representations are a poor substitute for the experience of life itself, and that both artists and consumers of art would do better to get out and see the world than to ignore it in favour of a few dabs of paint within a frame.[57] This notion of the estrangement of art from life forms one of the cornerstones of Cendrars's art-critical stance in *Dan Yack*. Indeed, much later in his career, in his 1950s radio interviews with Michel Manoll, Cendrars stated in relation to the novel that 'les artistes vivent à côté, en marge de la vie et de l'humanité' [artists live apart, on the margins of life and of humanity], and added that he did not consider himself to be an artist.[58]

Dan Yack is also resolutely not an artist: he even prides himself on never having read a book. In the first part of the novel, *Le Plan de l'aiguille*, this rich heir to a shipping conglomerate is jilted by his lover and sets off from St. Petersburg to the Antarctic, in a bid to find himself, to establish himself anew. He takes with him on his journey three artists, against whom he is defined: André Lamont, a composer, Arkadie Goischman, a poet, and Ivan Sabakoff, a sculptor.[59] They resolve to stay on a remote, uninhabited island for a year, and the action centres on the inevitable self-destruction of the artists, whose creative resources are too weak or too ill-adapted to be able to survive the tough conditions, and whose demise speaks volumes of the state of the arts as Cendrars sees it. Lamont proves to be unable to live or to create without his habitual audience made up of fawning women. In the moment where he realizes that his symphony is a failure, he can think of no better than to cry for his lover — who, moreover, kills him by infecting him with syphilis. Lamont hence represents artistic decadence and the dangerous, emasculating influence of

women over the male artist. This is just one of many indications that Cendrars
subscribes to a broadly-held cultural conception of art as a fundamentally masculine
endeavour: indeed, throughout both parts of *Dan Yack* there is an obsessive interest
in artistic/sexual impotence or sterility that echoes the concerns of Apollinaire's 'Le
Poète assassiné' and *La Femme assise*. The poet Goischman, meanwhile, is seen to
be motivated entirely by money ('Il faut bien vivre' [We all have to live]), but the
irony is that his work has earned him 'pas un radis' [not a penny].[60] Creatively and
sexually impotent, his scurvy-ridden body begins to disintegrate, and he finally cuts
off his nose in a pathetic parody of Van Gogh, his creative achievement amounting
to no more than a 'plagiat [...] raté' [a failed [...] act of plagiarism] (*TADA*, IV, 94).
In Goischman, Cendrars provides a portrait of the artist who pursues art for all the
wrong reasons — not only for money, but also because he is seduced by the myths
surrounding avant-garde creation, of which Van Gogh was so emblematic in this
period.[61] Goischman's symbolic castration and concomitant impotence bespeak the
vacuity and failure that such myths serve to conceal.

Sabakoff, the sculptor, is a rather more complex and appealing figure. While
his companions are motivated by more base concerns, he declares, 'Moi, moi, je
travaille pour l'Art' [I work for Art's sake] (*TADA*, IV, 18). He is not impotent or
weak, and he busies himself with practical tasks on the island, while his fellow
artists wither away. Unlike Lamont and Goischman, who immediately become
alienated from the vigorous and virile Dan Yack, Sabakoff forms a close friendship
with the latter; the material nature of his medium also contrasts with the abstract,
immaterial non-creation of the other artists, resurrecting the hope of an art that
remains grounded in the stuff of life itself. And yet Sabakoff, too, comes to a sticky
end, crushed by his own statue of Dan Yack. The question, of course, is why — and
what this death signifies within the novel's art-critical schema.

Cendrars's choice of sculpture as representative of the visual arts may move us
some way towards an answer to this question. This choice may, as Claude Leroy has
noted, be motivated partly by the fact that Cendrars had already explicitly 'taken
leave' of painting: 'À quoi bon la congédier une seconde fois?' [Why bother to
dismiss it a second time?].[62] But the representation of sculpture in narrative fiction
also inevitably raises the spectre of Pygmalion, the sculptor who, in Ovid's tale,
brought his statue to life. Sabakoff is closely linked to this myth of the artist in a
lengthy passage where he dreams of a sculpture representing a primordial creation
myth, and in which the artist himself is figured as a divine forger, giving life to
humanity. At the summit of this colossal monument is a single figure:

> Il se levait. Il faisait le tour du dernier pic de la montagne en s'élevant
> graduellement. Marche par marche, il montait de face, de trois quarts, de dos.
> Toujours plus haut, toujours plus haut. Enfin, il se détachait seul sur le vide. Il
> avait atteint le sommet. Une boule, une sphère, un globe, la terre, une lampe,
> le soleil, qu'il tentait d'arracher, de soulever et de maintenir, haut, très haut en
> l'air, à bout de bras, sans faiblir. Prométhée! (*TADA*, IV, 54)

> [He stood up. He circled the last peak of the mountain, rising up gradually. Step
> by step, he went up face-on, in profile, with his back turned. Always higher,
> always higher. Finally, he stood out alone against the void. He had reached the
> summit. A ball, a sphere, a globe, the Earth, a lamp, the sun, that he tried to

snatch, to lift up and hold, high, very high up in the air, on his outstretched arm, without faltering. Prometheus!]

The monument culminates, then, in a representation of the artist's own heroic effort of creation, and as he, like Prometheus, seizes divine power, his sculpture becomes animated — it is alive with movement.[63] The conflation of the myths of Prometheus and Pygmalion in this passage is one that, as Anne Geisler-Smzulewicz has demonstrated, was extremely common in nineteenth-century versions of the Pygmalion story: whereas in Ovid's tale the sculpted figure came to life through the intervention of Venus (and the sculptor himself, while skilled, remained a mere mortal), modern retellings attributed Galatea's animation to the artist's own quasi-divine creative powers.[64] The artist Pygmalion thus took on the heroic, rebellious quality of Prometheus, who had stolen divine powers from the gods. Sabakoff is situated very much within this mythical framework, and within a line of fictional artists whose creative ambitions reach towards the sphere of the ideal and the divine. But, like Prometheus, these artists may be punished for overstepping their bounds, and their creative projects may end in disaster or failure. As such, this intertextual connection raises the suspicion that, like so many other modern Pygmalions — like Frenhofer, like Claude Lantier, who aspire to ideal, life-giving creation yet find that this is out of their reach — Sabakoff cannot but fail to achieve his dream.

As the sun returns to Dan Yack's island after the long polar winter, Sabakoff resolves to make his vision a reality: looking around the stark Antarctic landscape, he resolves to 'peupler tout ça' [populate it all] (*TADA*, IV, 79). But his project quickly goes awry. It is not that Sabakoff fails to create — on the contrary, he is incredibly prolific — but rather that the idealism of the project itself leads the sculptor away from the material basis of his art. As Yvette Bozon-Scalzitti puts it, 'L'idéal de pureté absolue qui anime Ivan mène également à la mort au terme de la dématérialisation parfaite qu'il exige' [The ideal of absolute purity that drives Ivan also leads to death, as the outcome of the perfect dematerialization that it demands].[65] The people over whom Sabakoff reigns as divine creator are increasingly abstract: he creates 'une statue monolithique, une borne humanisée, un glaçon anthropomorphique' [a monolithic statue, a humanized pillar, an anthropomorphic ice cube] (*TADA*, IV, 80), and represents Dan Yack through his monocle, symbolic of his own distorted artistic vision. This movement towards abstraction subsequently veers into the immaterial, and Prometheus's gift of light becomes a curse as the artist misguidedly seeks to sculpt with it: 'La seule sculpture possible, c'est la lumière. J'y arriverai. Comme un ange' [The only possible sculpture is light. I will get there. Like an angel] (IV, 83). This, clearly, is an artistic ideal taken to an untenable extreme, but Sabakoff's failure also seems inevitable within the conjuncture of the Pygmalion and Prometheus myths: the artist who attempts to transcend the limits of his creative powers must be punished for his hubris. The material accordingly reclaims its rights over the sculptor, and Sabakoff is killed by the statue that would have completed his monument. The latter, as Bozon-Scalzitti notes, is made from a dark 'glace fossile' [fossilized ice] (IV, 92) whose earthy materiality contrasts with his earlier works, sculpted in an ice described as 'fragile, pure, lumineuse, transparente, à peine opaque, presque immatérielle!' [fragile, pure, luminous, transparent, only slightly opaque, almost immaterial!] (IV, 80).[66] Moreover, as a figurative sculpture of a human form, the statue echoes another legendary narrative about sculpture: the story of the Golem, in Jewish legend an artificial man made of clay, who in some versions rebels against and crushes the creator who dared to bestow upon him the divine gift of life.[67]

Even if in the second part of the novel Dan Yack declares that all three artists had died of 'impuissance' [impotence] (*TADA*, IV, 250), it must be allowed that Sabakoff's impotence is of a different order to that of his fellow artists. His is not an aesthetic failure — Cendrars's aim is not simply to criticize sculptural abstraction — but rather a tragic inability to attain an impossible ideal, his struggle made all the more heroic by Cendrars's mobilization of myths of artistic creation. These myths also prepare the way for Dan Yack, the industrialist and the only one of the group to survive the Antarctic sojourn, to assert his own heroic creative power, and its superiority over art. It is thus highly significant that the statue that kills Sabakoff represents Dan Yack, and (within the context of his broader sculptural project) positions him as a divinity — indeed, as Prometheus. The industrialist's creative power thus displaces that of the artist, and the remainder of *Le Plan de l'aiguille* deals with Dan Yack's astonishing entrepreneurial achievements, and in particular his rapid construction of a whaling station on the site of 'Port-Déception' in the desolate South Shetlands, the name of its antecedent being redolent of the failure of the three artists, while the process of populating the new settlement, the utopian 'Community-City', provides an ironic echo of Sabakoff's thwarted desire to play God, to 'peupler tout ça'. The implication, it seems, is that if art is to continue in any form — and it does, in the form of the novel itself — then Dan Yack's materialist *art de vivre*, and his technologically assisted creative acts, may provide a model, where poetry, music, and sculpture have failed.

Alongside industrial forms of creation, an alternative model for art may be provided by new sound technologies, a source of endless fascination to Dan Yack, who declares, 'Je n'aime que le ronron nasillard des phonographes et les cris géants des gramos' [I like only the nasal purring of the phonograph and the gigantic cries of the gramophone] (*TADA*, IV, 26). These technologies are adopted as an expressive medium by the protagonist in the second part of the novel, *Les Confessions de Dan Yack*. The 'confessions' narrate, in a jumbled chronological sequence, Dan Yack's return to Europe and participation in the First World War, his marriage to a young girl, Mireille, and her subsequent death; they consist of a number of sound recordings made by Dan Yack via dictaphone, which he then sends to a typist to be transcribed.[68] Crucially, Cendrars also asks the reader to believe that his own creative process was similarly mediated by sound recording, claiming in a foreword that, 'Cette Deuxième Partie a été *parlée* au Dictaphone; elle n'a pas été écrite' [this Second Part was *spoken* into a Dictaphone, and not written], and emphasizing that the printed form of the novel is a poor translation of its sonorous essence ('Quel dommage qu'on n'*entende* pas la voix de Dan Yack entre ces pages' [What a shame that we can't *hear* the voice of Dan Yack in these pages]).[69] Might this new technology be able to replace the sterile and overly idealized forms of art that had been dismissed in *Le Plan de l'aiguille*, as a mode of representation more responsive to the reality of modern life?

Clearly, recording technology does not suffer from an excess of idealism: it is attractive to Dan Yack, and to Cendrars, precisely because it is close to life, providing a direct trace of reality. In terms of Cendrars's own work, the concern to record and document experience is in evidence as early as *La Prose du Transsibérien*,[70] and is pursued further in the author's increasing turn to reportage and memoir in his work after *Dan Yack*. In the novel itself, sound recording is conceived by the protagonist not just as a way to document life but as a way to preserve it, and even to reanimate the past: 'Pour moi,' Dan Yack says, 'le dictaphone est un appareil qui réveille tous les échos' [For me, the dictaphone is a device that reawakens echoes] (*TADA*, IV, 172). His fascination with the trademark 'la voix de son Maître' [His Master's Voice], associated with the image of the gramophone and 'le petit fox qui lui obéit' [the little terrier obeying it] (IV, 163), reveals that part of the appeal of this technology lies in the illusion of mastery that it affords — the ability to overcome temporal boundaries, and to bring back what is irrevocably lost. Dan Yack thus attempts to reanimate his dead wife, by reading out and recording her notebooks. But Mireille cannot truly come to life, since she is unable to speak for herself: Mireille's voice is replaced by 'la voix de son Maître', who in reading her words appropriates them and asserts control over her (sonorous) image. Dan Yack's project of reanimation through representation, like Pygmalion's statue, of which this aspect of the novel provides yet another distant echo, is thus seen to be grounded in narcissism, rather than love.

But it is not merely because Dan Yack neglected to record Mireille's own voice before her death that his project fails: the recording technology itself is also fragile, meaning that the human voice may be scrambled, distorted, or disrupted. The 'confessions' are frequently fragmentary, and Dan Yack warns his typist that 'ce rouleau est fêlé. [...] Il est fendu de bout en bout' [this cylinder is cracked. [...] It is broken from one end to the other] (*TADA*, IV, 171). The needle of the recording apparatus appears as an obsessive motif, which crops up throughout the novel in a variety of substituted forms: in the mountain peaks of the Plan de l'aiguille (an area of the Alps where some of Dan Yack's 'confessions' are recorded), in chimneys, in pine needles even. But the 'Plan de l'aiguille', the ruse of recording, is not without its dangers, since a needle may be harmful as well as salutary. It is frequently associated with death: with the harpoon that pierces the whale's flesh, with the slaughter of sea-lions, whose recorded cries Dan Yack frequently listens to on his gramophone. It is also associated with the key traumatic event of the early twentieth century: the First World War. Recalling the mass destruction of human life in the trenches, Dan Yack muses:

> Il me semblait qu'une fulgurante épée tombait du haut du ciel et battait des étincelles rugissantes, et sabrait et massacrait tout à la surface du monde comme une aiguille aiguisée de gramophone qui érafle, raie à tort et à travers un vieux disque déjà usé, remonté à fond et dont toutes les voix humaines sont définitivement condamnées. (*TADA*, IV, 250)

> [It seemed to me that a flaming sword was falling from the sky, producing fiery sparks, and stabbing and massacring everything on the surface of the Earth like a sharpened gramophone needle that scrapes and scratches every which way

an old record, already worn out and reset, and on which all human voices are
already definitively condemned]

Like the face that stares out from a faded photograph, the recorded voice is
condemned — merely a trace of what is dead or irremediably lost to time.

Cendrars's ambivalence towards sound recording is mirrored in his treatment of
another technological means of representation in the second half of the novel, where
cinema emerges as a further alternative to the obsolete modes of expression dismissed
in *Le Plan de l'aiguille*. Dan Yack puts his wife Mireille in front of the camera, a
move which perhaps reflects the author's own involvement in film-making, and his
view of cinema as a universal, popular language uniquely appropriate to expressing
the modern sensibility.[71] It is also motivated by an attempt to please Mireille (who
in her notebooks gives a lengthy account of the couple's afternoons spent at rowdy
popular cinemas), to make her laugh — metaphorically, to 'animate' her, to bring
her to life, and to cure her of the mysterious illness that will eventually consume
her (and which is characterized by frigidity: like a cold, immovable statue, *elle reste
de marbre*). Dan Yack's ambition, then, is once again to give life through art, but
implicit in this ambition is also the desire to create an ideal woman, responsive to
his own desires and obedient to 'la voix de son Maître': the Golem of the first part
of the novel thus gives way to Galatea, and the Pygmalion myth raises its head
once again. Through cinema Mireille becomes endlessly malleable, pliant to the
role she is given. Many of her film roles are multiple, consisting of a combination
of different female types which appeal to a range of possible male desires and
fantasies: in the film on Edgar Allen Poe, she is an amalgam of Eleonora, Ligeia, and
Ulalume, while in the *Contes d'Hoffmann* she is dressed up 'en sylphide, en reine de
Saba, en princesse lointaine, en Cendrillon, en fée, en magicienne, en bonne petite
servante' [as a sylph, the Queen of Sheba, a distant princess, Cinderella, a fairy, a
sorceress, a good little servant girl] (*TADA*, IV, 231).[72] Alongside Mireille's other
Pygmalion, the director Lefauché, Dan Yack frequently assumes the role of director
and producer, coaching her on her gestures, and turning her into a film star with
mass appeal. Like Galatea, Mireille owes her identity — on and off screen — to her
creator, as she confesses in one of her notebooks:

> Je lui dois tout. Tout ce que je sais, c'est lui qui me l'a appris. Il m'a appris à
> m'habiller. Il m'a appris à marcher. Il m'a appris à me maquiller. Je dois avouer
> que, sans lui, je n'aurais jamais su rendre tout ce que j'ai fait dans *L'Ève future*.
> (*TADA*, IV, 235)

> [I owe him everything. Everything I know, he taught me. He taught me to
> dress. He taught me to walk. He taught me to do my makeup. I must admit
> that, without him, I wouldn't have been able to achieve everything I did in
> *L'Ève future*]

Mireille is presented not as an artist with her own creative power, but as a passive
material onto which Dan Yack's own creative impulses are projected.

Mireille's role as the artificial woman Hadaly in a film version of Villiers de
l'Isle-Adam's *L'Ève future* is particularly significant in the context of Cendrars's
reworking of the Pygmalion myth. Villiers's novel is itself informed by that myth,

and provides, as Marie Lathers has argued, 'an idealist response to the artist-model plots of realism and naturalism', replacing the real, physiological artist's model with an ideal woman 'modelled' to the desires of her creator.[73] Like *Dan Yack*, *L'Ève future* also deals with the question of art in the machine age: Villiers's Edison, like Dan Yack, may be considered as part of a new breed of artist, imagining new forms and profoundly changing human life with their inventions. Dan Yack's project for a giant gramophone, to be mounted in the central square of Community-City, would seem to be a conscious echo of Edison as inventor of the phonograph, while the scale of the machine in question recalls some of Edison's more extravagant discoveries as presented in *L'Ève future*. If these new artists undeniably change human life, however, they do not necessarily change it for the better: the technologies they invent and promote present threats and dangers as well as revitalizing capacities. Nowhere is this more apparent than in the cinematic 'animation' of Mireille: placed in relation to Edison's animation of the android Hadaly, whose demise at the end of Villiers's novel appears as a punishment for the inventor's Pygmalionesque attempt to meddle with the divine, this project appears ill-fated from the outset.

For her role as Hadaly, Dan Yack moulds or sculpts Mireille into an artificial, mechanical woman, just as he has already taught her to correspond to the type of artificial feminine ideal that the cinematic 'machine' (*TADA*, IV, 236) demands. She is made up for the camera, and coached to move in a deliberately mechanical way: 'Il me réapprenait à marcher, géométriquement, pour le cristallin gradué des objectifs et non plus pour la sensibilité des yeux' [He taught me to walk again, geometrically, for the graduated cristalline lens and not for the eyes] (IV, 237). Whereas Edison's sculpted android comes to life, this process is almost reversed as Mireille takes on the role of Hadaly, and she complains:

> J'ai souffert le martyre durant des mois et des mois, je devais retenir mon souffle, la circulation de mon sang, freiner tous mes sens pour paraître blême, inanimée, sentimentalement amorphe tant que durait la mise au point de la femme artificielle. (*TADA*, IV, 233)

> [I suffered for months and months: I had to hold my breath, stop my blood from circulating, rein in all of my senses to appear pale, inanimate, sentimentally amorphous for as long as the artificial woman was being perfected]

Mireille has to become inanimate for this particular role, but more generally her on-screen representation fails to bring her to life, for the cinematic image is only an image, and in the era prior to sound film, a silent image, one that is unable to laugh as Dan Yack so desperately wants it to. As in Dan Yack's dictaphone recordings, Mireille's cinematic representation is unable to speak for itself, or to come to life as anything other than a sterile product of Dan Yack's narcissistic desire, and it is no doubt highly significant in this respect that the couple's marriage remains sexless until the end. As Dan Yack implicitly recognizes when he tells Mireille, 'Tu devrais tourner dans la vie' [You should film in real life] (*TADA*, IV, 235), the cinematic image is sterile, artificial, and, like the other art forms explored in the novel, utterly estranged from life.

Rather than giving life, the camera seems to drain it from its subjects. In this respect, Cendrars's novel may be seen to look back to certain art narratives of the previous century, in which the painted representation is conceived as a parasite and rival to the model, whose life it usurps. In Zola's *L'Œuvre*, for example, Christine senses that posing for Claude's portrait of her means 'prêter sa chair, pour que l'autre naquît' [lending her flesh, to allow the other to be born].[74] Another possible intertext, suggested by Mireille's role as the female lead in a film on Poe, is the latter's *The Oval Portrait*, where the painted image comes to life, but at the cost of the model's death. (Indeed, for the film on Poe Cendrars may have had in mind Jean Epstein's 1928 film *La Chute de la Maison Usher*, which includes key elements from *The Oval Portrait*.)[75] In invoking these nineteenth-century fictional representations of painting, Cendrars's representation of cinema questions whether this technologically mediated art form — in the 1920s still felt to be a relatively recent development — could truly be considered to be modern, or whether it might suffer from the same pathologies as more traditional visual art forms. It simultaneously looks forward, I think, to Walter Benjamin's insistence that the filmic image robs the actor of his aura, his authentic individual presence: Benjamin cites Pirandello, for whom the actor's body 'loses its corporeality, it evaporates, it is deprived of reality, life, voice, and the noises caused by his moving about, in order to be changed into a mute image, flickering an instant on the screen, then vanishing into silence'.[76]

Cendrars's representation of Mireille's cinematic dissection similarly comes as a kind of rewriting of the symbolic violence inflicted on the female model in art narratives of the nineteenth century: *L'Œuvre*, in which Christine is sacrificed to an art which 'la ravalait' [swallowed her up], once again comes to mind — as perhaps does Edison's lengthy dissection of his 'model' woman, which exposes the intimate physiological/mechanical makeup of Hadaly's body to his guest Lord Ewald's gaze, and to that of the reader.[77] But it also provides a curious anticipation of Benjamin's analogy between surgeon and cameraman.[78] The director Lefauché (aptly named, since 'faucher' can mean to kill, to destroy, to cut down, and is suggestive of a Grim Reaper figure) is described by Mireille in the following violent terms:

> Il savait me tirer des larmes, me faire verser de véritables larmes pour ses gros plans. [...] Ces séances m'exténuaient. Alors il s'acharnait, et quand je n'en pouvais plus, que j'allais m'évanouir, il me retenait encore un instant au tournant de ma défaillance, M. Lefauché, pour faire braquer sur moi un objectif monstrueux, les plus cruels éclairages du studio et fouiller ainsi impitoyablement mon malaise jusqu'au dernier degré de l'exténuation. (*TADA*, IV, 234)

> [He knew how to extract tears, make me cry real tears for his close-ups. These sessions exhausted me. Then he would pounce, and just when I couldn't take any more, when I was about to faint, he would keep me at breaking point, Mr Lefauché, and pointing a monstrous lens and the cruellest lights in the studio at me, pitilessly seek out my malaise until I was at the ultimate point of exhaustion]

One should note that 'un objectif' can mean a viewfinder for a gun as well as for a camera, while 'braquer' similarly contains the threat of violence as the camera is trained on its subject/victim. Mireille is tortured, the most intimate areas of her self exposed to the gaze of the camera for the benefit of a cinematic art based on scopophilic pleasure. This passage echoes a contemporaneous text by Cendrars, *Une nuit dans la forêt*, in which the narrator (in this instance identified as Cendrars himself) casts himself as a film director, and says of Pompon, his prospective leading lady, 'je l'aurais plantée au bout d'un projecteur comme on épingle un insecte et j'aurais braqué sur elle tous mes objectifs' [I would have planted her in front of a projector as one pins down an insect and I would have trained all my lenses on her].[79] He goes on to describe the instruments of cinematic vivisection:

> Le 170 *Dallon-Téléphoto* qui vous capte un individu et le ligote brusquement comme au lasso, le 120 *Dallmeyer* qui le dope, le leurre et le transforme en patient, le 100 *B&L Tessar* qui l'endort comme au chloroforme et le désanime, le 75 *Carl Zeiss Matched* qui fend et écartèle les muscles, le 50 *Vérito* qui griffe et pince les nerfs, le 28 Ultrastigmate qui colore les pensées et le 12 *Goerz-Hypar* qui compénètre insensiblement votre victime pour se substituer à sa personnalité.[80]

> [The *Dallon-Telephoto* 170 which captures a subject and binds him as if with a lasso, the *Dallmeyer* 120 which drugs him, lures him in and turns him into a patient, the B&L Tessar 100 which puts him to sleep like chloroform and deanimates him, the *Carl Zeiss Matched* which cuts and tears apart the muscles, the *Verito* 50 which scrapes and pinches the nerves, the Ultrastigmate 28 which colours the subject's thoughts and the *Goertz-Hypar* 12 which imperceptibly penetrates the victim and substitutes itself for his personality]

Despite this gruesome description, which equates the camera lens to an instrument of torture, the cinematic 'cut' is conceived as a salutary one: Cendrars insists that his role is like that of the surgeon, talks in the passage just cited about his 'patient' (as well as his 'victim'), and regrets that Pompon refused to be filmed, since 'à elle, cela lui aurait fait du bien' [it would have done her some good].[81] Pompon needs to have the traumatic events of her past quasi-surgically excised from her psyche. As in Benjamin's analysis, Cendrars believes that the camera's gaze allows the 'optical unconscious', the unseen elements of reality, to be exposed, but this optical unconscious is also analogous to the psychological unconscious.[82] The camera is thus able to 'fouiller [...] mon malaise', as Mireille puts it. In *Dan Yack*, as in *Une nuit dans la forêt*, the incision inflicted by the camera on its subject is intended to reveal, and thereby remove, the psychological trouble that haunts her. Instead, it simply exposes it to her in all its unbearable reality — 'je me voyais révélée à moi-même' [I was revealed to myself] (*TADA*, IV, 239) — and Mireille dies as a result.

Dan Yack's enthusiastic embrace of the cinema, and of technologies allowing sound to be recorded and replayed, thus gives way to a troubling ambivalence. As arts based on mechanical reproduction, they provoke the same excitement and the same anxiety as all machines in Cendrars's work: potentially generative and productive, they are also registered as a threat, presenting a danger to the human body, and a force that may escape human control.[83] In *Dan Yack*, this threat is present in the 'détraquement' [breakdown] of an automated slot machine with which the hero is fascinated (*TADA*, IV, 126); it is present in the violence of the factory equipment at Community-City, which cuts and processes whale carcasses, but also rips off the limbs of inattentive workers, and in the monstrous anthropomorphic form of the factory itself, a terrifying melding of human and machine: 'L'usine, la gueule ouverte sur le port, les entrailles à nu, colérique, rageante, avec des explosions brusques de vapeur, des renâclements, le bruit continu de ses formidables mâchoires' [The factory, its mouth open to the port, its entrails exposed, angry, raging, with sudden snorts and explosions of steam, and the continual noise of its terrifying jaws] (IV, 141). But it is most vivid, as we have seen, in Cendrars's exploration of technologically mediated modes of representation, whose products are seen, at best, to amount to no more than a sterile, artificial imitation of life, and at worst to represent a deadly parasite.

As Dan Yack abandons cinema, and his dictaphone, at the end of *Les Confessions,* one may detect a certain nostalgia for the traditional arts which were literally and symbolically killed off in *Le Plan de l'aiguille*: while poetry, music, and sculpture may have been fatally ill-adapted to the realities of life, they are innocuous in comparison to the threat to life presented by mechanical art forms. Related to this, I think, is the fact that Cendrars's text is shot through with intertexuality, constantly glancing back to a rich tradition of narratives about art.[84] The novel is, in this respect, firmly anchored in the past, a fact that sits awkwardly alongside Dan Yack's insistence that 'Il faut nous moderniser, c'est de notre âge. Notre génération doit tout recommencer' [We must make ourselves modern, it's part of our age. Our generation must begin everything again] (*TADA,* IV, 122). It is also arguably at odds with Cendrars's own literary image, and his position at the forefront of the 'Futurist Moment'. Claude Leroy has argued that the central dynamic of *Dan Yack* concerns the modernist imperative to break with the past: the novel is about freeing oneself from the symbolic influence of the father, and establishing a new, distinctly 'modern' identity (hence why Dan Yack chooses a new name, rejecting that of his family).[85] Within the framework of this analysis, traditional artistic expression fails because it is unable to detach itself from the past. By extension, the mechanical arts fail to come alive because they are constructed so as to reproduce reality, rather than to create it; cinema, moreover, is seen simply to rehash literary classics — Poe, Hoffmann, Villiers — rather than to forge new narratives. Turning back on itself, meaninglessly repeating, and ultimately sterile, mechanical reproduction can neither resuscitate the past, nor breathe new life into the present: as Dan Yack laments, 'Ah! Pourquoi est-ce que tout se répète, puisque rien ne revient?' [Why does everything repeat itself, when nothing comes back?] (IV, 267).

Dan Yack itself certainly does not 'tout recommencer': far from breaking with the past, it recycles and reuses well-worn narrative patterns, and inscribes modern experience within tradition. But this does not necessarily imply that it, too, is a failure. Cendrars's intertextual strategy does not amount to a mechanical repetition or reproduction of other stories, and it stands in contrast to the more direct cut-and-paste techniques used to construct *Kodak* out of Gustave Le Rouge's *Le Mystérieux Docteur Cornélius*, and to 'Dernière heure', one of the *Dix-neuf poèmes élastiques*, which was 'copied' from *Paris-Midi*.[86] Cendrars's strategy in *Dan Yack* consists, rather, in rewriting, or in the adaptation of past narratives to the particular problems of the age of mechanical reproduction. And it may be better understood if we pay attention to Cendrars's own presentation of the novel, in a short text that accompanied the 1929 publication of *Le Plan de l'aiguille*. Starting from the premise that 'La modernité a tout remis en question' [modernity has called everything into question], Cendrars explains that technology has changed not only our surroundings, but the psychological makeup of the human subject: 'sa sensibilité, son émotion, sa façon d'être, de penser, d'agir, tout son langage, bref, la vie' [his sensibility, his emotion, his way of being, of thinking, of acting, his whole language: basically, his life]. He goes on:

> Cette transformation profonde de l'homme d'aujourd'hui ne peut pas s'accomplir sans un ébranlement général de la conscience et un détraquement intime des sens du cœur: autant de causes, de réactions, de réflexes qui sont le drame, la joie, l'orgueil, le désespoir, la passion de notre génération écorchée et comme à vif...
>
> Seule la formule du roman permet de développer le *caractère actif* d'événements et de personnages contemporains qui, en vérité, ne prennent toute leur importance qu'en *mouvement*.
>
> Depuis quelque cinq ans, le roman français sert dans le monde à la mise au point du nouveau régime de la personnalité humaine. (*TADA*, IV, 292)[87]

> [This profound transformation of modern man cannot come about without transforming consciousness and upsetting our intimate sense of ourselves: these are so many causes, reactions, reflexes which are the drama, the joy, the pride, the despair, the passion of our skinned and raw generation...
>
> Only the formula of the novel can allow one to develop the *active character* of contemporary events and characters which, in truth, only take on their true magnitude when seen *in movement*.
>
> For some five years, the French novel has served the purpose of clarifying the new regime of the human personality]

Cendrars conceives of his novel, then, as a response to modernity and to changes in human consciousness. This may mean attempting to translate the fast-moving nature of modern life into the form of the novel (which the wide-ranging, fragmented narrative of *Dan Yack* arguably does), but it does not, as we have already seen in relation to Apollinaire's particular take on 'modern' art, have to mean a naïve, Futurist-tinged hymn to modern technology. As the above passage shows, Cendrars is attentive to the shocks and traumas of modern experience; his phrase 'notre génération écorchée et comme à vif' reminds one, once again, of Benjamin, and in particular his exploration of neurasthenia, or mental hypersensitivity, as a modern psychopathology to which Baudelaire had responded in his urban poetry.[88] And so it may be that part of Cendrars's intention, in his 'mise au point du nouveau régime de la personnalité humaine', is not only to describe or explain the modern psyche, but also to treat it — *mettre au point* in the sense of fixing or fine-tuning a malfunctioning machine. If, according to Benjamin, the modern era's generalized rupture with the past produces an 'increasing atrophy of experience', this must be remedied by reinscribing the present into a continuous narrative that connects it with tradition. That is, relating the present to the past turns the raw experience of the present (*Erlebnis*) into something meaningful, into 'experience in the strict sense of the word' (*Erfahrung*), where individual experiences 'combine with material of the collective past'.[89] Relating Dan Yack's attempts at technologically mediated creation (whether through industrial production, through sound, or through cinema) to tales of pre-technological creation thus parries the shock of the modern, and works to inscribe the narrative within a meaningful framework of tradition.

This is, however, about as far as Cendrars's optimism about art goes in *Dan Yack*. While the text's inscription within literary tradition suggests that art in the modern age may function to give a sense of meaning to an otherwise impoverished experience of the present, its intertexts simultaneously function to indicate the dangers and limits of artistic creation. The Pygmalion myth (in its modern forms, where the possibility of attaining divine creative power is resolutely closed), the legend of the Golem, *The Oval Portrait*, *L'Ève future*, and the other narratives about art whose ghosts haunt *Dan Yack* all tell of the ultimate failure of art to overcome human limits, to change human life, to act as a saviour: in each case, the artist seeks to create life through art, but this culminates in disaster. The anxiety about the power of art that is present in these stories is transposed, in *Dan Yack*, to the age of mechanical reproduction, where it becomes all the more acute, as traditional forms of art seem ill-adapted to the present, and technologically-mediated forms bring new fears to light. The novel circulates around questions concerning the nature of modern art, how it might differ (if at all) from industrial production, and what it can and cannot achieve. As we have seen, Cendrars's novel insists very much on art's limits rather than its possibilities, and even while the text attempts to give some sense of meaning to modern experience, it pessimistically casts doubt on its own ability to achieve this, and leaves many of its own questions about art in the age of mechanical reproduction worryingly unsettled.

Notes to Chapter 3

1. Perloff, *The Futurist Moment*.
2. See Guillaume Apollinaire, *Calligrammes*, in *Œuvres poétiques*, ed. by Marcel Adéma and Michel Décaudin (Paris: Gallimard, Bibliothèque de la Pléiade, 1965), 163–314 (hereafter referred to as *Po*); Blaise Cendrars, *Dix-neuf poèmes élastiques*, TADA, I, 63–94.
3. Guillaume Apollinaire, 'L'Esprit nouveau et les poètes', *Pr*, II, 943–54 (p. 954).
4. See Linda Goddard, '"Poésie plastique?" The Competition between Art and Literature in Early Twentieth-Century France', in *The Art Book Tradition in Twentieth-Century Europe*, ed. by Kathryn Brown (Farnham: Ashgate, 2013), pp. 117–29 (p. 124). For a review of early twentieth-century sources situating painting ahead of literature, see also Goddard, *Aesthetic Rivalries*, pp. 233–35.
5. André Derain created woodcuts for Apollinaire's 1909 *L'Enchanteur pourrissant*, while Raoul Dufy illustrated *Le Bestiaire* (1911).
6. Anna Boschetti, *La Poésie partout: Apollinaire, homme-époque (1898–1918)* (Paris: Seuil, 2001), p. 268; see for example 'Le Roi-lune', *Pr*, I, 303–19, 'Le Gastro-astronomisme ou la cuisine nouvelle', *Pr*, I, 401–04, and 'Mon cher Ludovic', *Pr*, I, 497–99.
7. On this expanded definition of poetry, see 'L'Esprit nouveau et les poètes', *Pr*, II, 950: 'On peut être poète dans tous les domaines: il suffit que l'on soit aventureux et que l'on aille à la découverte' [One can be a poet in all domains: one just needs to be adventurous and to explore new things].
8. The novella was first published within a collection of short stories bearing the same name; I have followed the practice of referring to the novella as 'Le Poète assassiné', while *Le Poète assassiné* refers to the collection as a whole. All references to the text are to the version published in *Pr*, I, 225–302.
9. For reasons of scope, I have been unable to examine Apollinaire's synopsis for *L'Abbé Maricotte* (*Pr*, I, 945–58), an unrealized novel that would have engaged with sculpture and with the Pygmalion myth. On this, see Daniel Delbreil, 'Portrait du portraitiste dans les récits de fiction

d'Apollinaire', in *Guillaume Apollinaire 21: Apollinaire et le portrait*, ed. by Michel Décaudin (Paris: Lettres modernes/Minard, 2001), pp. 249–68 (pp. 263–64), and 'Statue et statut du poète dans l'œuvre de Guillaume Apollinaire', in *Écrire la sculpture (XIXᵉ–XXᵉ siècles)*, ed. by Ivanne Rialland (Paris: Classiques Garnier, 2012), pp. 171–85 (pp. 183–84).

10. Blaise Cendrars, 'Quels seront les maîtres?' (*La Rose Rouge*, 1919), *TADA*, XI, 55–56 (p. 56).

11. Blaise Cendrars, 'De la parturition des couleurs', *TADA*, XI, 71–72. On Cendrars's engagement with Survage's (unrealized) project, see Jean-François Thibault, 'Cendrars et Survage: rythmes colorés', in *Blaise Cendrars 20 ans après*, ed. by Claude Leroy (Paris: Klincksieck, 1983), pp. 183–88. Apollinaire was also interested in Survage's invention: see 'Le Rythme coloré', *Paris-Journal*, 15 July 1914, *Pr*, II, 826–27.

12. On Cendrars's career in the 1920s, see 'Pro domo: comment j'ai écrit *Moravagine*', *TADA*, VII, 240–42: Cendrars describes 'mes débuts non pas tant dans l'art du roman que dans l'art du... chevalier d'industrie qu'exerce le romancier moderne depuis Balzac et qui consiste à savoir se procurer de l'argent avec du vent' [my beginnings not so much in the art of the novel as in the art of... the knight of industry, which has been practised by novelists since Balzac and consists in knowing how to conjure money from thin air] (p. 242).

13. This collection was announced in *Les Soirées de Paris*, nos. 26–27 (July–August 1914), but not realized during the poet's own lifetime. See the recent edition based on the original maquette: *Et moi aussi je suis peintre*, ed. by Daniel Grojnowski (Cognac: Le Temps qu'il fait, 2006).

14. Guillaume Apollinaire, 'Les Cubistes et les poètes', *La Vie anecdotique (Mercure de France)*, 12 March 1912, *Pr*, III, 130–31.

15. Guillaume Apollinaire, *Journal intime 1898–1918*, ed. by Michel Décaudin (Montpellier: Éditions du Limon, 1991), p. 142 (entry for 27 February 1907).

16. Guillaume Apollinaire, *Les Peintres cubistes: méditations esthétiques*, *Pr*, II, 5–52 (p. 19). The beginning of the section on Picasso, dealing with his early painting (*Pr*, II, 19–22), was published as 'Picasso, peintre' in *La Plume* in 1905. For further analysis, see Rosemary Eberiel, 'Clowns: Apollinaire's Writings on Picasso', *Res*, 14 (Autumn 1987), 143–59 (pp. 143–52), and Éliane Formentelli, 'Écrire "Picasso" d'Apollinaire', *Études françaises* (Montréal), 21.1 (Spring 1985), 9–29.

17. Jennifer Pap, 'The Cubist Image and the Image of Cubism', in *The Image in Dispute: Art and Cinema in the Age of Photography*, ed. by Dudley Andrew (Austin: University of Texas Press, 1997), pp. 155–80 (esp. pp. 162–69). On Apollinaire's art criticism, see also L. C. Breunig, 'Les Phares d'Apollinaire', *Cahiers du Musée National d'Art Moderne*, 6 (1981), 63–69, and Étienne-Alain Hubert, 'Georges Braque selon Guillaume Apollinaire', in *L'Esprit nouveau dans tous ses états, en hommage à Michel Décaudin*, ed. by P. Brunel and others (Paris: Minard, 1986), pp. 265–74.

18. *Pr*, II, 24–25; cited by Pap, 'The Cubist Image and the Image of Cubism', p. 168.

19. See Boschetti, *La Poésie partout*, p. 310.

20. See Peter Read, *Picasso and Apollinaire: The Persistence of Memory* (Berkeley: University of California Press, 2008), pp. 91–92. Read also notes that the 'Benin Bird' refers to a West African metal sculpture owned by Apollinaire.

21. Marie-Jeanne Durry suggests that Apollinaire's scurrilous portrait of Irène Lagut in *La Femme assise* was revenge for her rejection of Picasso: see 'Irène Lagut', *Les Lettres françaises*, no. 1270 (12–18 February 1969), 6–7, 9 (p. 9). Willard Bohn, *Apollinaire, Visual Poetry and Art Criticism* (Lewisburg, PA: Bucknell University Press/London & Toronto: Associated University Presses, 1993), p. 129, cites correspondence with Lagut in which she refers to 'une déception amoureuse' concerning herself and Apollinaire, which suggests that any sour grapes may be Apollinaire's own.

22. Caroline Levitt, 'Raoul Dufy, Pierre Alechinsky and Jim Dine: Depicting the Arts in Guillaume Apollinaire's "Le Poète assassiné"', in *Art in French Fiction since 1900*, ed. by Katherine Shingler, *Nottingham French Studies*, 51.3 (2012), 232–47 (p. 234).

23. On Picasso as a divine or 'orphic' figure, see 'De Michel-Ange à Picasso', *Pr*, II, 396–98 (p. 398); Apollinaire uses similar imagery in his 1908 catalogue preface on Braque, *Pr*, II, 110–12 (p. 112): 'Georges Braque ne connaît point le repos' [Georges Braque knows no rest].

24. Daniel Delbreil, *Apollinaire et ses récits* (Fasano and Paris: Didier/ Schena, 1999), p. 301. Apollinaire does suggest that Paris is a new Rome in *La Femme assise*, *Pr*, I, 409–94 (p. 430): 'la cité géante qui a remplacé Rome à la tête du monde' [the gigantic city that has replaced Rome at the head of the world].

25. See Levitt, 'Raoul Dufy, Pierre Alechinsky and Jim Dine', p. 232; also Read, *Picasso and Apollinaire*, p. 93. For more on the emblem of the mirror in Apollinaire's work, see Katherine Shingler, 'Apollinaire's Mirror', in *The Book of the Mirror*, ed. by Miranda Anderson (Newcastle: Cambridge Scholars, 2007), pp. 166–80.

26. Delbreil, *Apollinaire et ses récits*, pp. 301–02.

27. Michel Décaudin, 'Sur la composition du *Poète assassiné*', *Revue des sciences humaines*, 84 (October–December 1956), 437–56 (p. 443), shows that the passage relating Croniamantal's first meeting with Tristouse actually came from an early version of *L'Enchanteur pourrissant* and thus predates Apollinaire's relationship with Laurencin, but the resemblance between Tristouse and Laurencin is nevertheless very striking.

28. See Christine Poggi, *In Defiance of Painting: Cubism, Futurism, and the Invention of Collage* (New Haven, CT: Yale University Press, 1992), pp. 10, 36–37, & 107–08.

29. This is, as Peter Read notes, a reference to Rodin as 'Maître de Meudon', which points up the statue's departure from sculptural traditions. See ' "Et moi aussi je suis sculpteur": Movement, Immobility and Time in the Fictional Sculptures of Apollinaire', in *From Rodin to Giacometti: Sculpture and Literature in France, 1880–1950*, ed. by Keith Aspley and Elizabeth Cowling (Amsterdam: Rodopi, 2000), pp. 76–83 (p. 83).

30. Daniel Oster, 'Statue et statut du poète dans *Le Poète assassiné* d'Apollinaire', *Stanford French Review*, 3 (1979), 161–72 (p. 167).

31. Read, *Picasso and Apollinaire*, p. 184.

32. Guillaume Apollinaire, ' "L'Écrivain le paria" ', *Paris-Midi*, 25 February 1917, *Pr*, II, 1316.

33. *Pr*, I, 284 ('elles vont tuer tous les poètes sur cette terre'). Further references to the disruptive, proto-feminist figure of Lilith occur in 'Le Poète assassiné', *Pr*, I, 242, and *La Femme assise*, *Pr*, I, 491.

34. Margaret H. Darrow, *French Women and the First World War: War Stories of the Home Front* (Oxford: Berg, 2000) (see especially pp. 195–99 on the 1916–17 'grèves de femmes' and the idea of women as profiting unjustly from the war). For a more general overview of gender relations and the First World War, see Susan R. Grayzel, 'Women and Men', in *A Companion to World War I*, ed. by John Horne (Oxford: Wiley-Blackwell, 2010), pp. 263–78.

35. Guillaume Apollinaire, 'Le Salut militaire aux femmes enceintes', *La Vie anecdotique* (*Mercure de France*), 16 January 1917, *Pr*, III, 246. On Apollinaire's pronatalism, see Mihailo Pavlovic, 'La Repopulation et *Les Mamelles de Tirésias*', in *Guillaume Apollinaire 6: Images d'un destin*, ed. by Michel Décaudin (Paris: Lettres modernes/Minard, 1967), pp. 133–50.

36. The section on artistic Montparnasse, for instance, reuses Apollinaire's article for his column *La Vie anecdotique*, in *Mercure de France*, 16 March 1914. On the novel's genesis and publication, see Michel Décaudin's notes in *Pr*, I, 1329–35. For contemporary critical responses to the novel, see [Anon.], ed., 'Le Dossier de presse de *La Femme assise*', *Que Vlo-Ve?*, second series, no. 2 (April–June 1982), 12–22.

37. An early version of the novel was entitled *Irène de Montparnasse ou Paris pendant la guerre*; see *Pr*, I, 1331, and 'Le Dossier de presse de *La Femme assise*', p. 14.

38. Apollinaire insists on the French or Latin origins of Cubism in the article 'L'Art et la guerre: à propos d'une exposition interalliée', *Paris-Midi*, 9 December 1916, *Pr*, II, 861–62; and in 'L'Origine du cubisme', letter published in *Mercure de France*, 22 September 1917, *Pr*, II, 1342–43. For a discussion of Apollinaire's adherence to the concept of Latinity (and the notion that this was a strategy calculated to protect his position), see Amotz Giladi, 'Guillaume Apollinaire et la "latinisation" des avant-gardes parisiennes durant la Première Guerre mondiale', *ConTEXTES* (varia), <http://contextes.revues.org/5045?lang=en> [accessed 17 February 2015]. On Apollinaire's nationalist leanings, see Pierre Caizergues, 'Apollinaire et la politique pendant la guerre', *Guillaume Apollinaire 12: Apollinaire et la guerre (1)*, ed. by Michel Décaudin (Paris: Lettres modernes/Minard, 1974), pp. 67–101.

39. Perry, *Women Artists and the Parisian Avant-garde*, p. 110. Of course, this was not merely a matter of male critics imposing these 'feminine' qualities onto the work of women painters; as Perry demonstrates (pp. 109–10), artists such as Laurencin often deliberately played on these 'feminine' values in order to make their work more marketable.

40. Guillaume Apollinaire, 'Prenez garde à la peinture! Le Salon des indépendants: six mille toiles

sont exposées', *L'Intransigeant*, 18 March 1910, *Pr*, II, 140–45 (p. 143).

41. Guillaume Apollinaire, 'Le Salon des indépendants', *Revue des lettres et des arts*, 1 May 1908, *Pr*, II, 104–10 (p. 107).

42. Guillaume Apollinaire, 'Salon d'automne', *Les Soirées de Paris*, 15 November and 15 December 1913, *Pr*, II, 615–21 (p. 617).

43. Apollinaire's prose text for the exhibition catalogue is reproduced in *Po*, 1149–50 (p. 1149).

44. For further discussion of this imagery, see Breunig, 'Les Phares d'Apollinaire', pp. 66–68; see also Bohn, *Apollinaire, Visual Poetry, and Art Criticism*, pp. 142–44.

45. Delbreil, *Apollinaire et ses récits*, p. 356.

46. *Les Mamelles de Tirésias*, *Po*, pp. 863–962 (p. 908). On the link between creation and procreation in Apollinaire's work, see Peter Read, *Apollinaire et 'Les Mamelles de Tirésias': la revanche d'Éros* (Rennes: Presses universitaires de Rennes, 2000), pp. 168–71.

47. Guillaume Apollinaire, 'Réponse à une enquête', *La Vie*, June 1914, *Pr*, II, 984–85 (p. 984).

48. For a discussion of falseness in Apollinaire's work, see Read, *Apollinaire et 'Les Mamelles de Tirésias'*, p. 64.

49. Guillaume Apollinaire, 'À travers le Salon des indépendants', *Montjoie!*, 18 March 1913, *Pr*, II, 529–39 (p. 535).

50. Guillaume Apollinaire, 'Le Douanier', *Soirées de Paris*, 15 January 1914, *Pr*, II, 627–41 (p. 630).

51. Guillaume Apollinaire, 'Georges Braque' (1908 catalogue preface), *Pr*, II, 110–12 (p. 112).

52. Guillaume Apollinaire, 'Des faux', *La Revue blanche*, 1 April 1903, *Pr*, II, 74–77.

53. Philippe Renaud, 'Latnamaïnorc, déchiffreur de Croniamantal, ou La leçon des formes et des mots', in *Guillaume Apollinaire 8: Regards sur Apollinaire conteur (Stavelot 1973)*, ed. by Michel Décaudin (Paris: Lettres modernes/Minard, 1975), pp. 101–39 (p. 107).

54. Elaine Showalter, *The Female Malady: Women, Madness and English Culture, 1830–1980* (London: Virago, 1987), pp. 167–74. In France, the terms 'pithiatisme', 'obusite', and 'sinistrose' were used to describe nervous conditions brought on by trench warfare: see Pierre Darmon, 'Des suppliciés oubliés de la Grande Guerre: les pithiatiques', *Histoire, économie, société*, 20.1 (2001), 49–64 (pp. 50–51).

55. See Apollinaire's rather ambivalent 'Futurist' manifesto *L'Antitradition futuriste*, *Pr*, II, 937–39.

56. See especially 'Quelle sera la nouvelle peinture?', *TADA*, XI, 53–54, and 'Pourquoi le "cube" s'effrite?', XI, 57–60.

57. Blaise Cendrars, 'Pour prendre congé des peintres', *TADA*, XI, 81–86 (p. 81).

58. Blaise Cendrars, *Blaise Cendrars vous parle*, *TADA*, XV, 26.

59. These three figures are usually held to be fictional avatars for Stravinksy, Chagall, and Archipenko respectively: see Jay Bochner, *Blaise Cendrars: Discovery and Re-creation* (Toronto: University of Toronto Press, 1978), p. 170, and Pascaline Mourier-Casile, 'L'Œil de Cendrars', *Revue des sciences humaines*, 216 (1989), 111–32 (pp. 120–21).

60. Blaise Cendrars, *Dan Yack*, *TADA*, IV, 20. Subsequent page references are given in parentheses in the text.

61. See Heinich, *La Gloire de Van Gogh*, especially pp. 207–22.

62. Claude Leroy, 'L'Atelier du double: Cendrars et Léger en miroir', in *Dis-moi, Blaise: Léger, Chagall, Picasso et Blaise Cendrars*, exhibition catalogue (Paris: Réunion des musées nationaux, 2009), pp. 15–23 (p. 19).

63. That Cendrars conceives Sabakoff's sculpture as animated is also confirmed in his 1936 text, *Hollywood, La Mecque du cinéma* (*TADA*, III, 1–137), where he states that a cinematic song-and-dance number is 'une page arrachée à mon roman *Le Plan de l'aiguille*' [a page torn out of my novel *Le Plan de l'aiguille*], and cites this particular passage (pp. 96–97). The attainment of movement in sculpture is also a key concern in other texts, such as 'Dialogue sur la sculpture', in Blaise Cendrars, *Inédits secrets*, ed. by Miriam Cendrars (Paris: Club français du livre, 1969), pp. 388–94, and the poem 'La Tête', in *Dix-neuf poèmes élastiques*, *TADA*, I, 91: 'La sculpture d'Archipenko est le premier œuf ovoïdal | Maintenu en équilibre intense | Comme une toupie immobile | Sur sa pointe animée' [Archipenko's sculpture is the first ovoid egg | Maintained in intense equilibrium | Like a spinning top still | On its animated tip].

64. Anne Geisler-Smzulewicz, *Le Mythe de Pygmalion au XIXe siècle: pour une approche de la coalescence des mythes* (Paris: Honoré Champion, 1999), p. 73. The conflation between the two myths is also made possible by the fact that Prometheus, in some versions of the myth, was a sculptor,

variously seen as modelling humans and animals and, in later versions (Goethe and Voltaire), as the creator of Pandora. See Jacqueline Duchemin, *Prométhée: histoire du mythe, de ses origines orientales à ses incarnations modernes* (Paris: Les Belles Lettres, 2000), pp. 49–50 & 119–22; also Sitzia, *L'Artiste entre mythe et réalité*, pp. 29–30.

65. Yvette Bozon-Scalzitti, *Blaise Cendrars ou la passion de l'écriture* (Lausanne: L'Âge d'homme, 1977), p. 73.

66. Ibid., p. 75.

67. Claude Leroy comments on this connection in his notes on *Dan Yack*, *TADA*, iv, 308, n. 54. Cendrars may have been aware of the Golem legend via Gustav Meyrink's 1915 novel *Der Golem*, or Paul Wegener's 1920 film adaptation.

68. In the early twentieth century the technology of dictation, performed until the 1950s using wax cylinders, was highly gendered: a male dictator would speak into a recording device, while a female typist listened and transcribed. See David L. Morton, *Sound Recording: The Life Story of a Technology* (Westport, CI: Greenwood Press, 2004), p. 46. This clearly corresponds to a conception of artistic creation as a masculine endeavour, and of the work as passive, feminine, and formed by the male gaze, which underlies *Dan Yack*.

69. *TADA*, iv, 161 (author's emphasis); the list of locations and dates of composition appended to the end of the novel also includes the claim that it was 'enregistré au Dictaphone quelque part à la campagne: été 1929' [recorded by Dictaphone somewhere in the country, summer 1929] (*TADA*, iv, 289). On Cendrars's interest in the creative possibilities of sound technology, see also Philippe Bonnefis, *Dan Yack: Blaise Cendrars phonographe* (Paris: Presses universitaires de France, 1992), esp. pp. 8–9.

70. See Susan Taylor-Horrex, 'Cendrars, Delaunay, et le simultanéisme: évolution de l'esthétique simultanéiste', *Cahiers Blaise Cendrars*, no. 3 ('L'Encrier de Cendrars'), ed. by Jean-Carlo Flückiger (Neuchâtel: Éditions de la Baconnière, 1989), 209–17 (p. 214).

71. See especially 'L'ABC du cinéma', *TADA*, xi, 29–33, and also 'Le Principe de l'utilité', *TADA*, xi, 35–46 (p. 46). Cendrars collaborated with Abel Gance on *J'accuse* (1919), and *La Roue* (1923), although his accounts of his involvement in these films, and of his various other film-making projects, may be somewhat exaggerated: see *Blaise Cendrars vous parle*, *TADA*, xv, 96 & 189. In 1923 he did direct his own film, which survives only via its *scénario* (*La Perle fiévreuse*, in Blaise Cendrars, *Œuvres complètes*, 8 vols (Paris: Denoël, 1962–65), iv, 7–61); the film also apparently provided the basis for *Une nuit dans la forêt*. On Cendrars's engagement with cinema in practice and via writing, see Mikhail Iampolski, *The Memory of Tiresias: Intertextuality and Film*, trans. by Harsha Ram (Berkeley: University of California Press, 1998), pp. 125–61, and Francis Vanoye, 'Le Cinéma de Cendrars', *Europe*, 566 (1976), 183–96.

72. The mention of the *Contes d'Hoffmann* brings to mind yet another Galatea: the wax automaton Olimpia who features in the story 'Der Sandmann', and in Offenbach's opera. On Hoffmann's reworking of the Pygmalion myth, see Michelle E. Bloom, 'Pygmalionesque Delusions and Illusions of Movement: Animation from Hoffmann to Truffaut', *Comparative Literature*, 52.4 (Autumn 2000), 291–320 (p. 296).

73. Lathers, *Bodies of Art*, p. 197. As well as *L'Ève future*, the figure of the artificial woman may recall Fritz Lang's 1927 film *Metropolis*, whose ambivalent treatment of the industrial machine also bears resonances with Cendrars's text.

74. Zola, *L'Œuvre*, p. 348.

75. Francis Vanoye notes this as a possible intertext in his introduction to *TADA*, iii, xv. Cendrars's familiarity with Poe was long-standing, as is demonstrated by a 1907 'liste de lecture' that mentions the *Nouvelles histoires extraordinaires*, in Cendrars, *Inédits secrets*, p. 28; Villiers and Hoffmann are also mentioned here amongst Cendrars's early reading matter (pp. 208 & 280).

76. Benjamin, 'The Work of Art in the Age of Mechanical Reproduction', p. 223.

77. Zola, *L'Œuvre*, p. 344; Villiers de l'Isle-Adam, *L'Ève future*, ed. by Alan Raitt (Paris: Gallimard, 1993), *livre cinquième* (pp. 213–69).

78. Benjamin, 'The Work of Art in the Age of Mechanical Reproduction', pp. 226–27.

79. Blaise Cendrars, *Une nuit dans la forêt* (1929), *TADA*, iii, 147–201 (p. 197).

80. Ibid.

81. Ibid.

82. Benjamin, 'The Work of Art in the Age of Mechanical Reproduction', p. 230.

83. See Yvette Bozon-Scalzitti, 'Cendrars et la machine infernale', in *Cendrars aujourd'hui: Présence d'un romancier*, ed. by Michel Décaudin (Paris: Minard/ Lettres modernes, 1977), pp. 15–33; see also Carrie Noland, *Poetry at Stake: Lyric Aesthetics and the Challenge of Technology* (Princeton, NJ: Princeton University Press, 1999), Chapter 1, for a broad analysis of Cendrars's poetic responses to technology and industrialized capitalism.

84. Beyond the art narratives that inform *Dan Yack*, there may be many other intertexts: the Antarctic expedition in *Le Plan de l'aiguille* has been linked to Poe's *Arthur Gordon Pym* (see J. M. Santraud, 'Dans le sillage de la baleinière d'Arthur Gordon Pym: *Le Sphinx des glaces, Dan Yack*', *Études anglaises*, 25.3 (1972), 353–66), and may also be influenced by Jean Charcot's accounts of his expeditions (see *TADA*, IV, 304, n. 38).

85. Claude Leroy, 'Figures de *Dan Yack*: le jeu dans l'île', in *Cendrars aujourd'hui: présence d'un romancier*, ed. by Michel Décaudin (Paris: Minard/ Lettres modernes, 1977), pp. 109–44 (pp. 139–41).

86. Blaise Cendrars, *Dix-neuf poèmes élastiques*, *TADA*, I, 80. On the composition of *Kodak*, see Francis Lacassin, 'Les Poèmes du Docteur Cornélius', in *Le Mystérieux Docteur Cornélius et autres œuvres de Gustave Le Rouge*, ed. by Francis Lacassin (Paris: R. Laffont, 1986), pp. 1181–1247, and Bozon-Scalzitti, *Blaise Cendrars*, pp. 297–309, which reveals Maurice Calmeyn's *Au Congo belge* as another source.

87. This text was later incorporated into *Aujourd'hui* (1931) under the title 'Le Roman français' (*TADA*, XI, 49).

88. Walter Benjamin, 'On Some Motifs in Baudelaire', in *Illuminations*, trans. by Harry Zohn, ed. by Hannah Arendt (London: Pimlico, 1999), pp. 152–96 (esp. pp. 156–62).

89. Ibid., pp. 155–56.

Surrealism and Visual Culture

In the previous chapter, we read Apollinaire's and Cendrars's engagements with the visual arts as fundamentally anxious: Apollinaire looked across at painting as a potential ally to a beleaguered and culturally isolated poetic writing, but also expressed fears that it may stab the latter in the back; Cendrars, meanwhile, took leave of painting, dismissed sculpture, and flirted with the new art of the cinema before ultimately 'divorcing' it ('pour incompatibilité d'humeur' [due to irreconcilable differences], he later joked, but in *Dan Yack* the split is caused by the dangers of the new medium, which outweigh its creative potential).[1] As we move to look at the Surrealist generation that followed in the wake of the pre-war Futurist Moment, we find its key practitioners much more open and inclusive, and apparently less anxious about protecting the position of literature within the field of cultural production. Indeed, Breton and Aragon, the two central literary figureheads of the movement as it formulated itself in the years following the First World War, sought deliberately to situate themselves on the margins of this field, in a position of all-out opposition. This is of course reflected in their political stance (their allegiance to communism, and their refusal to so much as touch on the war, even if to express opposition to it), but also in their attitude to mainstream aesthetic currents: at a time when many writers and artists were turning away from Cubism and other avant-garde currents in the name of a 'retour à l'ordre' which privileged classical values, they renewed their interest in these; indeed, they expressed an interest in *any* type of art — whether it be primitive or popular or otherwise — that might give free expression to the hidden realms of the unconscious mind. Moreover, for the Surrealists, the task was not to protect 'literature' but instead to reconfigure its identity, to abandon anything that had the whiff of staid nineteenth-century literariness about it and seek out new forms of writing.[2] In this respect, they were genuinely on the lookout for generative influences from other media. They were particularly attracted to the model of cinema, as we shall see, but also to the myriad attractions of an expanded visual field, or to a broad concept of 'visual culture' as the term is now understood.[3]

What renders this apparent openness to the visual more problematic, however, is the fact that visual art appears to sit somewhat awkwardly within Surrealism's early theoretical elaborations of itself. In Breton's founding manifesto, Surrealism is famously defined in terms of an 'automatisme psychique pur par lequel on se propose d'exprimer, soit verbalement, soit par écrit, soit de toute autre manière, le fonctionnement réel de la pensée' [pure psychic automatism through which we propose to express, either verbally or in writing, or by any other means, the real workings of thought] (*BOC*, 1, 328). While this formulation admits (rather vaguely) that other means of expression might be possible, it privileges verbal language, and indeed throughout the manifesto it is clear that the principal mode of creation Breton has in mind is automatic writing, as practised by himself and Soupault in *Les Champs magnétiques* (1920) and other experiments. In a 1924 article in the first issue of the Surrealists' official organ *La Révolution surréaliste*, Max Morise wondered how the visual arts might fit in with this model: painting is a lengthy, reflective undertaking, in which the operations of taste and memory may intervene to interrupt a pure, direct expression of spontaneous thought.[4] Morise's article was not entirely pessimistic, however, proposing that early Cubist painting and collage, the drawings of mediums and madmen, and Man Ray's rayographs might be genuinely Surrealist visual expressions; moreover, Breton was quick to remedy the perceived gap in Surrealism's remit in his series of articles on 'Le Surréalisme et la peinture' (1925). And yet in the critical literature on Surrealism there remains a persistent view that the movement treated the visual arts as something of an afterthought, and, crucially, that it consistently judged the visual arts against the preconceived, and privileged, model of automatic writing.[5]

Kim Grant has countered this, arguing that automatic writing is itself fundamentally visual. The key example of automatic writing that Breton gives in the *Manifeste du surréalisme*, 'Il y a un homme coupé en deux par la fenêtre' [There is a man cut in two by the window] is itself a visual image: not merely a sentence, but an imaginative vision that Breton translates via words (*BOC*, 1, 324–25).[6] In *Le Paysan de Paris* (1926), Aragon goes so far as to provide the following definition of Surrealist activity: 'Le vice appelé *Surréalisme* est l'emploi déréglé et passionnel du stupéfiant *image*, ou plutôt de la provocation sans contrôle de l'image pour elle-même et pour ce qu'elle entraîne dans le domaine de la représentation de perturbations imprévisibles et de métamorphoses' [The vice known as Surrealism is the unfettered, passionate use of the image-drug, or rather the uncontrolled triggering of images for their own sake, and in order to bring about unexpected perturbations and metamorphoses in the domain of representation].[7] As such, Surrealism may be seen as trying to translate the activities of, and in turn to stimulate, the visual imagination, and it may do this either through visual images or through texts, or both. What this chapter seeks to show is that while the place of the visual might not have been fully thought through in Surrealism's initial theoretical statements, it is in fact very much built into the practice of Surrealist writing from the early stages of the movement. In the first instance, I will examine the relative roles of painting and cinema in Aragon's first novel *Anicet* (1921), a text that belongs to the period of 'unofficially designated' Surrealism preceding Breton's manifesto.[8] I will demonstrate that cinema, in Aragon's novel, ultimately wins out over painting, which in the context of the post-war 'retour à l'ordre' is associated with the staid conventions of academic art. In this analysis, cinema appears not only as a particularly potent source of inspiration or 'image-drug', but might also be seen to take its place alongside still photography as what Rosalind Krauss has called a 'condition of Surrealism': a model that may have helped the Surrealists to elaborate their conception of the surreal as rooted in the real. Cinema, then, is figured in *Anicet* not just as an attractive 'other', a potential rival or ally to writing, but as a properly generative influence for Surrealist writing, with the text itself aspiring to take on a cinematic visuality.[9]

While a full examination of Surrealist engagement with the visual is clearly beyond the scope of this study, the chapter will conclude with a brief examination of André Breton's *Nadja* (1928), not only as an example of a text that clearly sits within the thematic terrain of the art novel and yet pushes at the formal boundaries of that genre, but also as a text that engages with an expanded conception of visual culture which moves beyond the confines of the 'fine arts'. Surrealism, as we shall see, involves an openness not only to the hitherto neglected unconscious mind, but also to modernity, and to various forms of the visual that might be incorporated into the Surrealist text — in the case of *Nadja*, materially incorporated into the printed text in the form of photographic documents. Here, painting and sculpture remain as important generative influences but they are considered alongside other, more everyday sources of visual experience: street signs, cinema, found objects, and popular images.

Despite this apparent openness, which entails a radical democratization of art, of artistic creation, and of aesthetic experience, Breton's text seems somewhat less inclusive when it comes to the possibility of female creativity. As Susan Rubin Suleiman and others have noted, Surrealism is fascinated with the figure of Woman: Surrealist art obsessively represents the female body; it takes Woman as representative of a positively valorized, irrational 'Other'; and as Katharine Conley has shown, it even figures psychic automatism, the cornerstone of Surrealist creation, in 'female' terms.[10] And yet within these representations, the female figure often appears as a fetishized object of contemplation: an image, at most a muse for the male poet/artist, and never a creative subject. Suleiman sees as representative of this the well-known 1929 photomontage included in *La Révolution surréaliste* (Figure 4.1) in which the all-male members of the movement are shown, eyes closed, contemplating a woman (a painted woman, and a creation of a male artist, René Magritte). Woman here is placed 'at the center but only as an image, while any actual woman is now out of the picture altogether'; she is present only as an object of the male gaze, or, as the caption indicates, a figure borne of the male imagination.[11] Indeed, the ellipsis in 'Je ne vois pas la ... cachée dans la forêt' [I do not see the ... hidden in the forest] seems to consign Woman fully to the visual realm, shutting her out of male-dominated language.[12] This might, of course, work to valorize the figure of the woman within the Surrealist world-view, associating her with a fluid realm of visuality and irrationality alien to logical discourse. But the fact remains that in this and many other Surrealist images of women, as well as in the real organization of the Surrealist movement in the 1920s, women were silenced, pushed towards the margins, and figured as images rather than as creative subjects: as Whitney Chadwick asserts, 'there was no female subject in Surrealism'.[13] This claim is supported, as we shall see, by both of the texts examined in this chapter: while both propose female figures of creativity, neither allow Woman her own subjectivity, or to become a fully-fledged artist in her own right.

FIG. 4.1. Photomontage featuring René Magritte, *Je ne vois pas la ... cachée dans la forêt*, from *La Révolution surréaliste*, 12 (1929). © 2015. BI, ADAGP, Paris/Scala, Florence. © ADAGP, Paris and DACS, London 2015.

Painting and Cinema in Aragon's *Anicet*

Louis Aragon's first novel, *Anicet ou le panorama, roman*, provides an apt starting point for investigation of the Surrealist response to visual culture, as it combines in its very title the notion of visual spectacle with that of literary narrative. In his 1964 preface to the novel, Aragon indicated that he considered the generic marker 'roman' to be very much part of the title, but added that it had been included primarily 'par la consonance avec le mot *panorama*' [for its consonance with the word *panorama*].[14] As such, one might wish to read it, if not as a straightforwardly ironic reflection of the Surrealist generation's anti-literary stance — 'un défi aux conceptions mêmes de mes plus proches amis de ce temps' [a challenge to the very conceptions of my closest friends from this time] as Aragon put it (*ORC*, I, 14) — then as an indication of the inseparability of literary and visual impulses in this 'panorama-roman'. If, however, we examine the novel closely, considering the techniques or indeed (to borrow Mieke Bal's term once again) the 'subterfuges'[15] through which the visual domain is allowed to be present in the text, we discover that these do not give rise to a unified, global vision, and that the relatively outmoded technology of the panorama is marginalized as a visual model for writing, in favour of two alternatives whose expressive resources Aragon explores in *Anicet*: painting and cinema. Thus, while the novel's title may suggest that it offers a panoramic vision of early twentieth-century artistic culture, this vision turns out to be composed of a series of partial, subjective sketches or, alternatively, a series of *ciné-feuilleton* episodes.

As Aragon's first novel, *Anicet* is a crucial aesthetic testing ground, a space in which the writer reflects on the properties of his own medium and the ways in which the movement that would later be baptized 'Surrealism' might draw on these two visual models of writing: the static image associated with the traditional art of painting, and the moving images associated with the new art of the cinema.[16] As well as situating writing in relation to alternative genres and art forms, Aragon also reflects on its current position within the field of cultural production, thinking through his generation's struggle to develop its own distinctive identity in relation to key literary influences (especially Rimbaud).[17] The novel's plot is structured around a competition between different forms of creative expression, each struggling to innovate and to attain 'la beauté moderne' [modern beauty] (*ORC*, I, 7) — represented in the form of a woman, Mirabelle, whose favours the artist must seek to win. Through a chance encounter in an inn, the young Anicet, who aspires to be a poet, is witness to a strange ritual whereby Mirabelle is presented with gifts by seven masked men. These men are members of a secret society devoted to the cult of Mirabelle, and are all artists or creators of one sort or another, seeking literally to conquer Mirabelle and symbolically to conquer modern beauty by innovating in their respective artistic domains. All, moreover, have real-life referents, or at least models: Bleu, Aragon tells us in his 1964 preface to the novel, is 'indiscutablement Picasso' [indisputably Picasso], while Chipre is based on Max Jacob, Omme on Valéry, Baptiste on Breton, and Pol represents Charlie Chaplin (I, 6–7). Agreeing to join their organization, Anicet finds himself in competition with these other artists, and especially with the painter Bleu, quickly identified as his strongest rival: 'Anicet pensa tendrement à Mire. Quelle œuvre créerait-il pour mériter son amour? Il songea à l'attrait de la robe du faisan, et craignit que le peintre, maître des couleurs, ne gagnât avant lui le prix qu'il enviait' [Anicet thought tenderly of Mire. What work could he create to win her love? He thought of the peacock's attractive robes, and feared that the painter, master of colours, would win the prize he coveted] (I, 68).

The painter's resources are perceived to be more powerful and seductive than those of the poet, and there is a sense that literature is in crisis, under pressure from the stunning innovations of modern painting. This is reflected in the fact that Anicet, as the principal representative of modern literature in the novel, is singularly inactive: he has produced only one rather inferior poem, and harbours vague plans for an article on modern painting, a project which is ironically dependent on the endeavours of his rivals in the visual arts. The rivalry between literature and painting comes to a head in Bleu's studio, where Anicet, who has been recruited into a gang of art thieves, finds himself breaking in one night. Overcome with admiration and jealousy, Anicet is tempted to destroy Bleu's work, but resists this temptation in the hope that he may one day 'inventer des charmes plus puissants' [invent more powerful charms] by literary means. He seeks to channel 'des cris qui viennent de plus loin dans les cœurs des hommes que de cette zone facilement atteinte où règne l'amour des formes colorées' [cries that come from further within men's hearts than from that easily accessible zone where love of coloured forms reigns supreme], releasing unconscious currents of thought in a creative process that clearly recalls Breton and Soupault's early experiments in automatic writing. These attempts end in failure, however, and Anicet remains acutely aware of the limitations of verbal language relative to the immediate visual appeal of coloured forms, lamenting, 'Pauvre poète qui cherche à lutter avec tes malheureuses images verbales!' [Poor poet, struggling with your wretched verbal images!] (*ORC*, I, 120).

Anicet may resist the impulse to destroy Bleu's work, but earlier in the novel his first act in the pursuit of Mirabelle is one of vandalism: raiding Paris's museums, he burns their most celebrated masterpieces on top of the Arc de Triomphe. This daring feat is motivated not so much by the need to eliminate a competitor for Mirabelle's affections (the works in question, 'les Greuze, les Boucher, les Meissonnier, les Millet' (*ORC*, I, 56), are seen as obsolete and irrelevant) as by a desire to topple revered artistic monuments, and to create a spectacle whose beauty is grounded in violent destruction. Bleu's painting is initially aligned with these iconoclastic desires, and thus distanced from the stale forms of the past. Conceiving of artistic creation as the ability to conjure beauty from worthless materials, '*Bleu*, le génie de cette époque, se sert pour ses tableaux de papiers peints, de journaux, de sable, d'étiquettes' [*Bleu*, the genius of our times, uses in his paintings wallpaper, newspaper, sand, labels] (I, 62). In his fictionalized portrait of Picasso and his work, Aragon highlights the way in which the artist's collage aesthetic brought into question the values of uniqueness, authenticity, and the well-made object traditionally attached to high art, alongside the idea that the dual aesthetic and monetary value of an artwork derived partly from the materials used in its creation. The value of Bleu/Picasso's work lies instead in the process by which those materials are transformed, a process which combines creative and destructive impulses. Indeed, in the ritual where Anicet first encounters the masked men, Bleu's gift to Mirabelle is, significantly, a railway signal whose removal will cause a collision between two trains. This found object, apparently devoid of aesthetic value, is transformed into a potential art object through its causal relationship to an act of destruction, and this is suggestive of Picasso's dissection of objects and their contours, as well as of the more general iconoclasm of the Cubist aesthetic, as Anna Balakian notes: 'Here the conquest of modern Beauty demands the sacrifice of order and risks terrible destruction. Had not Picasso caused, indeed, the collision and explosion of long-established and orderly systems, the breakdown of standardization and of accepted relationships?'[18] Equally, the signal's value may be seen to derive from its multivalency, as Anicet compares it successively to 'une tache de sang, à un œil, à un sexe, à un chapeau de conte de fée' [a bloodstain, an eye, a sex, a fairytale hat] (1, 49). This signal or 'sign' which, once removed from its original context, is able to take on a variety of alternative, co-existing meanings, calls to mind the punning substitutions of Picasso's Cubist works and the multiple readings they generate, and suggests that their power lies in this semiotic proliferation.

The critical account of Picasso's work that Aragon articulates through the fictional text is, however, just as attentive to the perceived failings of Picasso's art at the beginning of the 1920s as it is to the successes of the earlier Cubist period. While his collages may have playfully highlighted and mocked the market forces governing the production of art, their market value has ironically increased, and the once-revolutionary Bleu is now incorporated into the bourgeoisie as 'l'Homme arrivé' [the Great Success], standing in contrast to Chipre, or Max Jacob's ascetic 'Homme pauvre' [Poor Man]. Now that Bleu has 'arrived', his primary interest is 'circulaire et dorée' [round and golden] (*ORC*, 1, 106), and his art begins to slip into the clichés of academic painting.[19] Having admired many of the works in Bleu's studio, Anicet comes across his much-trumpeted new work, entitled *La Louange du corps humain*, and discovers it to be:

> une parfaite académie, une figure de proportions avec ses cotes en chiffres connus. Anicet saisit subitement que Bleu en atteignant la perfection avait passé du domaine de l'amour à celui de la mort et de la gloire. Il prononça plusieurs noms de grands hommes et sourit. (*ORC*, 1, 121)
>
> [a perfect academic nude, a proportional figure done by numbers. Anicet suddenly understood that Bleu, in attaining perfection, had passed from the realm of love to that of death and glory. He muttered the names of several great men, and smiled]

At the conclusion of this episode, related within a chapter whose title, 'Décès', seems to signal the death of modern painting, Anicet is finally able to breathe a sigh of relief. Bleu is no longer a contender in the pursuit of modern beauty, and his name joins the ranks of those Salon painters whose works were destroyed earlier in the novel. Aragon's representation of Bleu culminates, then, in a thinly-veiled attack on Picasso's return to classicism, suggesting that such a move leaves the painter in an aesthetic dead-end, unable to respond adequately to modernity.[20] The moment of the painting's unveiling and Anicet's discovery of its failure explicitly recalls similar episodes in *Le Chef d'œuvre inconnu* and other art narratives in the nineteenth-century tradition, and this intertextual echo further consigns Bleu/Picasso's art — and, by implication, painting more generally — to the past, associating it with the unattainable, 'invisible' masterpiece that, according to Belting, characterized the idea of art throughout the nineteenth century. Interestingly, this critique of Picasso is one that Aragon did not pursue in his non-fiction writing on art, where he remained more or less silent on Picasso's work between 1918 and 1924, at the height of the artist's dalliance with classicism. It may be, then, that the veil of fiction provided Aragon with a safe space in which to present this critique, without obliging him to challenge directly a consecrated avant-garde master who would later be appropriated by Breton as a Surrealist trailblazer.[21]

The failure of painting is also, I think, reflected in the withheld visuality of Aragon's writing. Aragon refrains, in particular, from detailed ekphrastic description, giving only rough, deliberately enigmatic sketches of the works encountered in the studio. Anicet sees, in turn, 'une maison schématique qui fidèlement figurait la *Maison*, celle qu'on ne désigne que par ce nom tendre sans le nantir d'un possessif' [a schematic house which faithfully rendered the *Home*, the one we indicate with this affectionate name without spoiling it with a possessive]; 'un adolescent grand et maigre dont les mains souffrent d'être vides, un garçon qui n'a pas encore appris la beauté du corps, ni quel secret cache ce maillot trop large' [a tall, skinny young man whose hands suffer from their emptiness, a boy who has not yet learned the beauty of the body, and what secrets his too-large trunks might hide]; and 'une nature morte qui laissa voir au jeune homme dans le jeu ambigu de la guitare et des bouteilles au centre du guéridon les formes jointes d'un couple amoureux que le monde ne pouvait plus troubler ni le charme des objets usuels' [a still life in which the young man saw, in the ambiguous play of the guitar and the bottles in the centre of the table, the conjoined bodies of a couple in love whom neither the world nor the charm of everyday things could disturb] (*ORC*, I, 118). These poetic descriptions are of course extremely evocative, but they are very much focused upon what Anicet reads into the paintings: on their affect, which is not literally visible on the surface, rather than on the arrangement of painted elements on the canvas. Thus, while readers familiar with Picasso's work will certainly draw on their knowledge in order to visualize the paintings, Aragon does not fully expose them through his writing, providing only an enigmatic starting-point for imaginative visualization.[22] By focusing on the viewing subject and his responses, he moves the painted image itself to the sidelines. Furthermore, Aragon's sketched indications dwindle to almost nothing as Anicet approaches *La Louange du corps humain*. We know that it is an 'académie' (a nude), but are given no further details: reduced to a generic category by Aragon's verbal representation, the painting's visual impact is denied, and visualization rendered all but impossible.

Since painting is ultimately revealed to fail in its attempt to capture modern beauty, it ceases to be either a rival in Anicet's quest, or a potential model for Aragon's own writing in the novel. There is a single instance in *Anicet* where the fragmentation of narrative perspective might be compared to the multiple viewpoints of Cubist painting — but Aragon quickly cancels this association by making it clear that the effect is a 'photographic' one:

> Les quatre interlocuteurs n'envisagèrent plus le paysage du même point de vue, de telle façon qu'un spectateur impartial qui n'aurait pas su choisir entre leurs quatre visions, n'eût plus obtenu de la scène qu'une photographie brouillée par la superposition des clichés. (*ORC*, i, 66)

> [The four speakers no longer saw the scene from the same perspective, so that an impartial spectator who could not choose between their four visions would have obtained from the scene a sort of blurred photograph in which different shots were superimposed]

What is 'seen' here is conceived in terms of an effect of superimposition used in still photography, but particularly common in early twentieth-century film, especially the trick-films of Georges Méliès.[23] Indeed, allusions to such special effects are, as we will see, one means by which Aragon places the novel's action within a specifically filmic universe. More generally, *Anicet* is peppered with references to film, tapping directly into the cinematic culture of the period.[24] Pol is involved in a series of Chaplin-esque chase scenes, Nick Carter (the fictional detective to whom a series of films had been devoted) features as a character, and many episodes within the novel (the antics of the art thieves, for instance) inescapably call to mind Feuillade's *Fantômas* and *Les Vampires*.[25] The aesthetic potential of the seventh art is also explicitly discussed during Baptiste and Anicet's visit to the cinema, an episode in which the unusual spectatorial behaviour of the characters looks forward to Breton's description of his cinema-going habits in *Nadja*:

> Sans se préoccuper des voisins, ils parlaient à voix haute et mêlaient à leurs discours des jugements sur les films. Ainsi vous regardez passer la vie, vous y intéressez votre sensibilité, vous vous en détournez pour explorer votre esprit et vous reportez de nouveau les yeux sur les spectacles quotidiens. (*ORC*, i, 82)

> [Without worrying about their neighbours, they spoke loudly and sprinkled their conversations with critiques of the films. In this way you see life pass by, you engage your senses, you turn away from them to explore your own mind and you then cast your gaze back upon the spectacles of everyday life]

Just as Breton describes himself entering screenings at random and never fully following the film, Aragon places emphasis here on the possibility of engaging and disengaging one's attention from the film at will, and represents the cinema as a social space, the setting for a new type of collective experience which Anicet and Baptiste happily disrupt as they pursue their discussions.[26] Moving beyond these elements common to both Aragon's and Breton's representations of cinema-going — beyond the Surrealist 'bravo pour les salles obscures' [bravo for dark movie theatres][27] — *Anicet* suggests that the status of film as the modern art form *par excellence* is closely bound up with the formal qualities of the medium itself, countering Michael Richardson's suggestion that the Surrealists were not interested so much in film *per se*, as in the collective experience of cinema-going.[28] Watching a film starring Pearl White (probably the extremely popular *Mystères de New-York*), Anicet notes that it is fundamentally non-literary, in that its fast-moving action eliminates the need, and indeed the opportunity, for verbal discourse or analysis. He concludes, 'Voilà bien le spectacle qui convient à ce siècle' [This is the spectacle that suits our century] (*ORC*, 1, 83). A similar view is expressed in Aragon's 1918 article on film, 'Du décor', where he argues that cinema 'doit être dépouillé de tout ce qui est verbal' [must be stripped of all that is verbal] and that it must hence liberate itself from the example of theatre.[29] It may be precisely because film was, prior to the advent of the sound film, an essentially visual medium, and because it was therefore opposed to literary forms (such as the *roman d'analyse*) which emphasized discourse at the expense of pure action, that it seemed to Aragon to supply a viable model for a new form of writing — a visual form of writing appealing to the sensibilities of the cinema-going public.[30]

Anna Balakian has contested the influence of film on *Anicet*, reading it as an overwhelmingly pessimistic novel in which cinema, like painting, is seen to be incapable of meeting the demands of modern beauty, and, by extension, incapable of providing new impetus for literary experimentation. Balakian cites as evidence of this the gift given by Pol, an avatar for Charlie Chaplin, to Mirabelle. The gift in question is a mandarin, which Pol steals from a cinema usherette, triggering the first of many comical chases. Balakian interprets the gift as follows:

> Much valor is displayed, and stunningly succulent is the fruit, but rapidly consumed. Aragon gives a succinct indictment of the value of cinema to aesthetics: brilliant, gilded, savory but ephemeral — so much effort for so short a satisfaction. We are here very far from the high hopes that Apollinaire had entertained for film as an eventual replacement for the word in the making of poetry, i.e. the Beautiful.[31]

It is true that Pol's gift is not enough to win Mirabelle, but none of the other artists' gifts are either, and it is the businessman Gonzalès whom she marries, beauty ending up 'aux mains des marchands' [in the hands of merchants] (*ORC*, 1, 100).[32] It is also true that the novel expresses some reservations about cinema, as Anicet's glowing assessment of its aesthetic potential is countered by Baptiste's complaints about the passivity of the film spectator. Nevertheless, it remains the case that filmic references permeate the novel, and that these go beyond superficial nods to popular film at the level of plot, and discussions between characters of the aesthetic merits of cinema. The properties of the filmic medium are incorporated into the very techniques of Aragon's writing, so that the experience of reading the novel is brought into close contact with the experience of the filmgoer.

Aragon achieves this primarily by identifying narrative perspective with the camera's gaze, which in turn invites the reader to conceive of the narrative as a cinematic sequence, projected onto a screen for us to 'see'. Often this effect is achieved by quite subtle means, as in the following sentence, where it hinges on the reference of the pronoun 'on': 'À ce moment, on s'aperçut que les interlocuteurs se trouvaient dans un Biard près de Saint-Philippe-du-Roule' [At that moment, we noticed that the speakers were located in a café near Saint-Philippe-du-Roule] (*ORC*, 1, 58). Since we know from the context of this sentence that 'on' does not refer to observers located within the diegetic frame, the reader is obliged to posit an audience whose presence is exterior to and does not affect the story world, and who are not omniscient or privy to all facts about that world: as such, they discover the location in which the conversation is taking place only as the 'camera' zooms out or cuts to a long shot revealing the café setting.[33] Similarly, when Anicet realizes that it is in fact Bleu's studio he has broken into, we are told 'il y avait un siècle que tout le monde le savait' [everyone else had known this for a hundred years] (1, 118). Here it is 'tout le monde' that introduces the idea of an audience observing the action, and once more the reference is not to a solitary reader, but to a collective spectatorship, whose privileged position of knowledge in this instance contrasts with the obliviousness of the observed character, creating suspense characteristic of the *film policier*.[34]

Aragon also draws attention to the way in which the action is visually presented to the reader/spectator — to the composition of his 'shots' and the transitions between them. During a scene at Mirabelle's mansion, 'tout à coup les valeurs se renversèrent':

> Les protagonistes devinrent les spectateurs, le sens de la chambre changea. Le haut de la page se trouva vers le seuil. D'en bas, Anicet et Mirabelle virent se dresser, la main gauche sur le battant ouvert, un grand personnage masqué de velours, coiffé d'un haut-de-forme et drapé dans une cape à collet. (*ORC*, 1, 99)[35]

> [The protagonists became spectators, the orientation of the room shifted. The top of the page was near the doorway. From below, Anicet and Mirabelle saw, with his left hand on the open shutter, a larger-than-life character with a velvet mask, wearing a top hat and draped in a collared cape]

The equation between 'page' and screen explicitly inviting us to visualize the action as if it were being projected in front of us as we read, we cut from one shot to another. Anicet and Mirabelle, who had been the protagonists — the focus of the camera's gaze — now become spectators. From the bottom of the page/screen, or the foreground of the space which is now viewed from a different angle, they observe the dramatic entrance of Omme (another of the seven masked men), whose costume recalls Fantômas as he appears in the famous Gaumont posters (Figure 4.2). This initially appears to render Omme as dashing and mysterious as Feuillade's criminal mastermind, but this implication is quickly undermined and the filmic reference takes on a parodic aspect as Mirabelle mockingly comments, 'Mon Dieu, qu'est-ce que cette mascarade? Mon cher Omme, vous faites vos entrées sans grand art. Mais vous devez étouffer, un après-midi d'été, sous un tel accoutrement' [Good god, what is this mascarade? My dear Omme, your entrances really are clumsy. You must be suffocating in that costume on this summer's afternoon] (*ORC*, 1, 99).

The most important filmic sequences in the novel, however, occur when two films are projected, within the fictional world, for the characters to see. The first of these is a newsreel which Anicet and Baptiste see during the cinema excursion mentioned earlier, and from which they learn of Mirabelle's marriage to Gonzalès. Aragon is once again attentive to framing, and describes the camera singling out Omme, who has observed Mirabelle's wedding, broken-hearted. The camera follows Omme as he leaves the church, enters a café, and plots to get Mirabelle away from her new husband: observing this lengthy sequence of actions, the reader is likely to forget that it is presented via the cinema screen, which Anicet and Baptiste are watching. At the end of the chapter, Anicet and Baptiste also enter the action,

FIG. 4.2. Gino Starace, poster for *Fantômas* (1913). Private collection. © 2015. White Images/Scala, Florence.

but although they have left the cinema, we (as readers/spectators) have not. Aragon reminds us of this by concluding the chapter with the following image: 'En haut, dans un coin de la toile, les bras croisés, le sourire énigmatique, Baptiste semblait le génie directeur de l'aventure' [At the top, in a corner of the screen, with his arms folded and an enigmatic smile, Baptiste appeared as the genius presiding over the action] (*ORC*, I, 92). We are still observing the action via the cinema screen, and this is brought to our attention through the use of a special effect of superimposition which allows multiple shots representing simultaneous events to be shown at once (and which once again draws on the vocabulary of adventure and mystery films, with Baptiste being cast as the dastardly genius shown plotting his enemy's downfall). The fantastic effects obtainable by the manipulation of the cinematic medium are even more stunning in the film screening at the Gonzalès house, which tells the assembled guests of Mirabelle and her new husband's respective life stories. Here, one of Mirabelle's former lovers performs the Méliès-esque feats of lighting his cigarette on the sun, and catching a cloud which he attaches to his buttonhole (I, 126).

Such special effects are also present in scenes which are not explicitly framed as film — that is, they are not films which the characters themselves watch — but which are, as Gindine notes, 'prêts à être enregistrés tels quels par une caméra, grâce à leurs indications précises de mouvements et d'éclairages' [camera-ready, thanks to their precise stage directions and lighting instructions].[36] This is the case in the following passage, in which Anicet dreams of seeing Mirabelle perform in a music hall:

> La rampe bleuâtre permet de voir le rideau se fendre comme un cœur. Il s'ouvre sur un autre rideau sombre, uni, lourd, aux plis droits. Un cercle lumineux apparaît tout en haut à gauche, et dans ce cercle une tête de femme. Sans étonnement Anicet reconnaît Mirabelle: il l'attendait. Elle a l'air d'une jolie réclame pour dentifrice. Elle chante en anglais, il ne peut la comprendre parce qu'elle ne va pas assez lentement. Cependant au passage, il accroche le mot *Darling* pareil à une clochette d'argent. Tout à coup, la tête s'éteint. Mais elle se rallume plus bas, à droite; la chanson continue et Anicet s'émeut de saisir le mot *lèvre*. Après une nouvelle éclipse, la tête reparaît plus bas encore et à gauche [...].
>
> Maintenant la tête est au milieu de la scène au ras du sol comme si Mirabelle s'était couchée à plat ventre. (*ORC*, I, 186)

> [The blue-tinged footlights allow us to make out the curtain splitting open like a heart. It opens onto another curtain, dark, heavy, with straight pleats. A circle of light appears at the very top left, and in this circle a woman's head. Unsurprised, Anicet recognizes Mirabelle: he was expecting her. She looks like something from a pretty advert for toothpaste. She is singing in English, and he can't understand because she's going too fast. He does manage to catch the word *Darling*, which rings out like a silver bell. All of a sudden, the head disappears into darkness. But then it is lit up again, lower down, on the right; the song continues and Anicet is moved by the word *lip*. After another eclipse, the head reappears even lower down on the left.
>
> Now the head is in the middle of the stage at floor level, as if Mirabelle were lying on her stomach]

As Gindine's comment suggests, this passage is eminently visual, Aragon's attention to *mise en scène* and lighting allowing us to imagine the action unfolding before our eyes. What links the passage to cinema, and what makes us conceive of the action as taking place not simply on a music hall stage, but a filmed music hall stage, is the trick effect of Mirabelle's head disappearing in one location, only to suddenly reappear in another. The lack of *vraisemblance* may be explained by the fact that the scene is taking place within a dream, but equally, the effect is one that could be realized in a film, through the use of straight cuts. Contemporary readers would have been extremely familiar with this technique, thanks to its use in a number of films of the period (alongside the many examples from Méliès, the fleeting apparition of Fantômas before Juve in the first episode of Feuillade's serial is one that Aragon would certainly have known).[37] It is in filmic sequences such as this that Aragon's writing really attains visuality, giving the reader full access to visual experience, while withholding it in the passages relating to painting.

Aragon's *Anicet* relates an allegorized quest for modern beauty, and asks how the novel might attain this, looking to the visual arts for inspiration. Painting, as we have seen, fails in this quest, and is displaced as a model for writing by cinema. The latter, meanwhile, is not conceived as a rival to literature that must be defeated or dispatched, but rather as a complementary resource that may be appropriated and adapted to the needs of the narrative text. As such, the 'competition' between the arts represented in the novel contrasts with the more pressurized, anxious rivalries played out in texts by Apollinaire and Cendrars: while the artists in the first part of *Dan Yack* are pitted against one another in a struggle which only the fittest will survive, the relationships between the players in Anicet's novel are characterized, initially at least, by 'de l'émulation sans jalousie' [emulation without jealousy] (*ORC*, I, 53), and they are free to collaborate and form alliances, becoming comrades more than rivals. Of course, the question remains: why cinema? The glamour and excitement of the new cinematic medium, combined with literature's need to look beyond itself for inspiration, might alone provide sufficient explanation for Aragon's *rapprochement* between novel and film. Indeed, in one of the novel's most self-conscious filmic episodes, we find Anicet imagining his break-in at Bleu's studio as if it were being filmed, and indeed as if he were the star, his exploits calling to mind images of 'Belles affiches des films américains!' [Handsome posters for American films!] (I, 116). Anicet has been seduced by the cinema to the extent that it mediates his own experience, and the episode demonstrates an awareness of the powerful hold of the seventh art over the popular imagination — something that Aragon was clearly keen to exploit through a literary incursion into cinematic culture.

A rather more nuanced response, however, and one that pushes further at the question of what exactly it might have been about film that appealed to the nascent Surrealist aesthetic, might be gained by reconsidering Aragon's attention to special effects, or more generally to the manipulations that may be performed on the filmic image. David Trotter has claimed that modernist writers in early twentieth-century Britain were interested in the cinema as pure mechanism, as a non-art, consisting in the recording of reality rather than its representation.[38] For the Surrealists, in contrast, the filmed image is already potentially 'truqué' or manipulated. As

Aragon commented in 'Du décor', film is 'maître de toutes ses déformations' [the master of all its deformations], and this is certainly borne out by *Anicet*, where the reader is frequently made aware of techniques used to distort the filmed image so as to create visual experiences not possible in reality.[39] Nevertheless, the conception of cinema as a mechanical, entirely neutral form of representation remains present in the novel, although it reveals itself only fleetingly, in 'slips' such as Baptiste's dismissive branding of cinema as 'cette mécanique' [that machine] (*ORC*, I, 84) and the representation of Pol/Chaplin as a robotic 'marionette' (I, 45).[40] And what is crucial to understanding the appeal of cinema, both to Aragon and to the Surrealist movement as it was to develop later in the 1920s, is that these two conceptions of cinema are only apparently at odds with one another. Cinematic tricks and illusions of the type frequently mobilized in *Anicet* rely for their power and effect on the spectator's unconscious acceptance of the idea that film constitutes a neutral, undistorted record of reality. Like Surrealist photography, which, as Rosalind Krauss has observed, 'exploits the special connection to reality with which all photography is endowed', Aragon's text plays on the fact that the filmed image gives a seamless and convincing impression of reality.[41] The illusion of Mirabelle's head moving around the stage, of a suitor catching a cloud and attaching it to his buttonhole: these derive their aesthetic value from their combination of, on the one hand, the creation of marvellous feats, and, on the other, the status of the filmed image as an unproblematic, unmediated 'deposit of the real'.[42] Putting this in rather crude terms, one may say that the spectator knows that what he is seeing is impossible, and yet the idea that film is not *representation* (mediated by a subjectivity), but rather direct, neutral *recording*, works against this, encouraging the spectator to accept the marvellous as part of reality — or at least as part of the reality of the film. This paradoxical quality was particularly appealing to the nascent Surrealist aesthetic, which hinged on a conception of the surreal not as detached from but as very much rooted in the real. (As Breton put it, he leant towards 'une philosophie [...] de l'immanence d'après laquelle la surréalité serait contenue dans la réalité même, et ne lui serait ni supérieure ni extérieure' [a philosophy of immanence according to which the surreal is contained within the real itself, and is neither superior nor exterior to it].)[43] It is the ability of film to stage what Aragon refers to as 'les spectacles quotidiens' [the spectacles of everyday life], to do so within a medium that is indelibly associated with indexicality and neutral, objective recording (even though it might in reality involve a great many manipulations of the image), and *at the same time* to give rise to a sense of the marvellous within everyday reality, that is crucial here, providing a model for Aragon's writing in *Anicet* but also, potentially, a touchstone for Surrealist creation more generally. The cinematic aspects of Aragon's novel might, as such, provide grounds for a reappraisal of the role of film in the genesis of the Surrealist aesthetic, suggesting that its influence was profound, and indeed that it might be placed alongside still photography as what Krauss calls a 'condition of Surrealism'.

Breton's *Nadja*: Woman as Artist, Woman as Work of Art

Breton's *Nadja* might perhaps be seen as the culmination of three decades of shifts and ruptures in the art novel, shifts which, as we have seen over the course of this study, have carried it far beyond the form and concerns of the genre's nineteenth-century foundational texts. Let us start with the obvious: *Nadja* is not a novel. It is, instead, an autobiographical text corresponding to Breton's demand for '[des] livres qu'on laisse battants comme des portes' [books left open like swinging doors], or books conceived along the lines of a 'maison de verre', a glass house in which the author is exposed to the direct gaze of the reader (*Nadja*, BOC, I, 651). One might even say that it is not a coherent narrative: it is made up of three distinct sections, and includes loosely connected anecdotes and diary entries alongside poetic and literary-theoretical passages, as well as a well-known diatribe against the ills of contemporary psychiatry. This heterogeneous texture is heightened by the inclusion of forty-four photographic illustrations, the majority of which represent real scenes, objects, and people mentioned in the text, while others reproduce works of art, including works by well-known contemporary artists allied with the Surrealist movement, 'primitive' sculptures, and drawings and collages by the eponymous Nadja.[44] Breton meets Nadja while wandering the streets of Paris and has a brief relationship with her, a relationship that is not so much romantic but intellectual: in her, he finds the living embodiment of Surrealism, an irrational (indeed, as it turns out, 'mad') female Other whose creative powers derive from her ability both to surrender herself to chance encounters and to pursue the spontaneous associations of the unconscious mind. Despite *Nadja*'s apparent distance from the art novel, it merits inclusion in this study because through it, Breton not only examines the figure of the artist (in this case, Nadja herself), but also formulates a response to many of the questions that plagued other early twentieth-century examples of the genre: questions of artistic identity (what constitutes or defines the ideal artist?); of reception or spectatorship (what is aesthetic experience and what kind of person can have it?); and of the essence of art (what is art, or more to the point, what is *authentic* art, as opposed to pale imitations?). *Nadja* gives a distinctly Surrealist response to all of these questions, responses which rest on the Surrealist conception of art as automatic (that is to say, spontaneous, uncontrolled, giving expression to the workings of the unconscious mind), but which also seek to open art up, to bring it down from its high-culture pedestal, and to make it continuous with the Surrealist experience of everyday life.

With Aragon's *Anicet*, we find the Surrealist art novel not only reflecting on cinema and its aesthetic potential, but enthusiastically embracing it as a model for its own narrative writing. This openness to cinema as an invigorating, popular form of expression that maintains close links with the everyday (via the staging of what Aragon calls 'les spectacles quotidiens' (ORC, I, 82)) is unsurprising given the openness of the Surrealist movement as a whole to objects and artefacts originating from beyond the confines of high culture or the traditional 'fine arts'. A key example of this is Pierre Naville's short text 'Beaux-arts', published in the third issue of *La Révolution surréaliste*, in which he flatly put down the controversy over the place of painting within Surrealism by stating, 'Plus personne n'ignore qu'il n'y a pas de *peinture surréaliste*' [no one is now ignorant of the fact that there is no such thing as *surrealist painting*]. In the place of the culturally privileged art of painting, he proposes as objects of aesthetic experience a series of popular, everyday visual 'spectacles':

> Le cinéma, non parce qu'il est la vie, mais le merveilleux, l'agencement d'élements fortuits.
> La rue, les kiosques, les automobiles, les portes hurlantes, les lampes éclatant dans le ciel.
> Les photographies: Eusèbe, l'Etoile, Le Matin, Excelsior La Nature, — la plus petite ampoule du monde, chemin suivi par le meurtrier. La circulation du sang dans l'épaisseur d'une membrane.[45]

> [Cinema, not because it is life, but the marvellous, the manipulation of fortuitous elements.
> Streets, kiosks, automobiles, screaming doorways, lights sparkling in the sky.
> Photographs: Eusèbe, l'Étoile, Le Matin, Excelsior, La Nature — the smallest lightbulb in the world, the path taken by a murderer. The circulation of the blood in a membrane.]

Cinema is positioned here as the Surrealist art form *par excellence*: it is characterized by a sense of the marvellous, which itself arises out of unforeseen, 'fortuitous' combinations of elements. These characteristics also apply, implicitly, to the everyday street experiences Naville goes on to enumerate, as well as to photography. The types of photographs he mentions here are those published in newspapers and scientific journals, so the reference is to 'straight' photography, rather than the kind of manipulated images one might associate, for instance, with Man Ray. Their content ranges from recent inventions to scientific discoveries to *faits divers*, and it is partly no doubt their very variety — the engineering of unforeseen combinations within the pages of the newspaper — that inspires Naville. But the photographs also give a sense of the marvellous as rooted within the real: a strange, undiscovered world latent in everyday experience, and revealed by the 'neutral' eye of the documentary camera. This idea of the marvellous, or the surreal, as rooted within everyday experience, and indeed within photographic images of everyday scenes and objects, was to be crucial for Breton in *Nadja*.

Breton was to push back against Naville's denial of a specifically Surrealist painting by publishing the first instalment of 'Le Surréalisme et la peinture' in the following issue of *La Révolution surréaliste*, yet even while he stated the case for an alliance of various forms of painting and drawing with the Surrealist movement, he admitted that he had himself become wary of painting, abandoning the halls of museums in favour of more quotidian spectacles: 'Dehors la rue disposait pour moi de mille plus vrais enchantements' [Outside, the streets offered me a thousand more real marvels] (*BOC*, IV, 351). *Nadja* certainly bears out the idea that painting was no longer considered a privileged form of expression, and that it could be just one source of poetic inspiration amongst many, not all of which might be 'art' per se, but rather visual artefacts — indeed visual 'spectacles', experiences, and encounters — of various sorts. Breton gives a number of examples of these in the first part of *Nadja*, where he relates a series of encounters that seem to have an aesthetic or poetic function, acting as 'signals' which give rise not so much to a sense of *beauty*, but rather to a sense of elusive, hidden significance, to 'la sensation très nette que pour nous quelque chose de grave, d'essentiel, en dépend' [the clear sensation that for us something very serious and essential depends on it] (*BOC*, 1, 652). These include encounters with people (Éluard, Péret), with statues (of Rousseau and Étienne Dolet), with street signs, with popular film (*L'Étreinte de la pieuvre*, a film from the Nick Carter series) and theatre (*Les Détraquées*), and with found objects, such as the mysterious cylindrical object discovered at the Saint-Ouen flea market, where Breton tells us he goes often, 'en quête de ces objets qu'on ne trouve nulle part ailleurs, démodés, fragmentés, inutilisables, presque incompréhensibles, pervers enfin au sens où je l'entends et où je l'aime' [in search of those objects that one cannot find anywhere else, outmoded, fragmented, unusable, almost incomprehensible, perverted in the sense I understand and love the term] (*BOC*, 1, 676). In each case, the object of the encounter provokes a feeling of shock or unease, which remains unexplained but is held, nevertheless, to reveal of an aspect of Breton's self, of his unconscious mind. All of these encounters pave the way for the encounter with Nadja herself: a young woman who wanders the city at random, giving herself up to chance encounters, and who will provide Breton with a deeper understanding of Surrealism, and also, crucially, a deeper understanding of himself. As such, Nadja functions within the text very much along the lines of the visual spectacles that precede her: we are invited to consider her as an image or found object, albeit a walking and talking one.

Breton's embrace of everyday visual spectacles, or a broadly defined visual culture that includes high and low, popular and distinguished, of course implies a democratization of aesthetic experience: this is no longer something accessible only to the museum goer with enough high-cultural knowledge to understand the works of art presented to him. For Breton, almost anything can trigger such experiences; by the same token, anyone can have them, provided that they are sufficiently receptive to the unconscious associations awakened by the visual spectacles of everyday life. Nadja herself is exemplary in this respect: a drifting, impoverished woman without formal education or cultural capital, she nevertheless appears as the ideal Surrealist spectator, open as much to the unconscious associations and visions provoked by a street scene as to the hidden meanings of a work of contemporary art. On a visit to Breton's apartment, she responds spontaneously to items from his heteroclite collection: she immediately identifies and connects with motifs in works by Braque and de Chirico that appear in her own imaginative visions; she greets a mask from Papua New Guinea as if it were an old friend, while another from Easter Island seems to tell her it loves her; she is able to unpack the meaning of a particularly enigmatic painting by Max Ernst in a way that turns out to accord perfectly with an explanatory text stuck to the back of the canvas (*BOC*, 1, 727). There is of course no preconceived framework for these free-flowing, automatic responses, the implication being that Nadja does not need expertise in art history or knowledge of any codified aesthetic principles in order to connect with and appreciate the art object. In this respect, *Nadja* might be seen to participate in a Surrealist vision of art and aesthetic experience that effectively throws out the notion of the connoisseur as it was explored by Proust or Bourget at the beginning of the century, and as it tended to imply a narrow, elitist conception of art appreciation as something of which only a select few were truly capable. Indeed, Surrealism might also be said to dispense with the very notion of art criticism, which depends on the existence of a more or less stable set of values and codes that may be used to evaluate the work of art and on the authority of the critic or 'expert' spectator.[46] If the Surrealist is to engage with the work of art and translate his or her experience of it into writing, then this will be within a mode that privileges the sensuous and the imaginary, and that avoids traditional description and critical evaluation in order to occupy a generically fluid space close to poetry and narrative fiction.[47]

Just as anyone can, in principle, respond fully to works of art and to visual spectacles if they only free up their imagination, so can anyone create works of art. This view is evidenced in the *Manifeste du surréalisme* where Breton gives clear instructions to the reader on how to produce his or her own automatic writing (*BOC*, I, 331–32), and in the 1933 text 'Le Message automatique', where he proclaims 'l'égalité totale de tous les être humains normaux devant le message subliminal' [the complete equality of all normal human beings before the subliminal message], and sees automatism as 'un patrimoine commun dont il ne tient qu'à chacun de revendiquer sa part et qui doit à tout prix cesser très prochainement d'être tenu pour l'apanage de quelques-uns' [a common asset in which each of us should stake a claim, and which must at all costs stop being seen as the preserve of a select few] (*BOC*, II, 387). Nadja, like the lay reader of the manifesto, is completely untrained and inexperienced in either poetic writing or in the visual arts and yet her utterances, 'prononcées devant moi ou écrites d'un trait sous mes yeux' [pronounced before me or written out quickly before my eyes], are carefully recorded by Breton as examples of automatic creation. Her drawings and collages, similarly, are done 'avec une grande inhabilité' [a great lack of skill] (*BOC*, I, 719), a quality that Breton seems to prize precisely because it indicated that the artist's imaginative vision — the 'œil sauvage' [untamed eye] celebrated in the opening lines of 'Le Surréalisme et la peinture' — was uninhibited by technical training (*BOC*, IV, 349). Although they were sometimes corrected or altered after the fact, Nadja's images respond to Breton's desire for a direct, spontaneous translation of the workings of the unconscious, and are characterized by a number of enigmatic symbols that speak, in mysterious terms, of Nadja's innermost self and her relationship with Breton. Not only is Nadja, as 'la créature toujours inspirée et inspirante qui n'aimait qu'être dans la rue, pour elle seul champ d'expérience valable' [the always inspired and inspiring creature who liked only to be in the street, for her the only valid field of experience] (*BOC*, I, 716), held up as a living embodiment of Surrealist principles, treating everyday life itself as a form of automatic art; not only is she an ideal spectator; she is also an ideal creator, her openness to chance encounters, spontaneity, and ability to release and respond to the unconscious characterizing all of these functions. And her status as creator, or as artist, is confirmed by the fact that her works are not only described but also reproduced within the text, displayed alongside the works included in Breton's own collection and, as such, implicitly placed on a level pegging with the works of contemporary and primitive art that he revered.

Seen from this point of view, Breton's text may be the first twentieth-century French art narrative in which female creativity is not only acknowledged, but unreservedly celebrated and placed centre-stage within the narrative rather than sidelined in favour of male creative endeavours which are implicitly registered as somehow more authentic, more valuable. On the face of it, Breton paints Nadja as an artist in her own right, and allows her images to speak for themselves. However, a consideration of the multiple purposes to which the photographic images in *Nadja* are put, and the implications of these for the inclusion of Nadja's artworks, might lead us to a reading, or to a number of readings, that contradict this.

It is often noted that the photographs in *Nadja* are there to provide documentary evidence, and to convince the reader that the marvellous events related in the narrative are real. The photographed street scenes, in particular, root the marvellous within the very real setting of the Paris streets, and the fact that these are very much 'straight' photographs of the type celebrated by Naville, free of any obvious manipulations, feeds into Krauss's suggestion that photography is valued by the Surrealists for its indexicality, for its status as a direct trace of the real akin to 'automatic' representation.[48] If we follow this reasoning through to Nadja's drawings, these might also be seen to operate as supporting documents, convincing us that Nadja was a real person (and not a fiction, or a figment of Breton's own creative imagination): so far, so good. In the preface to the 1963 edition of *Nadja*, however, Breton attests that the photographs were included to 'éliminer toute description — celle-ci frappée d'inanité dans le *Manifeste du surréalisme*' [eliminate all description, the latter being dismissed as inane in the *Surrealist Manifesto*] (*BOC*, I, 645). The assumption underlying this move seems to be to do with the primacy of the visual: literary description for Breton is not only tedious, but provides us with an impoverished, indirect representation of visual experience. The photographs included in *Nadja*, ostensibly in place of written descriptions, counter this by exposing the objects of these experiences directly to the reader's gaze. This seems to follow on quite naturally from the democratization of aesthetic experience for which *Nadja* seems to militate: by giving the reader direct access to these objects, Breton frees us to formulate our own automatic, and highly personal, responses. Another statement contained towards the end of the text belies this, however, indicating that Breton's intention was in fact to allow the reader to consider scenes and objects 'sous l'angle spécial *dont je les avais moi-même considérés*' [from the particular angle *from which I myself had considered them*] (*BOC*, I, 746, my emphasis). That is to say, Breton's intention is that the reader should share in *his* particular experience, partake of his personal vision. And what might otherwise appear to be a simple attempt to 'put the reader in the author's shoes' begins to look like an attempt to impose a totalizing personal vision when one considers that *Nadja* — a text that announces itself as being about someone else, a woman — begins with the question 'Qui suis-je?' (*BOC*, I, 647), takes us through the various 'signals' (including Nadja herself) that might lead Breton to a firmer sense of himself, and culminates, towards the end of the text, with an affirmation of stable identity in the form of Breton's own photographic portrait.

When we acknowledge that the text announces itself as a quest for the author's identity, the photographic documents begin to resemble nothing so much as items in a 'musée personnel', as indeed Magali Nachtergael has suggested.[49] Just like Breton's real collection at his rue Fontaine apartment, the heteroclite objects exhibited to the reader in *Nadja*, via photographic representations, do not simply showcase the collector's 'distinction' or 'artistic sensibility' (although they do speak volumes about his aesthetic standpoint as a lover of both primitive and modern art); these items are included in the collection because they reflect on and even exteriorize aspects of his identity.[50] If Breton's quest for identity might be solved by knowing 'qui je "hante"' [who it is that I 'haunt'] (*BOC*, I, 647), as he suggests at the beginning of *Nadja*, then by a similar token he might also come to know himself, and make himself known to the reader, through the objects that he haunts or frequents, and which haunt his imagination. Nadja's works are one element in this complex elaboration, or exhibition, of identity: subsumed into this very personal creative project, it is difficult to read them as speaking on their own terms or as affirmations of an autonomous creative subject. Rather, they are reduced to facets of Breton's own totalizing creative vision.

Nadja is thus not so much the subject of Breton's text as she is its object — or one object amongst the many included in the collection. There is no full photographic portrait of her in the text (although a portrait is often given of even the most minor character); she is seen only via a fragmented photograph of her 'yeux de fougère' [fern eyes], where her eyes, instead of offering up the possibility of a distinctive creative vision, are reduced to an image — an isolated body-part, fetishistically repeated (Figure 4.3). Her subjectivity, her status not only as a creative agent but as a *whole person*, is thus elided, in a way that parallels the disintegration of her personality and descent into madness. This of course is in direct contrast with Breton, whose position as creative subject remains stable throughout, despite the initial question mark over his identity. As Roger Cardinal has shown, this is typical of the Surrealists' engagement with outsider art, or art created by the mentally ill: the Surrealist author may be fascinated by madness, may value 'mad' or irrational productions, but he always holds the mad subject at a distance, refusing to relinquish his own hold on reason or to embrace fully an irrationality that always holds an element of danger.[51] This is the principal reason for the end of Breton's relationship with Nadja: her creativity, while positively received at the beginning of their relationship, is soon found to be out of control, and therefore dangerous and aberrant. It is aberrant because it is *mad*, because it is *female*, but also because it stakes a claim to subjectivity, because it tries to speak on its own terms, and this is unacceptable within the terms of Breton's own totalizing vision. Vincent Kaufman has argued that Breton's women (Nadja, and later Jacqueline Lamba) are valued primarily as readers, or as passive recipients of Breton's creative vision. What triggers Breton's rejection of Nadja, according to Kaufman, is the realization that Nadja has her own personal history, certain more sordid elements of which do not fit in with his vision of her as ideal recipient; this autonomy means that she cannot be made a vessel for his own vision.[52] By rejecting the real Nadja, but turning her into a text, he appropriates her creativity for his own purposes, annexing her creative subjectivity to his own. A found object or visual spectacle, she is ultimately Breton's work of art, his version of Galatea: a passive recipient of the meanings he invests in her.

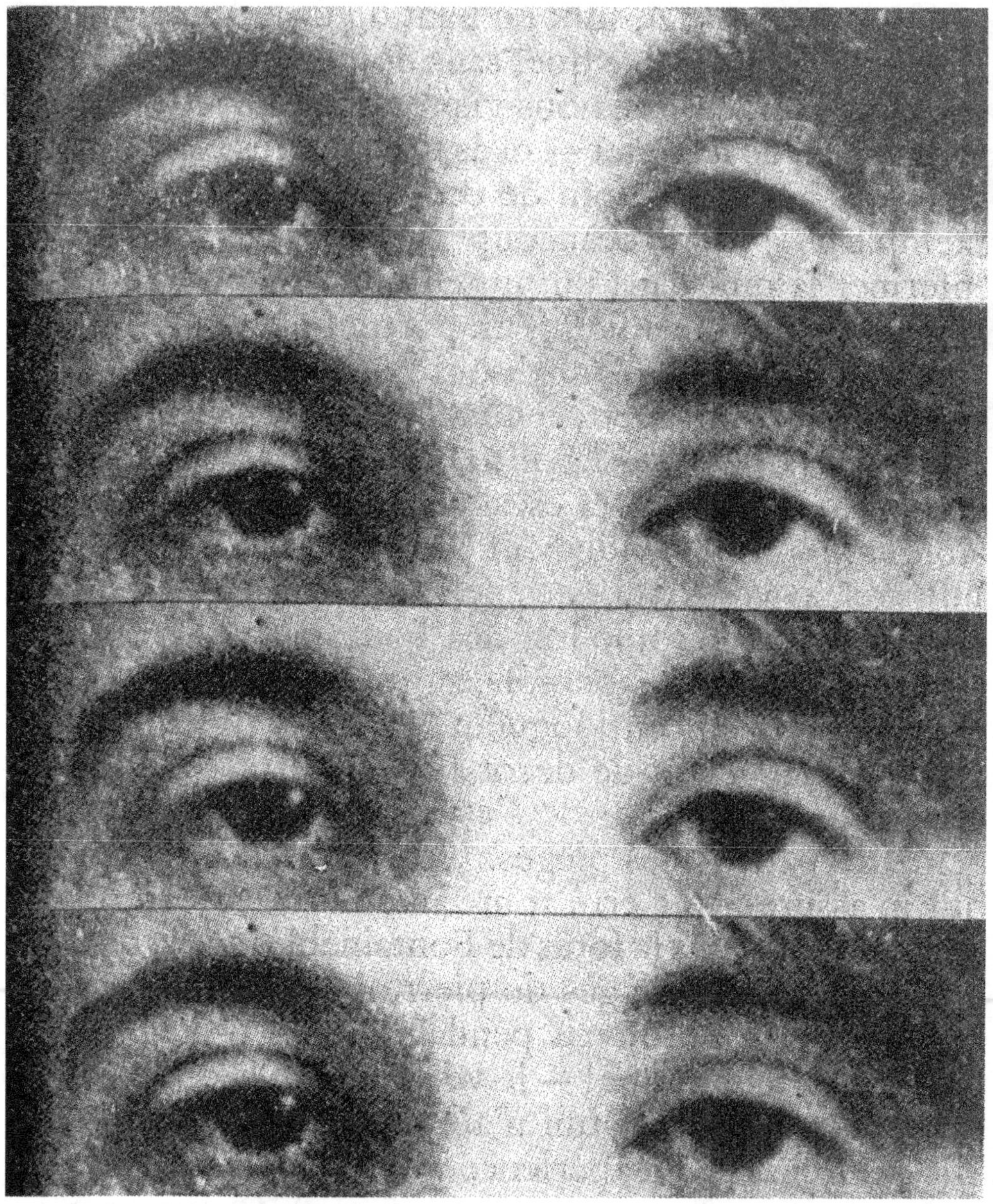

FIG. 4.3. 'Ses yeux de fougère', from André Breton, *Nadja* (1928). © ADAGP, Paris and DACS, London 2015. © Éditions GALLIMARD.

Once it becomes apparent that Nadja has crossed over from the charmingly unhinged into full-blown insanity, Breton exits the relationship; when he learns from others that she has been committed to an asylum, he does little to help her. Much has been written about Breton's moral failings in this instance, but the question of whether the real Breton acted morally, and whether he could or should have acted differently, is not my primary concern here.[53] What is extremely important, however, is the fact that within the framework of the text itself, his moral disengagement reinforces a conception of Nadja not as a fully-fledged subject but, once again, as object, a found object who has served her purpose within Breton's creative search for himself, and is now cast aside. Once madness explicitly enters the narrative frame, moreover, Nadja's drawings and collages seem retrospectively to lose their status as works of art, and revert to the status of supporting documents, attesting to the state of Nadja's mental health, much like the drawings and writings of the mentally ill that were used as diagnostic evidence by psychiatrists around the turn of the century.[54] Despite Breton's diatribe against contemporary psychiatry, his relationship with Nadja thus comes to look very much like a doctor-patient one, with Breton approaching her verbal and visual creations with a sympathetic eye, but from the analyst's position of authority.

Susan Rubin Suleiman has compared *Nadja* fruitfully to the images of Charcot's patient Augustine originally published in the *Iconographie photographique de la Salpêtrière*, and which were republished in *La Révolution surréaliste* in the same year as *Nadja*.[55] In the accompanying text, 'Le Cinquantenaire de l'hystérie', Breton and Aragon jointly laud the expressive potential of hysteria, but, as is indicated by the six photographs of Augustine in various provocative 'attitudes passionnelles', as well as by the mention of the sexual liberties taken by Charcot's interns with their female patients, they remain transfixed by it not as an expression of a subjectivity, but because it provides them with a visual stimulus for male fantasy.[56] They do not, in other words, want to hear the 'mad' or hysterical woman speak, to hear the workings of her unconscious mind; they want her to remain the silent object of their gaze. The same is true of Nadja. Breton's Surrealist take on the art novel thus offers us the tantalizing possibility of a liberated female creativity: in the person of Nadja, madness and femininity come together as the ultimate irrational 'Other', the embodiment of an idealized automatic creation. And yet Breton backs away from fully embracing this in order to assert his own creative power, and his own (male) subject position as author of *Nadja* — and, perhaps, as author of Nadja herself. She might take on various guises in our reading and re-reading of Breton's text: she might stand as the irrational voice of the unconscious speaking from within the male subject, who maintains control at all times; she might be figured in terms of a found object or image carefully stored in Breton's highly personal cabinet of curiosities; she might be a muse, or inspiration to creation. She might, of course, also be compared to Mirabelle in Aragon's *Anicet*, a figure who seems to be an abstraction, an ideal of 'modern beauty', but is also a real, flesh-and-blood woman; who appears to be the object of a quest, and who stands to be 'won' by the creative endeavours of the male artists who surround her, in a kind of parodic version of courtly love, and yet cannot be construed as entirely passive.[57] Whether she is an object of the artistic quest or merely (as in Nadja's case) a signpost pointing the artist towards something or someone else, what is clear is that the Surrealist Woman of the 1920s is not (yet) an artist: across all our readerly imaginings of her, she remains shut out of full creative subjecthood, which remains an exclusively male preserve.

Notes to Chapter 4

1. *Blaise Cendrars vous parle*, *TADA*, xv, 135.
2. Breton defines Surrealism against the nineteenth-century novel in the *Manifeste du surréalisme* (1924), in André Breton, *Œuvres complètes*, ed. by Margueritte Bonnet et al., 3 vols (Paris: Gallimard, Bibliothèque de la Pléiade, 1988–1992), i, 309–46 (pp. 313–16). Hereafter referred to as *BOC*.
3. I use the term 'visual culture' here as it designates an object of study, as opposed to a discipline or theoretical approach (where 'visual culture' is synonymous with 'visual (culture) studies').
4. Max Morise, 'Les Yeux enchantés', *La Révolution surréaliste*, 1 (December 1924), 26–27.
5. See Elza Adamowicz, *Ceci n'est pas un tableau: les écrits surréalistes sur l'art* (Lausanne: L'Âge d'homme, 2004), esp. pp. 9–30; Grant, *Surrealism and the Visual Arts*, esp. pp. 89–115. Goddard, ' "Poésie plastique?", pp. 117–24, usefully situates Surrealism's attitude to the visual arts within the broader historical context of debates around hierarchies of the arts.
6. Grant, *Surrealism and the Visual Arts*, pp. 80–82. Breton states in a note that had he been a painter, he might have translated the image in visual terms (*BOC*, i, 325), which suggests that the verbal expression is just one material translation of thought amongst many.
7. Louis Aragon, *Le Paysan de Paris* (Paris: Gallimard, 1953), p. 82.
8. I have followed the critical consensus identified by Witkovsky, according to whom the period between the First World War and the publication of the *Manifeste* 'continues to be understood as one of cohabitation between an unofficially designated Surrealist movement and an official banner, Dada'. Matthew S. Witkovsky, 'Dada Breton', *October*, 105 (Summer 2003), 125–36 (p. 127). While I read *Anicet* as a Surrealist text, this is not to deny its Dadaist leanings, evident notably in its lack of deference towards its filmic references.
9. In this respect, it might be aligned with what Christophe Wall-Romana has recently branded 'cinepoetry'; see *Cinepoetry: Imaginary Cinemas in French Poetry* (New York: Fordham University Press, 2013). The interactions between early film and literature are of course complex and extend beyond the Surrealist movement: see *Le Spectateur nocturne: les écrivains au cinéma, une anthologie*, ed. by Jérôme Prieur (Paris: Éditions de l'étoile/Cahiers du cinéma, 1993); Roland-François Lack, 'First Encounters: French Literature and the Cinematograph', *Film History*, 20 (2008), 133–43; Richard Abel, 'American Film and the French Literary Avant-Garde (1914–1924)', *Contemporary Literature*, 17.1 (1976), 84–109. Alan Spiegel, *Fiction and the Camera Eye: Visual Consciousness in Film and the Modern Novel* (Charlottesville: University Press of Virginia, 1976), proposes a somewhat looser notion of 'cinematographic literature', many examples of which precede the 1895 invention of the cinematograph.
10. Suleiman, *Subversive Intent*, pp. 11–32; Katharine Conley, *Automatic Woman: The Representation of Woman in Surrealism* (Lincoln: University of Nebraska Press, 1996), pp. 1–2, 10. See also Robert J. Belton, *The Beribboned Bomb: The Image of Woman in Male Surrealist Art* (Calgary: University of Calgary Press, 1995).
11. Suleiman, *Subversive Intent*, p. 24.
12. In this respect, the photomontage clearly corresponds to a long-standing tradition, going back at least to Lessing, which genders images as female and language as male. See W. J. T. Mitchell, 'Space and Time: Lessing's *Laocoon* and the Politics of Genre', in *Iconology: Image, Text, Ideology* (Chicago & London: University of Chicago Press, 1986), pp. 95–115.
13. Whitney Chadwick, 'Mythic Woman/Real Woman: Embodying Desire in 1938', in *Twilight Visions: Surrealism and Paris*, ed. by Therese Lichtenstein (Berkeley: University of California Press, 2009), pp. 145–82 (p. 176). Women were not officially integrated into the Surrealist movement until the 1930s; see Suleiman, *Subversive Intent*, pp. 29–32.
14. Louis Aragon, *Anicet ou le panorama, roman*, in *Œuvres romanesques complètes*, ed. by Daniel

Bougnoux and others, 5 vols (Paris: Gallimard, Bibliothèque de la Pléiade, 1997–2012), I, 1–182 (pp. 3 & 6); hereafter referred to as *ORC*. Further page references for this edition of the novel will be given in parentheses.

15. Bal, *The Mottled Screen*, p. 3.

16. *Anicet* is certainly not the only fiction text in which Aragon engages closely with the visual: one might compare the treatment of painting and cinema in another of Aragon's early fiction texts, the short story 'Madame à sa tour monte' from *Le Libertinage* (1924), in *ORC*, I, 297–305. On the role of painting in the later *monde réel* cycle of novels, see Marc Chiassaï, *Aragon/Peinture/ Écriture: la peinture dans l'écriture des 'Cloches de Bâle' à 'La Semaine Sainte'* (Paris: Kimé, 1999).

17. At the beginning of the novel, Anicet kills a woman who turns out to have been the mistress of a certain 'Arthur' (Rimbaud); Philippe Forest has read this as a kind of fictional *règlement de comptes* with the preceding generation of writers; see 'Anicet, panorama du roman', *L'Infini*, 45 (Winter 1987), 79–102 (p. 87).

18. Anna Balakian, 'Anicet, or the Search for Beauty', in *The Snowflake on the Belfry: Dogma and Disquietude in the Critical Arena* (Bloomington: Indiana University Press, 1994), pp. 199–213 (p. 204).

19. 'Selling out', or more generally the relationship between art and the market, is a frequent concern in Surrealist criticism on contemporary art, including Aragon's article 'Au bout du quai, les Arts Décoratifs!', *La Révolution surréaliste*, 5 (October 1925), pp. 26–27, and the 1926 instalments of Breton's 'Le Surréalisme et la peinture', repr. in André Breton, *Le Surréalisme et la peinture*, in *Œuvres complètes IV: écrits sur l'art et autres textes*, ed. by Margueritte Bonnet and others (Paris: Gallimard, Bibliothèque de la Pléiade, 2008), 357–70 (henceforth *BOC*, IV). For commentary on these texts, see Grant, *Surrealism and the Visual Arts*, pp. 137–40 & 157–69.

20. Jean Arrouye proposes a similar reading in 'Bleu et *La Louange du corps humain*', in *Écrire et voir: Aragon, Elsa Triolet et les arts visuels*, ed. by Jean Arrouye (Aix-en-Provence: Publications de l'Université de Provence, 1991), pp. 23–37. Aragon's view of Picasso's work of course changed as the latter moved away from classicism; on the range of Aragon's art-critical responses to Picasso, see André Daspre, 'Écrits d'Aragon sur Picasso', in *Hommage à Claude Digeon* (Paris: Les Belles Lettres, 1987), pp. 233–47. The fact that Picasso illustrated *Anicet* for its republication in the second volume of Aragon and Elsa Triolet's *Œuvres romanesques croisées*, 42 vols (Paris: Robert Laffont, 1964) is also evidence of a subsequent turnaround in attitude.

21. Aragon mentions Picasso in his article 'Du décor', *Le Film*, 16 September 1918, repr. in *Écrits sur l'art moderne*, ed. by Jean Ristat (Paris: Flammarion, 1981), pp. 5–9 (p. 5). He does not mention him again until 1924, when he defends his set designs for the ballet *Mercure* (see *Écrits sur l'art moderne*, pp. 16–17). That Aragon may have been wary of attacking the master is suggested by an early 'key' to *Anicet* in which he seems to excuse the critical stance articulated in the novel by distancing Bleu from Picasso ('son pseudo-modèle'), and explains that his information about Picasso at the time of writing was second-hand: see *ORC*, I, 167–71 (p. 169). Picasso's status as the leading authority in the visual arts for the Surrealists is stated most explicitly in the first installment of Breton's 'Le Surréalisme et la peinture', *BOC*, IV, 354–55; on Breton's attempts to align Picasso with Surrealism, see Elizabeth Cowling, ' "Proudly we claim him as one of us": Breton, Picasso, and the Surrealist Movement', *Art History*, 8.1 (March 1985), 82–104.

22. Aragon's technique here is in this respect typical of Surrealist writing on art, which refrains from straightforward description of the art object; as Adamowicz notes, 'si description il y a, il s'agit moins de ce que représente que de ce qu'évoque le tableau' [if there is description, it is a description not so much of what the painting represents as of what it evokes] (*Ceci n'est pas un tableau*, p. 26).

23. On Méliès's editing techniques, see for instance André Gaudreault, 'Theatricality, Narrativity, and Trickality: Reevaluating the Cinema of Georges Méliès', in *Fantastic Voyages of the Cinematic Imagination: Georges Méliès's 'Trip to the Moon'*, ed. by Matthew Solomon (Albany: State University of New York Press, 2011), pp. 31–47.

24. For a general analysis of the role of cinema in *Anicet*, see Yvette Gindine, *Aragon: prosateur surréaliste* (Geneva: Droz, 1966), pp. 18–22.

25. Aragon expressed his admiration for the latter in 'Les Vampires' (1923), in *Projet d'histoire littéraire contemporaine*, ed. by Marc Dachy (Paris: Gallimard, 1994), pp. 7–9. Michael Richardson has

argued that *Fantômas* is a quintessentially Surrealist work because in it the marvellous surges forth from everyday situations: see *Surrealism and Cinema* (Oxford: Berg, 2006), pp. 22–23.

26. André Breton, *Nadja*, in *BOC*, I, 643–753 (p. 663).

27. Breton, 'Manifeste du surréalisme', *BOC*, I, 345.

28. Richardson, *Surrealism and Cinema*, p. 8.

29. Aragon, 'Du décor', in *Écrits sur l'art moderne*, p. 9.

30. On Aragon's distaste for traditional literary forms, see Gindine, *Aragon: prosateur surréaliste*, p. 16.

31. Balakian, '*Anicet*, or the Search for Beauty', p. 203.

32. In his *Entretiens avec Francis Crémieux* (Paris: Gallimard, 1964), p. 47, Aragon notes that Gonzalès was a stand-in for the art dealer Léonce Rosenberg, and confirms that this was intended as a criticism of modern art's complicity in market forces.

33. 'On' is used in a number of other instances to refer to an audience: cf. *ORC*, I, 70 ('on comprit'), and *ORC*, I, 115 ('on n'entend pas les légers crissements').

34. Cf. also *ORC*, I, 120: 'personne n'avait envie d'en rire'.

35. Mary Ann Caws, *The Eye in the Text: Essays on Perception, Mannerist to Modern* (Princeton, NJ: Princeton University Press, 1981), pp. 180–82, also comments on this passage in the course of her discussion of 'the cinema of the Surrealist text'.

36. Gindine, *Aragon: prosateur surréaliste*, p. 20.

37. *Fantômas*, dir. Louis Feuillade. Gaumont, 1913.

38. David Trotter, *Cinema and Modernism* (Oxford: Blackwell, 2007).

39. Aragon, 'Du décor', in *Écrits sur l'art moderne*, p. 9.

40. Aragon also insists on 'la découverte de la mécanique et de ses lois' in Chaplin's films in 'Du décor', in *Écrits sur l'art moderne*, p. 8.

41. Rosalind Krauss, 'The Photographic Conditions of Surrealism', *October*, 19 (1981), 3–34 (p. 26 for both quotations).

42. Ibid. On photography as indexical, and Surrealist photography more generally, see also Krauss, 'Photography in the Service of Surrealism', in *L'Amour fou: Photography and Surrealism*, ed. by Rosalind Krauss and Jane Livingston (Washington, DC: Corcoran Gallery of Art/New York and London: Abbeville Press, 1985), pp. 15–54.

43. Breton, catalogue preface for 1927 exhibition by Arp, repr. in *Le Surréalisme et la peinture* (1928); *BOC*, IV, 404.

44. A further four photographs were included in the 1963 edition; see *BOC*, I, 1496.

45. Pierre Naville, 'Beaux-arts', *La Révolution surréaliste*, 3 (April 1925), 27.

46. See Breton's reflections on the impossibility of Surrealist art criticism in the March 1926 instalment of 'Le Surréalisme et la peinture', *BOC*, IV, 358–59; see also Aragon's lampooning of the figure of the art critic as 'policier de l'art' in *Anicet*, *ORC*, I, 65–68.

47. As Adamowicz puts it, Surrealist writing on art often provides 'un prolongement narratif de tableaux' [a narrative prolongation of paintings]; see *Ceci n'est pas un tableau*, p. 30.

48. Krauss, 'The Photographic Conditions of Surrealism'; on the status of the photographs in *Nadja* as authenticating documents, see also Dawn Ades, 'Photography and the Surrealist Text', in *L'Amour fou*, ed. by Rosalind Krauss and Jane Livingston (Washington, DC: Corcoran Gallery of Art/New York & London: Abbeville Press, 1985), pp. 155–89 (p. 161), and Ian Walker, *City Gorged with Dreams: Surrealism and Documentary Photography in Interwar Paris* (Manchester: Manchester University Press, 2002), pp. 48–67.

49. Magali Nachtergael, 'Nadja: images, désir et sacrifice', *Postures*, 7 (2005), 159–73 (p. 165).

50. Breton's collection was sold off in 2003; extensive documentation is provided on the website <www.andrebreton.fr> [accessed 24 July 2015]. On Breton's practices of collecting, see Dagmar Motycka Weston, 'Communicating Vessels: André Breton and his Atelier, Home and Personal Museum in Paris', *Architectural Theory Review*, 11.2 (2006), 101–28, and Katharine Conley, 'What Makes a Collection Surrealist? Twentieth-Century Cabinets of Curiosities in Paris and Houston', *Journal of Surrealism and the Americas*, 6.1 (2012), 1–23.

51. Roger Cardinal, 'Surrealism and the Paradigm of the Creative Subject', in *Parallel Visions: Modern Artists and Outsider Art*, ed. by Maurice Tuchman and Carol S. Eliel (Princeton, NJ: Princeton University Press, 1992), pp. 94–119 (p. 97).

52. Vincent Kaufman, 'What are (Breton's) Women for?', trans. by Sally Silk, *SubStance*, 16.3 (1987), 57–68 (pp. 60–62). Irmak Ertuna, 'The Mystery of the Object and Anthropological Materialism: Orhan Pamuk's *Museum of Innocence* and André Breton's *Nadja*', *Journal of Modern Literature*, 33.3 (Spring 2010), 99–111, interprets *Nadja* along similar lines, with Nadja's 'reality, or subjectivity' provoking Breton's rejection of her (p. 102).

53. Katharine Conley reviews this debate, and mounts something of a defence of Breton, in *Automatic Woman*, p. 117.

54. See Allison Morehead, 'The *Musée de la folie*: collecting and exhibiting *chez les fous*', *Journal of the History of Collections*, 21.1 (2011), 101–26; and my article 'Mad Puns and French Poets: Visual-Verbal Punning in Apollinaire's *Calligrammes*', in *Writing, Reading, Grieving: Essays in Memory of Suzanne Dow*, ed. by Ruth Cruickshank and Adam Watt, *Nottingham French Studies*, 53.1 (2014), 19–34. Jean Arrouye ('La Photographie dans *Nadja*', in *Mélusine IV: le livre surréaliste* (Lausanne: L'Âge d'homme, 1982), pp. 123–50) classes Nadja's drawings and collages amongst the authenticating 'documents' included in the text, rather than amongst the 'objets pervers/ objets d'art' (although he admits that the images may belong simultaneously to more than one category).

55. Suleiman, *Subversive Intent*, pp. 106–07.

56. Aragon and Breton, 'Le Cinquantenaire de l'hystérie', *La Révolution surréaliste*, 11 (March 1928), 20–22.

57. Walter Benjamin picked up on Breton's brief reference to courtly love in *Nadja*, arguing that Breton's relationship with Nadja should be conceived as courtly rather than sensual. See 'Surrealism: The Latest Snapshot of the European Intelligentsia', in *One-Way Street and Other Writings*, trans. by J. A. Underwood (London: Penguin, 2009), pp. 143–60 (p. 148).

CONCLUSION

Fiction and Criticism

In his review of literary responses to art, the critic François Fosca complained that Proust's style 'éblouissai[t] les auditeurs et les lecteurs, mais n'augmentai[t] pas en fait leur connaissance et leur compréhension des œuvres et des artistes' [wowed his audience, but did not in fact increase their knowledge or understanding of works of art or of artists]. He singled out for particular criticism Proust's representation of Vermeer's *View of Delft*: 'Celui qui ignorerait tout de Vermeer n'en saurait guère plus après avoir lu *À la Recherche du temps perdu*. [...] Proust n'a nullement expliqué pourquoi Vermeer [...] était digne d'être admiré' [A person completely ignorant about Vermeer would not know much more after reading *In Search of Lost Time*. [...] Proust has not explained why Vermeer [...] deserves our admiration].[1] Fosca's assumption here is that fiction about art should fulfill exactly the same function as art criticism: it should describe works of art, single out their unique qualities, and explain precisely what makes them worthy of aesthetic contemplation. Proust's representation of the *View of Delft* does not do this — not, at least, in the didactic, art-historical way that Fosca demands. But Bergotte's encounter with the painting does nevertheless teach us something about the work of art, and indeed about how to look more generally: like the critical article that Bergotte reads, Proust's text prompts us to look again, directing the reader-spectator's gaze towards the materiality of the painting, towards the 'petit pan de mur jaune', which we are encouraged to consider as 'pan', as marks on the canvas, before we consider it as 'mur'. But this is certainly not Proust's only intention here. Part of the purpose of the episode is to direct our attention back to writing: to consider, alongside Bergotte who wishes he had made the material of his own writing precious, the relationship between text and image.

This is, of course, part of a wider pattern in the early twentieth-century art novel. The writers we have examined over the course of this study are not only writing about art but also, often indirectly or implicitly, reflecting on writing and its relationship to the visual arts. We have seen this to be the case especially in those texts which, as part of an avant-garde attempt to reconfigure writing, to make it respond to modernity or to capture what Aragon calls a specifically 'modern beauty', stage encounters between figures representing different forms of expression — encounters that may take the form of 'competitions' between the arts, but where writing often also looks across to the visual arts to make alliances, or to find new models and generative stimuli. This is the case in Aragon's *Anicet* and in Cendrars's

Dan Yack, as well as in Apollinaire's 'Le Poète assassiné' — even if here the alliance between painting and poetry represented through the creative 'marriage' of Croniamantal and L'Oiseau du Bénin ultimately turns sour. We also find art novels reflecting on the ways in which various kinds of 'talk' or verbal discourse about art (which include criticism, but also fiction itself) inform or even constitute the work of art, and how this 'talk' often colludes with the commercial imperatives of the art market while at the same time somehow falling short of its main object: the work of art itself. This is the case in Georges-Michel's *Les Montparnos*, which self-consciously implicates itself in these processes, and in Mauclair's *La Ville lumière*, where art discourses are seen to be at best a mere distraction, a sideshow that does not really bear on the work of art itself, and at worst, a mis-representation or counterfeiting ('des théories circulant comme des pièces fausses' [theories doing the rounds like false coins], as Mauclair puts it).[2] These issues are also taken up by Bourget and Proust, for whom the Morellian theory of connoisseurship, which seeks to determine the attribution and hence the 'value' of the work of art, also fails to engage sensuously and imaginatively with the work of art itself.

While alliances between fictional artists and writers, and between image and text, may often be fruitful, what often emerges from these texts is a sense of the irreconcilable *distance* between the two media: a sense that text and image are not equivalent, that they serve different purposes, and may misunderstand one another. This is borne out by the fact that sustained ekphrastic description, of the sort that might allow us imaginatively to *picture* the work of art, is relatively rare, the texts in question implicitly acknowledging that words are no substitute for the image itself. When these descriptions do occur, however, they tend to be focalized via a spectator, and hence to focus on the viewing subject's reactions to the work of art, as is the case with Proust's Bergotte (and with Marcel too, when he views Elstir's paintings), and Aragon's Anicet. If, as Judith Labarthe-Postel has suggested, this type of narrative focalization is what distinguishes twentieth-century instances of ekphrasis from nineteenth-century ones (such as Balzac's description of Frenhofer's masterpiece, related by an omniscient and objective narrator), then the early twentieth-century art novel reflects a move away from literary realism (and from the illusion of 'direct' access to the work of art as object of description, or to the fictional world more generally), and concomitantly, a move away from any notion of objective truth or value in art.[3] Since, in the early twentieth-century art novel, we are made very much aware that all descriptions of the work are mediated via a subjectivity rather than made available to us directly, the work cannot be objectively known, judged, or criticized. This in turn may relate to the broader interrogation of aesthetic value that is pursued across the range of texts we have considered. Of course, this new emphasis on the spectator's subjective and very personal experience of the work of art may also be a response to what Paul Smith sees as one of the key purposes of the art novel: to provide a space in which to understand the experience of looking at a picture, a space 'inside which art makes particular and unusually cogent sense, and comes alive with especial vividness', in a way that it cannot in a dry piece of criticism.[4] While the art novel might resist any attempt to recreate the work itself via ekphrasis, it can and does capture what it is like to view a work of art: the way in which the immediate impression of the work mingles with memory; the way in which it awakens highly personal associations; its affective impact.

Throughout this study, we have approached the art novel as a vehicle for criticism, as a way to articulate art-critical positions that are often — but not always — consonant with those expressed in the author's critical writing on art. The art novel may on occasion provide a space in which to air views that cannot be expressed elsewhere: thus Aragon's critique of Picasso's turn to classicism, Apollinaire venting his suppressed grievances against painting as an art form that is perceived as more culturally privileged than poetic writing, and Mauclair implicitly targeting the dangerous influence of aesthetic cosmopolitanism on modern art (an influence that he would only explicitly attack in his criticism some time later) are all examples of the way in which fiction might provide the cover that is necessary for the writer to be able to say what is (as yet) unsayable. More generally, however, we have noted that the art novel and art criticism inhabit close quarters: not just that they 'say' similar things about art, but that authors working in both camps tend to operate genre-blurring tactics that bring them into close proximity with one another. Proust and Bourget's demand for a more sensuous and imaginative spectatorship brings with it a demand for more sensuous and imaginative writerly responses to the work of art: thus in the period examined here, and particularly in the hands of avant-garde writers, art criticism begins to move away from the kind of model Fosca had in mind, towards something more creative and which often looked more like prose poetry or imaginative fiction than conventional, essayistic discourse. We have seen that Apollinaire in *Les Peintres cubistes* develops a poetic-narrative mode of response, using Picasso's painting as a point of departure for the creation of mysterious fictional worlds; Cendrars, meanwhile, engages in a lyrical attempt to render, through 'des mots aussi *photogéniques* que possible' [words that are as *photogenic* as possible] (*TADA*, XI, 71), the effects of Survage's cinematic experiments in 'De la parturition des couleurs', a text whose generic indeterminacy allowed it subsequently to be incorporated into his hermetic fiction *L'Eubage*.[5] Surrealism's rejection of the contraints of reason and privileging of the imagination meant that it appeared to disallow the kind of art criticism that would assess the work against preconceived aesthetic principles, and tended towards a more poetic, instinctive response to the work of art that often resembled fiction or a poetic narrative. Of course, this did not prevent the Surrealists, or indeed Apollinaire or Cendrars, from adopting more conventional formal and critical approaches when this suited them. What is clear, however, is not only that fiction writing served as a potential model for new forms of criticism, but that the art novel is often a natural extension of a broader creative project that seeks to respond to art through writing — and, in addition, that it acts as a venue in which authors might self-consciously work through the function and form of 'critical' writing on art.

Just as art criticism is never ideologically neutral, the art novel is not just about aesthetics divorced from everything else. In engaging with the art and with the art-critical debates of their times, the novels we have considered also deal with the intersection of art, national identity, and gender. Many of the texts examined here reflect the agenda of the 'retour à l'ordre', seeking to privilege an art that can be identified with classical French or Latin traditions. They also seek rhetorically to protect a privileged relationship between art and masculinity: while the early twentieth-century art novel might have moved beyond the passive female models, objects of the creative male gaze, that predominate in nineteenth-century art narratives, they persist in identifying artistic creation as a fundamentally male endeavour. Female creativity is registered as threatening or disruptive; it is marginalized and dismissed; if it is valorized, this is done within an explanatory framework that puts the female artist's success down to the fact that she has taken on 'male' characteristics (as in Apollinaire's *La Femme assise*). Elsewhere, women are figured not so much as artists but as muses (as in Aragon's Mirabelle, a figure who arguably has her own power but still stands by while the men get on with the creative work), or as works of art (like Mireille in *Dan Yack*, a Galatea-like creation, or indeed Nadja as an element in Breton's all-encompassing Surrealist vision).

It is clear, then, that the art novel can teach us something about art: but it is more than a souped-up, sublimated form of criticism, and more than a simple art-historical document, a *roman à clef* serving up 'evidence' about artists and their work. What I hope to have demonstrated over the course of this book is that reading an art novel is a multi-layered experience, with the reader often having to negotiate a complex conjunction of fact and fiction; to read the text in relation to real works of art that he or she may or may not have seen, and to critical debates surrounding those works; to consider, finally, what the author is trying to say not just about art, but about everything that surrounds art and determines its authenticity and value: artists, spectators, dealers, galleries, collectors, models, muses, criticism... and art writing more generally. In doing so, the art novel draws attention to and questions the very terms within which it presents a 'critical' account of art, its creation, and reception.

Notes to the Conclusion

1. Fosca, *De Diderot à Valéry*, pp. 74 & 77.
2. Mauclair, *La Ville lumière*, p. 148.
3. Labarthe-Postel, *Littérature et peinture dans le roman moderne*, p. 243.
4. Smith, 'Literature and Art', p. 11.
5. Blaise Cendrars, *L'Eubage: aux antipodes de l'unité* (1926), in *TADA*, VII, 285–327 (pp. 303–05).

BIBLIOGRAPHY

Art Fiction

APOLLINAIRE, GUILLAUME, *La Femme assise*, in *Œuvres en prose complètes*, ed. by Pierre Caizergues and Michel Décaudin, 3 vols (Paris: Gallimard, Bibliothèque de la Pléiade, 1977, 1991, & 1993), I, 409–94

——'Le Poète assassiné', in *Œuvres en prose complètes*, I, 225–302

ARAGON, LOUIS, *Anicet ou le panorama, roman*, in *Œuvres romanesques complètes*, ed. by Daniel Bougnoux and others, 5 vols (Paris: Gallimard, Bibliothèque de la Pléiade, 1997–2012), I, 1–182

——'Madame à sa tour monte', in *Œuvres romanesques complètes*, I, 296–305

BALZAC, HONORÉ DE, *Le Chef-d'œuvre inconnu — Gambara — Massimilla Doni* (Paris: Garnier-Flammarion, 1981)

BLANCHE, JACQUES-ÉMILE, *Aymeris* (Paris: Éditions de la Sirène, 1922)

BOURGET, PAUL, *La Dame qui a perdu son peintre* (Paris: Plon, 1910; fasc. repr. Elibron Classics, 2006)

——'La Pia' [1896] in *Voyageuses* (Paris: Nelson, n.d.), pp. 13–79

——'La Seconde Mort de Broggi-Mezzastris', in *La Dame qui a perdu son peintre* (Paris: Plon, 1910; fasc. repr. Elibron Classics, 2006), pp. 135–68

BRETON, ANDRÉ, *Nadja*, in *Œuvres complètes*, ed. by Margueritte Bonnet and others, 3 vols (Paris: Gallimard, Bibliothèque de la Pléiade, 1988–92), I, 643–753

CARCO, FRANCIS, *Scènes de la vie de Montmartre, roman* [1919] (Paris: J. Ferrenczi & Fils, 1939)

CENDRARS, BLAISE, *Dan Yack*, in *Tout autour d'aujourd'hui*, ed. by Claude Leroy, 15 vols (Paris: Denoël, 2001–06), IV

FOSCA, FRANÇOIS, *Derechef* (Paris: Simon Kra, 1927)

GASQUET, JOACHIM, *Il y a une volupté dans la douleur...* (Paris: Bernard Grasset, 1921)

GEORGES-MICHEL, MICHEL, *Les Montparnos* (Paris: Livre de poche, 1976)

GONCOURT, EDMOND and JULES DE, *Manette Salomon* (Paris: Gallimard, 1996)

LYS, GEORGES DE, and ANDRÉ IBELS, *L'Arantelle: roman d'art* (Paris: J. Bosc, 1908)

MARGUERITTE, VICTOR, *La Garçonne* [1922] (Paris: Flammarion, 1949)

MAUCLAIR, CAMILLE, *La Ville lumière: roman contemporain* (Paris: Paul Ollendorff, 1904)

MURGER, HENRY, *Scènes de la vie de bohème*, ed. by Loïc Chotard and Graham Robb (Paris: Gallimard, 1988)

PROUST, MARCEL, *À la recherche du temps perdu*, ed. by Jean-Yves Tadié, 4 vols (Paris: Gallimard, Bibliothèque de la Pléiade, 1987–89)

——*Remembrance of Things Past*, trans. by C. K. Scott Moncrieff and Terence Kilmartin, 3 vols (London: Chatto & Windus, 1981)

RAMUZ, C.-F., *Aimé Pache, peintre vaudois* [1911] (Lausanne: Plaisir de Lire, 1973)

SALMON, ANDRÉ, *La Négresse du Sacré-Cœur* (Paris: Nouvelle revue française, 1920)

WARNOD, ANDRÉ, *Lily, modèle: roman de Montmartre* (Paris: L'Édition française illustrée, 1919)

——*Lina de Montparnasse* (Paris: Nouvelle revue critique, 1928)

ZOLA, ÉMILE, *L'Œuvre*, ed. by Marie-Ange Voisin-Fougère (Paris: Librairie Générale Française, 1996)

Other Material

[Anon.], 'Revue esthétique des journaux et des revues', *L'Esprit nouveau*, 3 (December 1921), 310

[Anon.], ed., 'Le Dossier de presse de *La Femme assise*', *Que Vlo-Ve?*, second series, no. 2 (April–June 1982), 12–22

ABEL, RICHARD, 'American Film and the French Literary Avant-Garde (1914–1924)', *Contemporary Literature*, 17.1 (1976), 84–109

ADAMOWICZ, ELZA, *Ceci n'est pas un tableau: les écrits surréalistes sur l'art* (Lausanne: L'Âge d'homme, 2004)

ADES, DAWN, 'Photography and the Surrealist Text', in *L'Amour fou: Photography and Surrealism*, ed. by Rosalind Krauss and Jane Livingston (Washington, DC: Corcoran Gallery of Art/New York & London: Abbeville Press, 1985), pp. 155–89

APOLLINAIRE, GUILLAUME, *Et moi aussi je suis peintre*, ed. by Daniel Grojnowski (Cognac: Le Temps qu'il fait, 2006)

——*Journal intime 1898–1918*, ed. by Michel Décaudin (Montpellier: Éditions du Limon, 1991)

——*Œuvres en prose complètes*, ed. by Pierre Caizergues and Michel Décaudin, 3 vols (Paris: Gallimard, Bibliothèque de la Pléiade, 1977, 1991, & 1993)

——*Œuvres poétiques*, ed. by Marcel Adéma and Michel Décaudin (Paris: Gallimard, Bibliothèque de la Pléiade, 1965)

ARAGON, LOUIS, *Écrits sur l'art moderne*, ed. by Jean Ristat (Paris: Flammarion, 1981)

——*Entretiens avec Francis Crémieux* (Paris: Gallimard, 1964)

——*Le Paysan de Paris* (Paris: Gallimard, 1953)

——*Projet d'histoire littéraire contemporaine*, ed. by Marc Dachy (Paris: Gallimard, 1994)

ARAGON, LOUIS, and ANDRÉ BRETON, 'Le Cinquantenaire de l'hystérie', *La Révolution surréaliste*, 11 (March 1928), 20–22

ARAGON, LOUIS, and ELSA TRIOLET, *Œuvres romanesques croisées*, 42 vols (Paris: Robert Laffont, 1964)

ARROUYE, JEAN, 'Bleu et *La Louange du corps humain*', in *Écrire et voir: Aragon, Elsa Triolet et les arts visuels*, ed. by Jean Arrouye (Aix-en-Provence: Publications de l'Université de Provence, 1991), pp. 23–37

——'La Photographie dans *Nadja*', in *Mélusine IV: le livre surréaliste* (Lausanne: L'Âge d'homme, 1982), pp. 123–50

AUBERT, JEAN, 'À propos d'une acquisition du Musée de Chambéry: Paul Bourget, amateur d'art', in *Paul Bourget et l'Italie*, ed. by M.-G. Martin-Gistucci (Geneva: Slatkine, 1985), pp. 13–21

BAL, MIEKE, *The Mottled Screen: Reading Proust Visually*, trans. by Anna-Louise Milne (Stanford, CA: Stanford University Press, 1997)

BALAKIAN, ANNA, '*Anicet*, or the Search for Beauty', in *The Snowflake on the Belfry: Dogma and Disquietude in the Critical Arena* (Bloomington: Indiana University Press, 1994), pp. 199–213

BALDWIN, THOMAS, *The Material Object in the Work of Marcel Proust* (Bern: Peter Lang, 2005)

BALES, RICHARD, 'Proust and the Fine Arts', in *The Cambridge Companion to Proust*, ed. by Richard Bales (Cambridge: Cambridge University Press, 2001), pp. 183–99

BELTING, HANS, *The Invisible Masterpiece*, trans. by Helen Atkins (London: Reaktion, 2001)

BELTON, ROBERT J., *The Beribboned Bomb: The Image of Woman in Male Surrealist Art* (Calgary: University of Calgary Press, 1995)

BENJAMIN, WALTER, 'On some motifs in Baudelaire', in *Illuminations*, trans. by Harry Zohn, ed. by Hannah Arendt (London: Pimlico, 1999), pp. 152–96

——'Surrealism: The Latest Snapshot of the European Intelligentsia' [1929], in *One-Way Street and Other Writings*, trans. by J. A. Underwood (London: Penguin, 2009), pp. 143–60

——'The Work of Art in the Age of Mechanical Reproduction', in *Illuminations*, trans. by Harry Zohn, ed. by Hannah Arendt (London: Pimlico, 1999), pp. 211–44

BERENSON, BERNARD, 'Amico di Sandro', *Gazette des beaux-arts*, 41 (1899), 459–71; 42 (1899), 21–36

——*Painters of the Italian Renaissance*, 3 vols (London: Phaidon, 1968)

BERGER, MAURICE, 'Epilogue: The Modigliani Myth', in *Modigliani: Beyond the Myth*, ed. by Mason Klein, exhibition catalogue (New York: Jewish Museum/New Haven, CT: Yale University Press, 2004), pp. 75–85

BIELECKI, EMMA, *The Collector in Nineteenth-Century French Literature: Representation, Identity, Knowledge* (Bern: Peter Lang, 2012)

BISSIÈRE, 'Notes sur Ingres', *L'Esprit nouveau*, 4 (January 1921), 388–400

BLOOM, MICHELLE E., 'Pygmalionesque Delusions and Illusions of Movement: Animation from Hoffmann to Truffaut', *Comparative Literature*, 52.4 (Autumn 2000), 291–320

BOCHNER, JAY, *Blaise Cendrars: Discovery and Re-creation* (Toronto: University of Toronto Press, 1978)

BOHN, WILLARD, *Apollinaire, Visual Poetry and Art Criticism* (Lewisburg, PA: Bucknell University Press/London & Toronto: Associated University Presses, 1993)

BONNEFIS, PHILIPPE, *Dan Yack: Blaise Cendrars phonographe* (Paris: Presses universitaires de France, 1992)

BOSCHETTI, ANNA, *La Poésie partout: Apollinaire, homme-époque (1898–1918)* (Paris: Seuil, 2001)

BOURDIEU, PIERRE, *La Distinction: critique sociale du jugement* (Paris: Minuit, 1979)

BOURGET, PAUL, *Essais de psychologie contemporaine*, 2 vols (Paris: Plon, 1901)

——*Sensations d'Italie (Toscane — Ombrie — Grande-Grèce)* (Paris: Lemerre, 1892)

BOWIE, MALCOLM, *Proust Among the Stars* (London: Harper Collins, 1998)

BOWIE, THEODORE, *The Painter in French Fiction* (Chapel Hill: University of North Carolina, 1950)

BOZON-SCALZITTI, YVETTE, *Blaise Cendrars ou la passion de l'écriture* (Lausanne: L'Âge d'homme, 1977)

——'Cendrars et la machine infernale', in *Cendrars aujourd'hui: Présence d'un romancier*, ed. by Michel Décaudin (Paris: Minard/Lettres modernes, 1977), pp. 15–33

BRETON, ANDRÉ, *Œuvres complètes*, ed. by Margueritte Bonnet and others, 3 vols (Paris: Gallimard, Bibliothèque de la Pléiade, 1988–92)

——*Œuvres complètes IV: écrits sur l'art et autres textes*, ed. by Margueritte Bonnet and others (Paris: Gallimard, Bibliothèque de la Pléiade, 2008)

BREUNIG, L. C., 'Les Phares d'Apollinaire', *Cahiers du Musée National d'Art Moderne*, 6 (1981), 63–69

BRIEFEL, AVIVA, *The Deceivers: Art Forgery and Identity in the Nineteenth Century* (Ithaca: Cornell University Press, 2006)

CAIZERGUES, PIERRE, 'Apollinaire et la politique pendant la guerre', *Guillaume Apollinaire 12: Apollinaire et la guerre (1)*, ed. by Michel Décaudin (Paris: Lettres modernes/Minard, 1974), pp. 67–101

CARCO, FRANCIS, *De Montmartre au quartier latin* (Monaco: Éditions Sauret, 1993)

——*La Légende et la vie d'Utrillo* (Paris: Bernard Grasset, 1928)

CARDINAL, ROGER, 'Surrealism and the Paradigm of the Creative Subject', in *Parallel Visions: Modern Artists and Outsider Art*, ed. by Maurice Tuchman and Carol S. Eliel (Princeton, NJ: Princeton University Press, 1992), pp. 94–119

CAWS, MARY ANN, *The Eye in the Text: Essays on Perception, Mannerist to Modern* (Princeton, NJ: Princeton University Press, 1981)

CENDRARS, BLAISE, *Inédits secrets*, ed. by Miriam Cendrars (Paris: Club français du livre, 1969)
——— *Œuvres complètes*, 8 vols (Paris: Denoël, 1962–65)
——— *Tout autour d'aujourd'hui*, ed. by Claude Leroy, 15 vols (Paris: Denoël, 2001–06)
CHADWICK, WHITNEY, 'Mythic Woman/Real Woman: Embodying Desire in 1938', in *Twilight Visions: Surrealism and Paris*, ed. by Therese Lichtenstein (Berkeley: University of California Press, 2009), pp. 145–82
CHASTEL, ANDRÉ, *La Gloire de Raphaël, ou le triomphe d'Eros* (Paris: Réunion des musées nationaux, 1995)
CHIASSAÏ, MARC, *Aragon/Peinture/Écriture: la peinture dans l'écriture des 'Cloches de Bâle' à 'La Semaine Sainte'* (Paris: Kimé, 1999)
COCKING, J. M., 'Proust and Painting', in *Proust: Collected Essays on the Writer and his Art* (Cambridge: Cambridge University Press, 1982), pp. 130–63
COCTEAU, JEAN, *Picasso* (Paris: L'École des lettres, 1996)
CONLEY, KATHARINE, 'What Makes a Collection Surrealist? Twentieth-Century Cabinets of Curiosities in Paris and Houston', *Journal of Surrealism and the Americas*, 6.1 (2012), 1–23
——— *Automatic Woman: The Representation of Woman in Surrealism* (Lincoln: University of Nebraska Press, 1996)
COWLING, ELIZABETH, '"Proudly we claim him as one of us": Breton, Picasso, and the Surrealist Movement', *Art History*, 8.1 (March 1985), 82–104
DARMON, PIERRE, 'Des suppliciés oubliés de la Grande Guerre: les pithiatiques', *Histoire, économie, société*, 20.1 (2001), 49–64
DARROW, MARGARET H., *French Women and the First World War: War Stories of the Home Front* (Oxford: Berg, 2000)
DASPRE, ANDRÉ, 'Écrits d'Aragon sur Picasso', in *Hommage à Claude Digeon* (Paris: Les Belles Lettres, 1987), pp. 233–47
DÉCAUDIN, MICHEL, 'Sur la composition du *Poète assassiné*', *Revue des sciences humaines*, 84 (October–December 1956), 437–56
DELBREIL, DANIEL, *Apollinaire et ses récits* (Fasano and Paris: Didier/Schena, 1999)
——— 'Portrait du portraitiste dans les récits de fiction d'Apollinaire', in *Guillaume Apollinaire 21: Apollinaire et le portrait*, ed. by Michel Décaudin (Paris: Lettres modernes/Minard, 2001), pp. 249–68
——— 'Statue et statut du poète dans l'œuvre de Guillaume Apollinaire', in *Écrire la sculpture (XIXe–XXe siècles)*, ed. by Ivanne Rialland (Paris: Classiques Garnier, 2012), pp. 171–85
DELEUZE, GILLES, *Proust et les signes*, 3rd edn (Paris: Presses universitaires de France, 2010)
DENIS, MAURICE, 'Paul Sérusier' (*L'Occident*, December 1908), repr. in *Du Symbolisme au classicisme: théories*, ed. by O. Revault d'Allonnes (Paris: Hermann, 1964), pp. 54–57
DIDI-HUBERMAN, GEORGES, 'Appendice: question de détail, question de pan', in *Devant l'image: question posée aux fins d'une histoire de l'art* (Paris: Minuit, 1990), pp. 273–318
DRUCKER, JOHANNA, *The Visible Word: Experimental Typography and Modern Art, 1909–23* (Chicago: Chicago University Press, 1994)
DUCHEMIN, JACQUELINE, *Prométhée: histoire du mythe, de ses origines orientales à ses incarnations modernes* (Paris: Les Belles Lettres, 2000)
DUNCAN, CAROL, 'Virility and Domination in Early Twentieth-Century Vanguard Painting', in *The Aesthetics of Power: Essays in Critical Art History* (Cambridge: Cambridge University Press, 1993), pp. 81–108
DURRY, MARIE-JEANNE, 'Irène Lagut', *Les Lettres françaises*, no. 1270 (12–18 February 1969), 6–7, 9
EBERIEL, ROSEMARY, 'Clowns: Apollinaire's Writings on Picasso', *Res*, 14 (Autumn 1987), 143–59
ERTUNA, IRMAK, 'The Mystery of the Object and Anthropological Materialism: Orhan Pamuk's *Museum of Innocence* and André Breton's *Nadja*', *Journal of Modern Literature*, 33.3 (Spring 2010), 99–111

FEUILLADE, LOUIS, dir., *Fantomas*. Gaumont, 1913.

FOREST, PHILIPPE, 'Anicet, panorama du roman', *L'Infini*, 45 (Winter 1987), 79–102

FORMENTELLI, ÉLIANE, 'Écrire "Picasso" d'Apollinaire', *Études françaises* (Montréal), 21.1 (Spring 1985), 9–29

FOSCA, FRANÇOIS, *De Diderot à Valéry: les écrivains et les arts visuels* (Paris: Albin Michel, 1960)

—— 'Les Montparnos', *La Quinzaine critique*, 1.3 (1929), 133–34

—— 'Le Salon des indépendants', *L'Amour de l'art*, 8 (1927), 33–37

FRANCESCATO, SIMONE, *Collecting and Appreciating: Henry James and the Transformation of Aesthetics in the Age of Consumption* (Oxford: Peter Lang, 2010)

FRANCK, DAN, *The Bohemians: The Birth of Modern Art, Paris 1900–1930*, trans. by Cynthia Hope Liebow (London: Phoenix, 2002)

FRAQUELLI, SIMONETTA, 'Montparnasse and the Right Bank: Myth and Reality', in *Paris Capital of the Arts, 1900–1968*, exhibition catalogue (London: Royal Academy of Arts, 2002), pp. 106–17

FREED-THALL, HANNAH, ' "Prestige of a Momentary Diamond": Economies of Distinction in Proust', *New Literary History*, 43.1 (2012), 159–78

FREUD, SIGMUND, 'The Moses of Michelangelo', in *The Standard Edition of the Complete Psychological Works of Sigmund Freud*, 24 vols (London: Vintage, 2001), XIV, 211–36

GAUDREAULT, ANDRÉ, 'Theatricality, Narrativity, and Trickality: Reevaluating the Cinema of Georges Méliès', in *Fantastic Voyages of the Cinematic Imagination: Georges Méliès's 'Trip to the Moon'*, ed. by Matthew Solomon (Albany: State University of New York Press, 2011), pp. 31–47

GEE, MALCOLM, *Dealers, Critics, and Collectors of Modern Painting: Aspects of the Parisian Art Market between 1910 and 1930* (New York: Garland, 1981)

GEISLER-SMZULEWICZ, ANNE, *Le Mythe de Pygmalion au XIXe siècle: pour une approche de la coalescence des mythes* (Paris: Honoré Champion, 1999)

GEORGES-MICHEL, MICHEL, *Ballets russes: histoire anecdotique, suivie d'un appendice et du poème de Shérérazade* (Paris: Éditions du monde nouveau, 1923)

—— *En Jardinant avec Bergson* (Paris: Albin Michel, 1926)

—— *La Bohème canaille* (Paris: La Renaissance du Livre, 1922)

—— *Les Grandes Époques de la peinture 'moderne': de Delacroix à nos jours* (New York: Brentano's, 1945)

—— *Peintres et sculpteurs que j'ai connus, 1900–1942* (New York: Brentano's, 1942)

GIDE, ANDRÉ, *Les Faux-monnayeurs* (Paris: Gallimard, 1997)

GILADI, AMOTZ, 'Guillaume Apollinaire et la "latinisation" des avant-gardes parisiennes durant la Première Guerre mondiale', *ConTEXTES* (varia), <http://contextes.revues.org/5045?lang=en> [accessed 17 February 2015]

GINDINE, YVETTE, *Aragon: prosateur surréaliste* (Geneva: Droz, 1966)

GINZBURG, CARLO, 'Morelli, Freud and Sherlock Holmes: Clues and Scientific Method', trans. by Anna Davin, *History Workshop*, 9 (Spring 1980), 5–36

GODDARD, LINDA, *Aesthetic Rivalries: Word and Image in France, 1880–1926* (Bern: Peter Lang, 2012)

—— ' "Poésie plastique?" The Competition between Art and Literature in Early Twentieth-Century France', in *The Art Book Tradition in Twentieth-Century Europe*, ed. by Kathryn Brown (Farnham: Ashgate, 2013), pp. 117–29

GOLAN, ROMY, 'From Fin de Siècle to Vichy: The Cultural Hygienics of Camille (Faust) Mauclair', in *The Jew in the Text: Modernity and the Construction of Identity*, ed. by Linda Nochlin and Tamar Garb (London: Thames and Hudson, 1996), pp. 156–86

GOLDSTEIN, CARL, 'French Identity in the Realm of Raphael', in *The Cambridge Companion to Raphael*, ed. by Marcia B. Hall (Cambridge: Cambridge University Press, 2005), pp. 237–60

GOMBRICH, E. H., 'Psychoanalysis and the History of Art', in *Meditations on a Hobby-Horse*, 4th edn (London: Phaidon, 1985), pp. 30–44

GOUX, JEAN-JOSEPH, *Les Faux-monnayeurs du langage* (Paris: Galilée, 1984)

GRANT, KIM, *Surrealism and the Visual Arts: Theory and Reception* (Cambridge: Cambridge University Press, 2005)

GRAYZEL, SUSAN R., 'Women and Men', in *A Companion to World War I*, ed. by John Horne (Oxford: Wiley-Blackwell, 2010), pp. 263–78

GUILLERM, JEAN-PIERRE, 'L'Avènement du détail pictural: de Balzac à Proust', in *Écrire la peinture*, ed. by Philippe Delaveau (Paris: Éditions universitaires, 1991), pp. 97–106

HAMON, PHILIPPE, 'Le *Topos* de l'atelier', in *L'Artiste en représentation*, ed. by René Démoris (Paris: Éditions Desjonquères, 1993), pp. 125–44

HEINICH, NATHALIE, 'Artistes dans la fiction: quatre générations', in *Images de l'artiste*, ed. by Pascal Griener and Peter J. Schneemann (Bern: Peter Lang, 1998), pp. 205–20

——*La Gloire de Van Gogh: essai anthropologique de l'admiration* (Paris: Minuit, 1991)

HEWITT, NICHOLAS, 'Images of Montmartre in French Writing, 1920–1960: "La Bohème réactionnaire"', *French Cultural Studies*, 4 (1993), 129–43

——'Shifting Cultural Centres in Twentieth-Century Paris', in *Parisian Fields*, ed. by Michael Sheringham (London: Reaktion, 1996), pp. 30–45

HIBBITT, RICHARD, 'Paul Bourget's Critique of *fin-de-siècle* Cosmopolitanism', in *The Cause of Cosmopolitanism*, ed. by Patrick O'Donovan and Laura Rascaroli (Bern: Peter Lang, 2011), pp. 173–87

HUBERT, ÉTIENNE-ALAIN, 'Georges Braque selon Guillaume Apollinaire', in *L'Esprit nouveau dans tous ses états, en hommage à Michel Décaudin*, ed. by P. Brunel and others (Paris: Minard, 1986), pp. 265–74

HUGHES, EDWARD J., *Proust, Class and Nation* (Oxford: Oxford University Press, 2011)

HUNEKER, JAMES, 'Literature and Art', in *Promenades of an Impressionist* (London: T. Werner Laurie, 1910), pp. 277–90

IAMPOLSKI, MIKHAIL, *The Memory of Tiresias: Intertextuality and Film*, trans. by Harsha Ram (Berkeley: University of California Press, 1998)

JOHNSON, J. THEODORE JR., 'From Artistic Celibacy to Artistic Contemplation', *Yale French Studies*, 34 (1965), 81–90

KARPELES, ERIC, *Paintings in Proust: A Visual Companion to Proust's 'In Search of Lost Time'* (London: Thames & Hudson, 2008)

KAUFMAN, VINCENT, 'What are (Breton's) Women for?', trans. by Sally Silk, *SubStance*, 16.3 (1987), 57–68

KNIGHT, DIANA, *Balzac and the Model of Painting: Artist Stories in 'La Comédie humaine'* (Oxford: Legenda, 2007)

KOLB, PHILIPPE, and JEAN ADHÉMAR, 'Charles Ephrussi (1849–1905); ses secrétaires: Laforgue, A. Renan, Proust; "sa" Gazette des beaux-arts', *Gazette des beaux-arts*, 6th period, 103.1380 (January 1984), 29–41

KRAUSS, ROSALIND, 'In the Name of Picasso', in *The Originality of the Avant-Garde and Other Modernist Myths* (Cambridge, MA: MIT Press, 1985), pp. 23–40

——'Photography in the Service of Surrealism', in *L'Amour fou: Photography and Surrealism*, ed. by Rosalind Krauss and Jane Livingston (Washington, DC: Corcoran Gallery of Art/ New York and London: Abbeville Press, 1985), pp. 15–54

——'The Photographic Conditions of Surrealism', *October*, 19 (1981), 3–34

KRIS, ERNST, and OTTO KURZ, *Legend, Myth, and Magic in the Image of the Artist: A Historical Experiment* (New Haven, CT: Yale University Press, 1979)

LABARTHE-POSTEL, JUDITH, *Littérature et peinture dans le roman moderne: une rhétorique de la vision* (Paris: L'Harmattan, 2002)

LACASSIN, FRANCIS, 'Les Poèmes du Docteur Cornélius', in *Le Mystérieux Docteur Cornélius et autres œuvres de Gustave Le Rouge*, ed. by Francis Lacassin (Paris: R. Laffont, 1986), pp. 1181–1247

LACK, ROLAND-FRANÇOIS, 'First Encounters: French Literature and the Cinematograph', *Film History*, 20 (2008), 133–43

LATHERS, MARIE, *Bodies of Art: French Literary Realism and the Artist's Model* (Lincoln: University of Nebraska Press, 2001)

——'"Tué par un excès d'amour": Raphael, Balzac, Ingres', *French Review*, 71.4 (1998), 550–64

LAUDE, JEAN, 'Retour et/ou rappel à l'ordre?', in *Retour au classicisme, 1917–1925*, exhibition catalogue (Saint-Tropez: Musée de l'Annonciade, 2002), pp. 17–56

LEROY, CLAUDE, 'Figures de *Dan Yack*: le jeu dans l'île', in *Cendrars aujourd'hui: présence d'un romancier*, ed. by Michel Décaudin (Paris: Minard/Lettres modernes, 1977), pp. 109–44

——'L'Atelier du double: Cendrars et Léger en miroir', in *Dis-moi, Blaise: Léger, Chagall, Picasso et Blaise Cendrars*, exhibition catalogue (Paris: Réunion des musées nationaux, 2009), pp. 15–23

LEVITT, CAROLINE, 'Raoul Dufy, Pierre Alechinsky and Jim Dine: Depicting the Arts in Guillaume Apollinaire's "Le Poète assassiné"', in *Art in French Fiction since 1900*, ed. by Katherine Shingler, *Nottingham French Studies*, 51.3 (2012), 232–47

MAINARDI, PATRICIA, *The End of the Salon: Art and the State in the Early Third Republic* (Cambridge: Cambridge University Press, 1993)

MANN, PAUL, *The Theory-Death of the Avant-Garde* (Bloomington: Indiana University Press, 1991)

MATHIAS, YEHOSHUA, 'Paul Bourget, écrivain engagé', *Vingtième siecle: revue d'histoire*, 45 (January-March 1995), 14–29

MAUCLAIR, CAMILLE, 'Auguste Rodin, son œuvre, son milieu, son influence', *La Revue universelle*, 1 (1901), 769–75

——*Idées vivantes* (Paris: Librairie de l'art ancien et moderne, 1904)

——'La Femme devant les peintres modernes', *La Nouvelle revue*, 2nd series, 1 (1899), 190–213

——'La Réaction nationaliste en art et l'ignorance de l'homme de lettres', *La Revue*, 54 (1905), 151–74

——'Le Besoin d'art du peuple', *La Revue bleue*, 5th series, 4.10 (2 September 1905), 306–10

——'Le Classicisme et l'académisme', *La Revue bleue*, 4th series, 19.11 (14 March 1903), 335–40

——'Les Deux Lions', *L'Aurore*, 16 May 1898, 1

——*Les États de la peinture française de 1850 à 1920* (Paris: Payot, 1921)

——*Les Mères sociales: romain contemporain* (Paris: Paul Ollendorff, 1902)

——*Le Soleil des morts* [1898] (Geneva: Slatkine, 1979)

——*Les Métèques contre l'art français: la farce de l'art vivant*, II (Paris: Nouvelle revue critique, 1930)

——*L'Impressionnisme: son histoire, son esthétique, ses maîtres* (Paris: Librairie de l'art ancien et moderne, 1904)

——*Trois crises de l'art actuel* (Paris: Charpentier, 1906)

MELIUS, JEREMY, 'Connoisseurship, Painting, and Personhood', in *Creative Writing and Art History*, ed. by Catherine Grant and Patricia Rubin, *Art History*, 34.2 (2011), 288–309

MELMOUX-MONTAUBIN, MARIE-FRANÇOISE, *Le Roman d'art dans la seconde moitié du XIXe siècle* (Paris: Klincksieck, 1999)

MITCHELL, W. J. T., 'Space and Time: Lessing's *Laocoon* and the Politics of Genre', in *Iconology: Image, Text, Ideology* (Chicago & London: University of Chicago Press, 1986), pp. 95–115

MODIGLIANI, JEANNE, *Modigliani sans légende* (Paris: Gründ, 1961)

MONNIER, GÉRARD, *L'Art et ses institutions en France: de la Révolution à nos jours* (Paris: Gallimard, 1995)

MONNIN-HORNUNG, JULIETTE, *Proust et la peinture* (Geneva: Droz, 1951)

MOREHEAD, ALLISON, 'The *Musée de la folie*: collecting and exhibiting *chez les fous*', *Journal of the History of Collections*, 21.1 (2011), 101–26

MORELLI, GIOVANNI, *Italian Painters: Critical Studies of their Works*, trans. by Constance Jocelyn Ffoulkes, 2 vols (London: J. Murray, 1892–93)

MORISE, MAX, 'Les Yeux enchantés', *La Révolution surréaliste*, 1 (December 1924), 26–27

MORTON, DAVID L., *Sound Recording: The Life Story of a Technology* (Westport, CI: Greenwood Press, 2004)

MOURIER-CASILE, PASCALINE, 'L'Œil de Cendrars', *Revue des sciences humaines*, 216 (1989), 111–32

NACHTERGAEL, MAGALI, 'Nadja: images, désir et sacrifice', *Postures*, 7 (2005), 159–73

NAVILLE, PIERRE, 'Beaux-arts', *La Révolution surréaliste*, 3 (April 1925), 27

NEAD, LYNDA, 'Seductive Canvases: Visual Mythologies of the Artist and Artistic Creativity', *Oxford Art Journal*, 18.2 (1995), 59–69

NEWTON, JOY, 'Camille Mauclair and Auguste Rodin', *Nottingham French Studies*, 30.1 (1991), 39–55

——'The Atelier Novel: Painters as Fictions', in *Impressions of French Modernity: Art and Literature in France 1850–1900*, ed. by Richard Hobbs (Manchester: Manchester University Press, 1998), pp. 173–89

NOLAND, CARRIE, *Poetry at Stake: Lyric Aesthetics and the Challenge of Technology* (Princeton, NJ: Princeton University Press, 1999)

OSTER, DANIEL, 'Statue et statut du poète dans *Le Poète assassiné* d'Apollinaire', *Stanford French Review*, 3 (1979), 161–72

PAP, JENNIFER, 'The Cubist Image and the Image of Cubism', in *The Image in Dispute: Art and Cinema in the Age of Photography*, ed. by Dudley Andrew (Austin: University of Texas Press, 1997), pp. 155–80

PAVLOVIC, MIHAILO, 'La Repopulation et *Les Mamelles de Tirésias*', in *Guillaume Apollinaire 6: Images d'un destin*, ed. by Michel Décaudin (Paris: Lettres modernes/Minard, 1967), pp. 133–50

PERLOFF, MARJORIE, *The Futurist Moment: Avant-Garde, Avant-Guerre, and the Language of Rupture*, 2nd edn (Chicago: Chicago University Press, 2003)

PETY, DOMINIQUE, 'Le Personnage du collectionneur au XIXe siècle: de l'excentrique à l'amateur distingué', *Romantisme*, 112 (2001), 71–81

POGGI, CHRISTINE, *In Defiance of Painting: Cubism, Futurism, and the Invention of Collage* (New Haven, CT: Yale University Press, 1992)

POLLOCK, GRISELDA, 'Artists, Mythologies and Media: Genius, Madness and Art History', *Screen*, 21 (Spring 1980), 57–96

PRIEUR, JÉRÔME, ed., *Le Spectateur nocturne: les écrivains au cinéma, une anthologie* (Paris: Éditions de l'étoile/Cahiers du cinéma, 1993)

PROUST, MARCEL, *Écrits sur l'art*, ed. by Jérôme Picon (Paris: Flammarion, 1999)

READ, PETER, *Apollinaire et 'Les Mamelles de Tirésias': la revanche d'Éros* (Rennes: Presses universitaires de Rennes, 2000)

——' "Et moi aussi je suis sculpteur": Movement, Immobility and Time in the Fictional Sculptures of Apollinaire', in *From Rodin to Giacometti: Sculpture and Literature in France, 1880–1950*, ed. by Keith Aspley and Elizabeth Cowling (Amsterdam: Rodopi, 2000), pp. 76–83

——*Picasso and Apollinaire: The Persistance of Memory* (Berkeley: University of California Press, 2008)

REARICK, CHARLES, *The French in Love and War: Popular Culture in the Era of the World Wars* (New Haven, CT: Yale University Press, 1997)

RENAUD, PHILIPPE, 'Latnamaïnorc, déchiffreur de Croniamantal, ou La leçon des formes et des mots', in *Guillaume Apollinaire 8: Regards sur Apollinaire conteur (Stavelot 1973)*, ed. by Michel Décaudin (Paris: Lettres modernes/Minard, 1975), pp. 101–39

RICHARDSON, MICHAEL, *Surrealism and Cinema* (Oxford: Berg, 2006)

RIVA, RAYMOND T., 'A Probable Model for Proust's Elstir', *MLN*, 78:3 (May 1963), 307–13

ROMNEY, JONATHAN, 'Forgery and Economy in Gide's *Les Faux-monnayeurs*', *Neophilologus*, 71.2 (April 1987), 196–209

SAISSELIN, RÉMY G., *The Bourgeois and the Bibelot* (New Brunswick, NJ: Rutgers University Press, 1984)

SALMON, ANDRÉ, 'Modigliani', *L'Amour de l'art*, 3.1 (1922), 20–22

—— *Modigliani: sa vie et son œuvre* (Paris: Éditions des Quatre Chemins, 1926)

SAMUELS, ERNEST, *Bernard Berenson: The Making of a Connoisseur* (Cambridge, MA: Belknap Press, 1979)

SANTRAUD, J. M., 'Dans le sillage de la baleinière d'Arthur Gordon Pym: *Le Sphinx des glaces, Dan Yack*', *Études anglaises*, 25.3 (1972), 353–66

SEIGEL, JERROLD, *Bohemian Paris: Culture, Politics, and the Boundaries of Bourgeois Life, 1830–1930* (Baltimore, MD: Johns Hopkins University Press, 1999)

SHAW, MARY, 'All or Nothing? The Literature of Montmartre', in *The Spirit of Montmartre: Cabarets, Humor, and the Avant-Garde, 1875–1905*, ed. by Phillip Dennis Cate and Mary Shaw (New Brunswick, NJ: Jane Voorhees Zimmerli Art Museum, 1996), pp. 111–57

SHIFF, RICHARD, *Cézanne and the End of Impressionism: A Study of the Theory, Technique, and Critical Evaluation of Modern Art* (Chicago: Chicago University Press, 1984)

SHINGLER, KATHERINE, 'Apollinaire's Mirror', in *The Book of the Mirror*, ed. by Miranda Anderson (Newcastle: Cambridge Scholars, 2007), pp. 166–80

—— 'Mad Puns and French Poets: Visual-Verbal Punning in Apollinaire's *Calligrammes*', in *Writing, Reading, Grieving: Essays in Memory of Suzanne Dow*, ed. by Ruth Cruickshank and Adam Watt, *Nottingham French Studies*, 53.1 (2014), 19–34

SHOWALTER, ELAINE, *The Female Malady: Women, Madness and English Culture, 1830–1980* (London: Virago, 1987)

SILVER, KENNETH E., *Esprit de Corps: The Art of the Parisian Avant-Garde and the First World War, 1914–1925* (Princeton, NJ: Princeton University Press, 1989)

SITZIA, EMILIE, *L'Artiste entre mythe et réalité dans trois œuvres de Balzac, Goncourt et Zola* (Turku: Åbo Akademi University Press, 2004)

SMITH, PAUL, *Impressionism: Beneath the Surface* (London: Everyman Art Library, 1995)

—— 'Literature and Art', in *The Nineteenth-Century Art Novel*, ed. by Paul Smith, *French Studies*, 61.1 (2007), 1–13

SPIEGEL, ALAN, *Fiction and the Camera Eye: Visual Consciousness in Film and the Modern Novel* (Charlottesville: University Press of Virginia, 1976)

STEINER, WENDY, *The Colors of Rhetoric: Problems in the Relation between Modern Literature and Painting* (Chicago: Chicago University Press, 1982)

STEWART, SUSAN, *On Longing: Narratives of the Miniature, the Gigantic, the Souvenir, the Collection* (Durham, NC: Duke University Press, 1999)

SULEIMAN, SUSAN RUBIN, *Subversive Intent: Gender, Politics, and the Avant-Garde* (Cambridge, MA: Harvard University Press, 1990)

TADIÉ, JEAN-YVES, *Marcel Proust* (Paris: Gallimard, 1996)

TAYLOR-HORREX, SUSAN, 'Cendrars, Delaunay, et le simultanéisme: évolution de l'esthétique simultanéiste', *Cahiers Blaise Cendrars 3: L'Encrier de Cendrars*, ed. by Jean-Carlo Flückiger (Neuchâtel: Éditions de la Baconnière, 1989), 209–17

THIBAULT, JEAN-FRANÇOIS, 'Cendrars et Survage: rythmes colorés', in *Blaise Cendrars 20 ans après*, ed. by Claude Leroy (Paris: Klincksieck, 1983), pp. 183–88

THUILLIER, JACQUES, 'Raphaël et la France: présence d'un peintre', in *Raphaël et l'art français*, ed. by J. P. Cuzin, exhibition catalogue (Paris: Galeries Nationales du Grand Palais, 1984), pp. 11–36

TOWNSEND, GABRIELLE, *Proust's Imaginary Museum: Reproductions and Reproduction in 'À la recherche du temps perdu'* (Oxford: Peter Lang, 2008)

TROTTER, DAVID, *Cinema and Modernism* (Oxford: Blackwell, 2007)

VALENTI, SIMONETTA, *Camille Mauclair, homme de lettres fin-de-siècle: critique littéraire, œuvre narrative, création poétique et théâtrale* (Milan: Vita e Pensiero, 2003)

VANOYE, FRANCIS, 'Le Cinéma de Cendrars', *Europe*, 566 (1976), 183–96

VASARI, GIORGIO, *Vies des artistes*, trans. by Léopold Leclanché and Charles Weiss, ed. by Véronique Gerard Powell (Paris: Grasset & Fasquelle, 2007)

VILLIERS DE L'ISLE-ADAM, *L'Ève future*, ed. by Alan Raitt (Paris: Gallimard, 1993)

WALKER, IAN, *City Gorged with Dreams: Surrealism and Documentary Photography in Interwar Paris* (Manchester: Manchester University Press, 2002)

WALL-ROMANA, CHRISTOPHE, *Cinepoetry: Imaginary Cinemas in French Poetry* (New York: Fordham University Press, 2013)

WARNOD, ANDRÉ, 'L'École de Paris', *Comoedia*, 27 January 1925, p. 1

——'Un âne chef d'école', *Le Matin*, 28 March 1910, p. 4

WATSON, JANELL, *Literature and Material Culture from Balzac to Proust: The Collection and Consumption of Curiosities* (Cambridge: Cambridge University Press, 1999)

WATT, ADAM, *Reading in Proust's 'A la recherche': 'Le délire de la lecture'* (Oxford: Clarendon Press, 2009)

WEISS, JEFFREY, *The Popular Culture of Modern Art: Picasso, Duchamp, and Avant-Gardism* (New Haven, CT: Yale University Press, 1994)

WESTON, DAGMAR MOTYCKA, 'Communicating Vessels: André Breton and his Atelier, Home and Personal Museum in Paris', *Architectural Theory Review*, 11.2 (2006), 101–28

WETTLAUFER, ALEXANDRA, *Pen vs. Paintbrush: Girodet, Balzac and the Myth of Pygmalion in Postrevolutionary France* (New York: Palgrave, 2001)

——*Portraits of the Artist as a Young Woman: Painting and the Novel in France and Britain, 1800–1860* (Columbus: Ohio State University Press, 2011)

WILSON, ELIZABETH, *Bohemians: The Glamorous Outcasts* (London: Tauris Parke, 2000)

WISER, W., *The Crazy Years: Paris in the Twenties* (New York: Atheneum, 1983)

WITKOVSKY, MATTHEW S., 'Dada Breton', *October*, 105 (Summer 2003), 125–36

WOLLHEIM, RICHARD, 'Freud and the Understanding of Art', in *On Art and the Mind* (London: Allen Lane, 1973), pp. 202–19

——'Giovanni Morelli and the Origins of Scientific Connoisseurship', in *On Art and the Mind* (London: Allen Lane, 1973), pp. 177–201

YOUENS, SUSAN, 'Le Soleil des morts: A Fin-de-siècle Portrait Gallery', *Nineteenth-Century Music*, 11.1 (Summer 1987), 43–58

ZOLA, ÉMILE, 'Proudhon et Courbet', in *Mes haines: causeries littéraires et artistiques* (Paris: Charpentier, 1879), pp. 21–40

INDEX